ACCOUNTING FOR FEMINISM

Although gender challenges in accounting are widely acknowledged, research often addresses the position of men and women in relation to various issues, without necessarily challenging the underlying structures and social constructions of gender. In contrast, this book takes a much more overtly feminist position, informed by feminist theory, feminist methodology and feminist activism, to challenge these constructs and resulting inequalities. The book addresses contemporary global feminisms and their potential emancipatory implications for accounting, as a profession and as a tool or technology.

It explores feminist theorisations of accounting, offering new insights into their relevance, and provides a rich theoretical and practical resource to advance knowledge in the discipline and stimulate further interdisciplinary research. Rather than being issue driven with chapters organised to address particular concerns that relate to gender and accounting, such as parenthood, career progression, accountability, etc., the structure of this book is such that the feminist theoretical position is the starting point for each chapter. The book highlights the range of ways that feminism, in its various forms and from numerous theoretical perspectives, can contribute to an understanding of the challenges relating to gender, race and class occurring within accounting, and the ways of overcoming them.

In this way, the book provides an integrated discussion of feminist theories and the emancipatory potential of applying them to accounting that will appeal to readers whatever their orientation to feminism.

Kathryn Haynes is Professor of Accounting, Northumbria University, UK.

ACCOUNTING FOR FEMINISM

Exploring Emancipation for Profession and Practice

Kathryn Haynes

Routledge
Taylor & Francis Group
LONDON AND NEW YORK

Designed cover image: Paper Trident/Getty Images

First published 2025
by Routledge
4 Park Square, Milton Park, Abingdon, Oxon OX14 4RN

and by Routledge
605 Third Avenue, New York, NY 10158

Routledge is an imprint of the Taylor & Francis Group, an informa business

British Library Cataloguing-in-Publication Data
A catalogue record for this book is available from the British Library

Library of Congress Cataloging-in-Publication Data
Names: Haynes, Kathryn, author.
Title: Accounting for feminism : exploring emancipation for profession and practice / Kathryn Haynes.
Description: Abingdon, Oxon ; New York, NY : Routledge, 2025. |
Includes bibliographical references and index.
Identifiers: LCCN 2024056396 (print) | LCCN 2024056397 (ebook) |
ISBN 9781032636597 (hbk) | ISBN 9781032634869 (pbk) | ISBN 9781032636603 (ebk)
Subjects: LCSH: Feminism. | Accounting.
Classification: LCC HQ1155 .H42 2025 (print) | LCC HQ1155 (ebook) | DDC 657.082—dc23/eng/20250213
LC record available at https://lccn.loc.gov/2024056396
LC ebook record available at https://lccn.loc.gov/2024056397

ISBN: 978-1-032-63659-7 (hbk)
ISBN: 978-1-032-63486-9 (pbk)
ISBN: 978-1-032-63660-3 (ebk)

DOI: 10.4324/9781032636603

Typeset in Sabon
by codeMantra

CONTENTS

FIGURES

TABLES

This book is a staggeringly good read and the outcome of impressive scholarship. Many scholars have tackled parts of this important topic, but not one of them has come close to providing an analysis that is as broad and deep as this work. It is, nevertheless, accessible to all and should be part of the canon for anyone working in business as well as academic members of the social science community more generally.

Professor Emerita Jane Broadbent, *Royal Holloway, University of London, UK*

In her landmark book, *Accounting for Feminism*, Professor Haynes has delivered a comprehensive analysis of leading edge research and practice into the role and importance of gender, race, class and culture for the accounting profession. The sweep of issues addressed, from expectations, choices and activism to accounting technologies, sustainability and research methodologies, will make an indelible mark on our global profession and its literature.

Professor Lee D. Parker, *Research Professor in Accounting, Adam Smith Business School, The University of Glasgow, UK, and Joint Founding Editor – Accounting, Auditing & Accountability Journal*

ACKNOWLEDGEMENTS

This book is the culmination of my long-held interest and research in the relationship between feminism and accounting. However, it could not have been written without the support of the Leverhulme Trust, whose award of a two-year Major Research Fellowship MRF-2021-084, entitled Contemporary Feminisms and Their Emancipatory Implications for Accounting, generously enabled me to have the time to carry out this programme of work. I was honoured to receive such a prestigious award, and I offer grateful thanks to the Leverhulme Trust.

I also extend my thanks to Elsevier for permission, under licence number 5750290778424, to reproduce some short extracts from my 2017 article: Haynes, K. (2017). Accounting as gendering and gendered: A review of 25 years of critical accounting research on gender. *Critical Perspectives on Accounting*, *43*, 110–124, in Chapters 1–4.

Thank you to colleagues at Routledge for support with the publishing process, including Kristina Abbotts, Senior Editor in Economics, Finance and Accounting, and Christiana Mandizha, Editorial Assistant.

Professionally, I am grateful to numerous colleagues who have offered support, friendship and encouragement over the years, but particularly in relation to this project: Professor Jane Broadbent, Professor Marcia Anisette and Professor Lee Parker, who supported my application to the Leverhulme Trust. Thank you to colleagues in the Department of Accounting and Financial Management at Northumbria University for your collegiality and support. Thanks also to Eller Everett who worked as Senior Research Assistant on this project, again funded by the Leverhulme Trust, and whose input was most helpful.

I offer my greatest thanks and love to all my family whose constant support and love throughout this work, and always in life, means so much. However, I offer particular thanks and love to my mother, Jean Saxton, and my daughters, Eleanor Taylor and Florence Reedy, for always supporting me in everything I have ever done. Ellie, thanks additionally for the advice on publishing books. Florence, thanks especially for all the discussions about feminism and for offering detailed feedback on this book. Finally, to my beloved husband, Alan Murray, thank you for your belief in me and in this project, for your encouragement and support, for discussion of feminism and offering feedback on this book, for cooking all the dinners, looking after the dogs and always caring for me.

1

THE CASE FOR FEMINISMS AND ACCOUNTING

Scoping the emancipatory potential of accounting

Introduction

Feminism and accounting are two terms that are rarely associated together. Accounting is a well-established practice of calculative practices, tools and techniques, as well as a global profession with standards and qualification requirements. Feminism, as an idea and a political movement, addresses the structures, systems, processes and power relations inherent in society that create, uphold or perpetuate inequity between genders. However, given the power of accounting in a globalised world, both as a practice and as a profession, it is arguably implicated in the power relations and systems addressed by feminism. Hence, considering accounting through a feminist lens is a means of understanding and potentially overturning some of those gendered systems that may be created or perpetuated by accounting.

Yet, feminism as a concept or political movement has many dimensions dependent on its contextualisation, positionality, historicisation or contemporality. Feminism may reflect a theory, an approach to knowledge production or an activism. Although feminism addresses the position of women in their various contexts, women are not a unitary category and they experience considerable difference between each other, dependent on social, economic, political or geographic positioning. Gender interacts with other characteristics, such as race, ethnicity, age or sexuality, that affect the identity and position of individuals and their experience of inequalities or multiple oppressions. One woman's feminist struggle is not necessarily identical to that of others, and yet feminism can support an understanding of difference amongst women, as well as commonality and solidarity. For these reasons, feminism can take a number of approaches to defining, experiencing

DOI: 10.4324/9781032636603-1

and *being* a woman in contemporary global societies. Hence it is more appropriate to discuss multiple *feminisms* than one unified movement. What these feminisms have in common, however, is an intention to identify, subvert or overcome the multiple oppressions that women face. They have an emancipatory intent.

Aims and scope

The purpose of this book is to examine the relationship between contemporary feminisms and accounting and thereby consider the emancipatory potential of accounting.

The overarching objectives of the book are to:

- Provide a comprehensive overview of contemporary feminist theories applied to accounting, in terms of accounting practice and the accounting profession;
- Advance feminist theorisations of accounting, offering new insights into their relevance;
- Illustrate how feminist accounting research can have emancipatory potential;
- Provide a rich theoretical and practical resource to advance knowledge in the discipline and stimulate further interdisciplinary research.

In addressing these objectives, the book is the first dedicated comprehensive study of feminisms within accounting.

This introductory chapter sets out the rationale and scope of the book. It defines key concepts, such as gender and emancipation, while identifying that feminism encompasses multiple meanings and theories. It provides some discussion of the nature, purpose and effects of accounting in our society, addressing the influence of accounting as a technology and as a globalised profession, and considers the role of accounting in creating, perpetuating or addressing inequalities. It then builds an argument of the relevance of multiple feminisms, covered by this text, within the context of accounting, and invokes their emancipatory potential. Different feminist theories take different approaches to gendered oppressions, and indeed some may even conflict with each other, but I illustrate how each theory can be applied to accounting, dependent on positioning and context. A summary of the subsequent chapters, their theoretical orientation and content is provided later in this introductory chapter.

This book aims to be of interest to both established scholars and early career researchers, including PhD students. I hope it will be read by feminists interested in how feminism relates to accounting and accountants interested in considering accounting as a feminist issue. However, it is also designed to be of interest to scholars from other disciplines, who are interested in the application of feminist theory to research or the politicisation of gender in professions and organisations. It is also designed to be accessible to managers and to practitioners of accounting. While I do include some practical outcomes for accounting, I have kept the technical details of accounting to a minimum, so that it is readable and accessible to all scholars.

Author positioning

Before proceeding, I want to set out my positionality as the author. I do not presume that I can detach myself from the experiences that influenced me to become and write as a feminist. Nor do I think this would be helpful in addressing the gendered challenges that this book addresses from a feminist perspective. Gender is felt, experienced, embodied and lived in everyday interaction. As the old adage suggests: 'the personal is political'. My background is as a White, British, working-class girl, growing up in a family with fairly traditional gender roles: my father, the main breadwinner, in a semi-skilled but not professionally qualified white-collar job, and my mother working part-time in administrative roles while I was a child. Education was a means to new opportunities and insights, and I was the first and only member of my family generation to go to university, supported by the availability of government grants. Despite an arts background, I trained to be a Chartered Accountant, lured by what seemed to be a varied career working with different organisations. Although Chartered Accountancy afforded me many opportunities and developed numerous lifelong skills, I soon realised that the profession and firms within it were inherently gendered. The culture was not conducive to career progression for someone in my position as a mother of young children and I found it rife with sexism. My intuitive sense of feminist injustice later became a more informed position on feminism when I left accountancy for academia and embarked on a PhD addressing motherhood and gender issues in the accounting profession (Haynes, 2005). The application of feminist theory to accounting has been of great interest to me since I first began academic research. Feminist praxis shaped my approach to education, leadership and research in academia. The generous award of a Major Fellowship by the Leverhulme Trust gave me the opportunity to examine and consolidate my interest in feminist theory and its relevance to accounting to produce this book.

However, while my feminist orientation was influenced by personal experience, I acknowledge that my experience is partial. Being a White, Western, cis-gendered woman academic accountant is also a position of privilege compared to many other women (and also many men and non-binary genders) in different contexts. Therefore, my aim in this book is to be reflexively aware of such privilege, attempting to be inclusive of wider experience, and drawing from multiple feminisms to recognise and learn from the experiences of others. In doing so, the book will provide insight into the role of accounting in a global context, with an awareness of the power of accounting as a concept of power and control.

Before addressing feminism specifically, I first discuss the nature of the social construction both of gender and of accounting.

The social construction of gender

The concepts of sex and gender are theoretically distinct but also closely related. Sex has traditionally been a largely essentialist notion, relating to biological difference between male and female, whereas gender is widely accepted to be socially constructed and informed by socially and culturally informed conceptions of masculinity and femininity. However, biological essentialism itself is also subject to social norms and understandings, and is partially gendered, such that gender relations are the outcomes of socio-cultural and historic conditions and processes in which people create and understand their social positioning (Haynes, 2017).

In the post-Enlightenment development of Western societies, Cartesian philosophy influenced an emergent understanding of human experience into dualisms: mind and body. These dualisms became associated with concepts of masculinity and femininity, since masculinity was linked with the mind, rationality, knowledge and science, and femininity was associated with the body, emotions, nurturing and nature (Haynes, 2005, 2008). The resultant binaries have influenced subsequent cultural understandings of biological sex differences, in which physical or mental strength, reproductive capacities and genitalia have been used to position women as subordinate to men (Rahman & Jackson, 2010). Moreover, anything that characterises human behaviour or identity by its 'essence', or the supposed essential or innate quality of the individual, becomes imbued with stereotypes and false claims of irreducibility. Essentialism can be associated with both biological sex (relating to male/female) and socially constructed gender (relating to masculine/feminine). Such essentialism has become pervasive in the majority of cultures around the world, with localised nuances dependent on context, religion, socio-economic or political position. Globally, all genders are subjected to gendering, although the focus of feminism has been on the position of women, as they have been subjected to more discrimination and oppression than men under patriarchal power relations (Haynes, 2017).

Gender is therefore the effect of social constructions and internalisations of being a man or a woman. However, in recent years the concept of gender has become more fluid. Gender binaries of male or female are not universally accepted or experienced. Individuals may self-identify along a spectrum of gender, as non-conforming, trans or non-binary. Gender fluidity is much more around how one identifies as a human being. Nonetheless, many people's perceptions of gender are still binary, and society tends to be divided in binary ways. There has been fierce debate among different types of feminists, for example, notably so-called gender-critical feminists, also known as trans-exclusionary radical feminists (Pearce, Erikainen, & Vincent, 2020), around trans women having access to women's only spaces and women's identities (Jones & Slater, 2020; Zanghellini, 2020). The argument put forward by gender-critical feminists is that women need to be considered separately due to the inequalities, violence and abuse they have experienced due to their biological status as women, somewhat returning to essentialism. However, trans women also experience significant inequality, violence and abuse in societies that render them 'other', outside of the norms of accepted identity and behaviour (Silva et al., 2022; Westbrook, 2023). In the majority of cases, violence and oppression towards women is perpetrated by cis-gendered men rather than people identifying as women. Given that I perceive feminism as standing up to structural and cultural oppressions based on gender, I therefore take an inclusive approach in this book to anyone identifying as women.

Reflecting the essentialism inherent in some feminisms, within society, and within the accounting profession, I have had to continue to use the binary terms women and men in this book although I acknowledge and respect the non-binary. I have continued to use the terms woman and women, rather than the term 'womxn', which some feminists use to signify the view that language is misogynistic by positioning wo*men* in relation to men (Alawattage et al., 2021). Some argue that womxn is more inclusive of non-White women and trans women in an intersectional value system. However, in doing so, there is a risk that trans women and non-White women are implicitly characterised as not being 'women', which negates their identity and causes deep offence. I am using the words woman and women to signify all the diversity of women, recognising differences between women, as illustrated in the various feminisms, rather than reducing women to their essential characteristics. In adopting this position, I am inspired by Judith Butler's inclusive stance on the nature of gender:

> What it means to be a woman does not remain the same from decade to decade. The category of woman can and does change, and we need it to be that way. Politically, securing greater freedoms for women requires that we rethink the category of 'women' to include those new possibilities. The historical meaning of gender can change as its norms are re-enacted, refused or recreated.
>
> So we should not be surprised or opposed when the category of women expands to include trans women. And since we are also in the business of imagining alternative futures of masculinity, we should be prepared and even joyous to see what trans men are doing with the category of 'men'.
>
> *(Butler, 2021)*

Having discussed the social construction of gender, I will now discuss the social construction of accounting, and its implications for inequalities, before then explaining why feminism is powerfully relevant to evaluating both accounting and gender.

The social construction of accounting

Accounting is also a social construction, as a concept which has been formulated by humans and become solidified and codified over hundreds, indeed, thousands, of years. As such, it is subject to the machinations, power relations, social norms and economic priorities of those who define, implement and use it.

Early forms of accounting apparently originated in ancient Mesopotamia, where it was closely associated with the development of writing, recording, counting and the development of concepts of money (Garbutt, 1984). Ancient peoples have always used counting mechanisms to understand what they have or have not, over many millennia. In Mesopotamia and ancient Egypt, people relied on primitive accounting systems to record the abundance of crops or monitor herding systems of animals (Carmona & Ezzamel, 2007). By the fourth century BC, there is evidence of accounting techniques being applied in Babylonia, Egypt and China (Jacobsen, 1983; Stone, 1969). The entry or exit of crops and goods to storehouses were given 'oral reports' to check their movements, which is where the term 'auditor' comes from, derived from the Latin 'audire', to hear (Meuwissen, 2014). The Roman Empire made use of accounting techniques within public expenditure and monetary policy, by recording revenues, cash, taxes and expenses of the emperor's personal finances and the state (Oldroyd, 1995).

By the fourteenth century, traders in Italy and Europe were using a system of double-entry bookkeeping, using debits and credits, to record ins and outs of goods, what was held in cash or goods, and what was owed. This was popularised by Luca Pacioli's book *Summa de Arithmetica* published in vernacular Italian for the common merchants (Smith, 2022). There is a raft of literature pointing to the origins of modern accounting occurring in Italy, although Walker (2005) suggests that the production and dissemination of accounting history knowledge is skewed towards Anglo-American settings in the age of modernity. In a sense there is a form of colonisation occurring here, as concepts from ancient Mesopotamia, Babylonia, in the East, in what is now part of Iran, were taken up by the West in trading activities in Europe and perpetuated around the globe. Accounting as a concept was being created as a worldwide phenomenon.

In modernity, the accounting discipline encompasses two significant areas: accounting practices and the accounting profession. Of the first, calculative practices – accounting tools, techniques and constructs – allow an account to be made and rendered. These are the internal and external measurements, metrics and calculations which determine revenues/costs, profit/loss or surplus/deficit without which an account of activity cannot be prepared. These practices occur in varying forms dependent on the accounting entity, which could be anything from a small business to a multinational company, a charity or a public sector organisation. Once an account is calculated within an organisation, it is usually reported, both internally to understand the position of the company and externally to its owners or trustees. Under capitalism and within the corporate field, directors have a duty to provide an account to the providers of capital, who are the shareholders. Accountability reflects that process of providing an account for actions, finances or acts for which one is held responsible. In order to standardise and make comprehensible these reporting practices, accounts are subjected to accounting principles, accounting standards and accountability processes, generated within an array of national, international or global reporting frameworks and regulation. Governance processes are then the structures or means through which the entity is directed and controlled, providing support for decision-making, accountability and control within the organisation. Hence, corporate governance has a strong relationship with accounting practices. Nonetheless, accounting practice has widened beyond the organisation or accounting entity to encompass accounting for, and reporting on, externalities, such as the natural environment, climate change, social value or social responsibility.

Given that accounting is a social construction, it is not a neutral activity. As Dillard (1991, p. 8) noted some decades ago, but which remains relevant in contemporary globalised societies, 'Accounting is a technology but it is not ideologically sterile'. The social construction of accounting informs what we apparently value, what we measure and how we measure it. Yet, these constructions are informed, consciously or unconsciously, by the assumptions and attitudes of the human beings who make them, human beings embedded in societal norms which influence perceptions of gender, race, class, and other personal characteristics. For this reason, accounting when viewed from this perspective, is referred to as 'accounting technology', to signify its value-driven, socially constructed and essentially political dimensions, rather than the more abstract 'tool' or 'technique'. Henceforth, in this text, I will refer to accounting as a technology or as a calculative practice, to recognise its non-neutral position.

The second area of significance within the discipline of accounting is the accounting profession. The modern accounting profession evolved from the nineteenth century with the development of accounting professional bodies, as discussed further in Chapter 2. Different schools of thought exist as to whether modern professions formed to represent the public interest, self-interest of their members or a combination of both. Professional accounting bodies acted as exclusionary bodies to make sure that only their members, who have passed the relevant exams, could practise accountancy, and when they gained a royal charter, only members could call themselves 'Chartered Accountants'. This ensured that the public could expect a member to have an appropriate level of professional competence and be subject to a professional code of ethics, while also excluding, for competitive purposes, any practitioners who were not suitably qualified. For many decades, those members not only excluded non-qualified people, but also excluded women (see Chapter 2). Even when women were admitted to the accounting profession, gendered challenges and inequalities remained.

The profession of accounting is dominated by global professional bodies and professional services firms, which support the development of, and influence the application of, accounting practices, principles and standards, governance and reporting frameworks. These firms also wield considerable influence in the socialisation of accounting professionals, their behaviours and career opportunities, and are themselves subject to scrutiny and critique on their performance on gender (see, for example, Anderson-Gough, Grey, & Robson, 2005; Edgley, Sharma, & Anderson-Gough, 2016; Haynes, 2012; Kumra & Vinnicombe, 2008). Hence, both accounting as a practice and accounting as a profession are arguably implicated in both the construction and perpetuation of inequalities underpinned by accounting (Haynes, 2025). As Hines (1988) highlighted some decades ago, by communicating 'reality' in financial reports, we are constructing a reality. We might also ask, in terms of the accounting profession, whether the profession reflects the shifting demographics of society or actively shapes that society through its culture and behaviours. I argue that accounting is both gendering and gendered, implicated in constructing and perpetuating gendered inequalities (Haynes, 2017).

Accounting as a socio-political construct implicated in inequality

Unequal distribution of power, property and wealth is inherent in modern capitalist societies and much inequality is structured along gendered lines.[1] Although poverty, for example, affects the world's poor irrespective of gender, there is extensive evidence that around the world women and girls continue to experience challenges and lack of rights, despite social and economic development, through the feminisation of poverty, disease and hunger; the burden of unpaid domestic and care work; adverse health and impacts from environmental degradation; vulnerability to conflicts and violence; lack of food security, asset and land ownership; water and sanitisation issues; lack of political representation, power and decision-making; and lack of access to education (United Nations Department of Economic and Social Affairs, 2010, 2020). Progress in achieving the United Nation's Sustainable Development Goal 5 on gender equality is significantly off-track after the Covid-19 pandemic, with weak access to leadership positions within political and economic spheres, endemic violence, poor funding of women's health and poor public financing aligned to gender equality objectives (United Nations Department of Economic and Social Affairs, 2022). Women tend to be disproportionately affected by challenges with hunger, education, access to decent work, political representation and health in both developed and developing countries (United Nations Department of Economic and Social Affairs, 2022). Moreover, as with poverty, there are claims that the effects of climate change will disproportionally affect women more than men. For example, in many countries in the continent of Africa, women's traditional roles as the primary users and managers of natural resources, primary caregivers and labourers engaged in unpaid labour mean they are involved in, and dependent on, livelihoods and resources that are put most at risk by climate change while simultaneously they are less likely to be involved in decision-making about solutions (United Nations Economic Commission for Africa, 2009). The pursuit of economic growth intensified after the financial crisis of 2008, and as economies recover from the pandemic there is a risk that this occurs at the expense of health and sustainability (Guerriero, Haines, & Pagano, 2020). This raises serious questions about the ability of the world to achieve a more sustainable future and stave off the effects of climate change and any inequalities it brings. Since climate change is now 'unequivocally' linked to human industrialised activity (IPCC, 2007, 2013, 2023), the role of organisations and business in solving or perpetuating the problem becomes more significant.

Accounting is implicated in creating and perpetuating these gender inequalities. Accounting has long been associated with supporting market capitalism and shareholder value (Bryer, 2000; Catchpowle, Cooper, & Wright, 2004; Chiapello, 2007), imbued in the late twentieth century with neoliberalist concepts of de-regulation, market power and privatisation (Morales, Gendron, & Guénin-Paracini, 2014). Decreasing power of organised labour, the dismantling of the welfare state and a focus on individual achievement and responsibility rather than redistributive justice is the focus of much of the politics of the Global North. The varied challenges facing women and men are interrelated with organisations and markets, and hence with accounting, as accounting processes, decisions and reports inform and support organisational decision-making, strategy and financing. Improvements in communications, IT and accounting systems, together with the expansion and, most significantly, the deregulation of capital markets, have led companies to consider new ways of structuring their activities, often by taking their manufacturing base to developing countries to make the most efficient use of low taxes, advantageous inward investment opportunities and cheap labour, often involving the sweatshop labour of the world's poorest women. Neoliberalism shapes the relationship between markets and politics, and accounting as a tool of neoliberalism is implicated in a host of practices which have gendered effects:

> The pursuit of profit, for a minority, affects accounting and financial practices in relation to division of labour, provision of capital, production of goods and services, identity politics, work within and without the home, maintenance of households and childcare, for the majority.
>
> *(Haynes, 2008, p. 540)*

The global accounting profession also has a role in maintaining neoliberal ideologies, not only in advising upon and regulating accounting and reporting systems, but also in relation to gender equality, politics and policies, reflecting the influx of women into the profession in recent decades. This raises questions about the representation of women in the profession, career opportunities and progression, and the degree to which the profession reflects the shifting gender demographics of society or actively shapes that society.

This discussion of accounting as a socio-political construct implicated in causing and perpetuating gender inequalities sets the scene for the chapters that follow and my argument for the need for a feminist approach to theorising on accounting. The gender challenges highlighted above epitomise the real and significant problems experienced by women, and men, differently and collectively, in both the Global South and the Global North. They resonate with Lehman's (2012, p. 256) call to tie 'the current rhetoric of global neoliberalism to contemporary feminist struggles [to]...illustrate the significant consequences of economic globalization on women, and accounting's connection'. They also represent why research on gender and accounting should not be experienced as a marginal, minority pursuit, as recounted powerfully by Dambrin and Lambert (2012), but should be central to the concerns of feminists, social scientists and accounting scholars in the interests of emancipation and social justice.

Relations between gender, accounting and feminism

There is a considerable interest in gender in accounting research, but this is not necessarily feminist in its nature. A great deal of research in the accounting literature, as well as other disciplines, continues to reflect a gender binary between male and female, which conflates sex identification with gender identities and roles. Research of this nature addresses gender as a binary variable in empirical studies that explore differences in attitudes and/or gender divisions between men and women on numerous issues, such as ethics, career drivers, behavioural attitudes or communication techniques. These studies may address issues of importance to women but, as I have argued above, there are clearly distinctions within and between identities of men, women or non-binary people, which this type of research does not address. Hence studies which consider gender as a variable within accounting research have been subject to critique for a considerable period. Gallhofer (1998) criticised research that uses the term 'woman' as if it were a universal and unitary category which results in the suggestion that concerns addressed and issues raised are of equal importance and relevance for all women, thereby resulting in a failure to address the differences between women themselves. In 2008, I argued that what these studies have in common is primarily an interest in gender as an *object* of study rather than as part of the research methodology and theoretical framework, tending to use quantitative research methods aimed at providing an objective and neutral assessment of an issue by eliminating irrational (prejudiced) elements such as gender stereotypes hidden in the research design or in ways of reasoning (Haynes, 2008). This results in research that settles for exploring gender divisions, while doing little to contest them. Despite Broadbent and Kirkham's (2008) plea for researchers to study gender as a fluid construct, with a feminist orientation, Hardies and Khalifa (2018) found that research where gender is a 'dummy variable' continues to be dominant in gender and accounting research, resulting in the fluidity and social construction of gender being ignored, women being represented as 'other' in opposition to men and other intersectional characteristics not being addressed.

Given my position on the social construction of gender and accounting, and the role of accounting as a socio-political construct implicated in inequality, I argue that feminism, or the wide range of possible forms of feminist theorising, are highly relevant to accounting. A feminist approach takes an overtly feminist position, informed by feminist theory and feminist methodology, to challenge and potentially overturn the underlying structures and social constructions of gender (Haynes, 2008, 2017) in the interests of greater equity, emancipation and social justice.

Feminism takes several forms dependent on theoretical perspective, historical, social or geo-political context. Women may have different understandings and experiences of gender inequality in varying political and geographical contexts, which require different solutions. Types of feminism may depend on the interaction of gender with other inequalities, or on the intersection of various characteristics or identities that may experience oppression. It may also depend on women's experiences of the outcomes of feminism and how they perceive its relevance to them. For example, feminists who have been relatively successful in organisations, careers or public life may have different understandings of priorities within feminism in relation to feminists who are fighting for political representation and access to education or against sexual violence. However, what many feminisms have in common is an understanding that gender inequality and oppression is not a natural given state, but has structural and cultural causes, necessitating a political and social rather than individual response.

The purpose of this book is not to promote one single approach to feminism in approaching an analysis and critique of accounting practice and the profession. Instead, I intend to illustrate and exemplify the rich potential of feminist theory in advancing knowledge of, and praxis within, accounting, in the hope that it will inspire other scholars to apply and extend feminist theory to accounting. Theories addressed include early, liberal, Marxist, Black, intersectional, postcolonial, decolonial, transnational, Islamic and Muslim, poststructuralist and eco feminisms. Each is discussed with relevance to literature and application to accounting. I draw extensively from my own research where applicable. The book thereby offers new insights into the relevance of feminist theorisations of accounting and their contribution.

Feminist accounting as an emancipatory project

The rationale for a feminist approach to accounting relates to the need to address the continued perpetuation of inequalities imbued in, or created by, accounting, both as a profession and as a practice. Hence, the title of this book *Accounting for Feminism: Exploring Emancipation for Profession and Practice*. One might ask who is being emancipated and from whom or what? However, as bell hooks[2] (2000, p. 1) puts it, 'feminism is a movement to end sexism, sexist exploitation, and oppression', which remains relevant in contemporary societies and is what emancipation is addressing. Although the struggles of early Western feminists for suffrage and property rights may have been attained, around the world women continue to be disadvantaged in land rights, monetary systems and positions of power. Gendered norms and stereotypes continue to constrain women, and also men and non-binary people, in roles and identities within domestic and workplace settings. Sexism, sexual violence and exploitation persist in all societies. My argument is that a feminist approach can support a deeper understanding of accounting's relationship with all of these issues, especially underpinned by globalisation and modern political capitalism (Haynes, 2017, 2024). Rather than considering accounting, and the organisations it serves, as gender-neutral, it can be considered as deeply partisan. Feminist accounting can be argued to be an emancipatory project supporting enhanced knowledge of the impact of accounting.

At the macro level of global capitalism, we need to know more about the effects of the interaction of accounting and gender on the global stage, especially when accounting is used by nation states and societies as a tool to perpetuate power and control, and where consumers are far removed from the impacts of their actions on other peoples around the globe. We still know very little, for example, about the role of accounting in supporting war and human rights abuses at the state and societal level, or the impact of accounting in perpetuating climate change and unsustainable business practices as they interlink with gender. At the meso level of the multinational professional services firm, particularly given the globalised expansion of such firms, there is a need for further research on the construction of gender and its effects, through career structures and policies, gendered histories, identities, embodiments and behaviours, in a variety of global contexts. At the micro level of the individual, we also need to know more about the subjective experience of women and men subjected to gendered social constructions and constraints (Haynes, 2017).

Feminist accounting research can elucidate these issues but also has substantial emancipatory potential, especially when laced with feminist intent to overturn power structures, promote a more equitable society and enable individual freedoms. A pre-existing body of work in accounting argues for its emancipatory potential (Gallhofer & Haslam, 2003, 2019). Accounting has been argued to emancipate through communicative practices (Gallhofer & Haslam, 2003), by rendering accountability (Bebbington et al., 2020), giving an alternative to traditional forms of account or narratives of accounting (Laine & Vinnari, 2017) or supporting activist practices and direct action (Martinez & Himick, 2023) or by expanding meanings of gender within the profession. However, feminist approaches to emancipatory accounting research draw attention to the possibilities of resistance, transformation and overcoming of power and control, which have detrimental gendered effects, in the interests of equity to all (Haynes, 2008; Lehman, 2019; Rumens, 2016; Tanima, Brown, & Dillard, 2020). This book will address the emancipatory potential of feminist accounting research, to overcome the inequities embedded in the use of accounting practices and within the accounting profession.

Overview of chapter content

The remaining chapters of the book are structured as follows:

Chapter 2: Early feminisms, accounting technologies and the professionalisation of accounting

This chapter expands on and contextualises the two key areas of focus in this text, to which feminist theories are applied: accounting as a technology and the accounting profession. It traces the history of early feminisms and their influence on the development of the accounting profession. The nature of accounting technologies is discussed together with critique of their gendered logic. The chapter addresses the professionalisation of accounting, drawing attention to the dearth of women admitted to the profession in its early years because of practices of social closure. Parallels with the women's rights movements for suffrage and economic rights of the late nineteenth and early twentieth century are explored, and the chapter gives accounts of some early women pioneers who gained entry to the profession. Both Western and non-Western histories of accounting are addressed. Finally, the chapter addresses wider structural and institutional male dominance over women in the form of patriarchy, which continues to have relevance to accounting.

Chapter 3: Liberal feminism and equal opportunities within the accounting profession

Chapter 3 addresses the influence and relevance of liberal feminism in understanding and challenging the position of women within the accounting profession, already established as a masculine context during its professionalisation process. Liberal feminism, sometimes referred to as mainstream feminism, emphasises equality legislation and equal opportunities. It represents a means of reform from within the moderate structures of society and within the organisation, although corporate liberal feminism tends to focus on the White, middle-class woman. While greater access to equal opportunities in relation to men has advanced women's career prospects, women continue to face multiple challenges and multiple burdens of responsibilities across domestic and working settings. Despite liberal feminism's rebuttal of essentialism, the socialisation processes, cultures, structures and career hierarchies of professional work remain highly gendered. For accountants who are mothers, liberal feminist ideals have failed to dismantle the problematic expectations placed on women in society and in the workplace, resulting in individualised responses and constrained choices rather than cultural shifts. Yet liberal feminism has become the dominant and acceptable face of feminism in the professional domain by reflecting a neoliberal, individualised responsibility under capitalist conditions, which deflects attention away from more radical feminist transformation.

Chapter 4: Feminist difference and resistance: class, race and intersectionality within accounting

Chapter 4 focuses on feminist resistance to embedded structures of inequality and forms of oppression, based on theories of difference, primarily arising from gender, class and race. arguing for more radical approaches to feminism which shift away from an individualised responsibility for representation to a more collective response, based on shared oppressions and shared solidarities of resistance. The chapter illustrates continuing and significant issues within the accounting profession arising from assumptions based on class or race. The role of accounting technologies in perpetuating the current constitution of gender, class and race is examined. The chapter evaluates how Marxist feminism, Bourdieusian feminist research that addresses class and

Black feminism can highlight embedded and institutionalised inequalities, and support resistance to existing structures of privilege, within accounting. Intersectional approaches supporting a more integrated analysis of structures and power relations are also addressed. However, the final call is for much more expansive feminist research that addresses racial injustice, in relation to the accounting profession and the use of accounting technologies, where there is currently much less focus than on gender injustice.

Chapter 5: Postcolonial, decolonial, transnational, Islamic and Muslim feminisms in accounting

This chapter addresses the relevance of non-Western feminisms – postcolonial, decolonial, transnational, Islamic and Muslim – to accounting. Accounting technologies have been implicated in the pursuit of colonialism and repressive regimes, resulting in the exploitation and dehumanisation of workers, indentured labourers or Indigenous Peoples. After some theoretical explanations of postcolonialism and decolonisation, the chapter explores their relevance to accounting technologies and the accounting profession. Despite the interaction of gender, race and class in the positioning of women as subaltern, oppressed and 'othered' under postcoloniality, and the repressive role of capitalism in exploiting women, feminist approaches to understanding these issues in the accounting context are underutilised. This chapter argues that transnational feminism, with its anti-racist and anti-capitalist stance, is highly relevant to accounting and provides six applications of transnational feminism to accounting. It also addresses the potential for the application of Islamic and Muslim feminisms to accounting, enabling women's agency within the interaction of religion, politics, society and gender. The chapter culminates with a discussion of the role of feminisms 'from the margins' in promoting social justice in accounting and outlines a set of principles for decolonising accounting research practice.

Chapter 6: Influences of poststructuralist feminisms on identities, sexualities and embodiment in accounting

This chapter evaluates the potential influence of poststructuralist feminism in accounting and its applications. It addresses performativity and 'doing gender'; identities and subjectivities in accounting; 'queer' and non-heteronormative identities in accounting; implications for bodies and embodiment, language and discourse. The chapter argues for the emancipatory potential of poststructuralist feminism and makes suggestions for five areas of its further potential in relation to accounting: revealing hierarchies of power in accounting technologies and the profession; combining these with feminist intent to change material realities of women's lives; extending deconstructive analysis to other areas such as race, class and dis/ability; expanding work on sexualities to include including non-cis accountants; and focusing on the inherent potential violence of discourses in constituting and symbolising cultural values.

Chapter 7: Ecofeminisms, ethics of care and accounting as *care*

This chapter addresses two key areas of feminist theory, ecofeminism and the ethics of care, and evaluates them in relation to accounting. Ecofeminism addresses the link between the oppression of women and the degradation and exploitation of the environment. The ethics of care concept focuses on relations of care, empathy and connectedness, rather than ethics of justice and rights, which underpin human and organisational behaviours. Although early ecofeminism and early ethics of care theory have been accused of being essentialist, the chapter re-evaluates their recent feminist credentials in addressing climate change, unsustainability and the need for a more relational, caring, global society. It discusses their interaction with accounting under capitalist neoliberalism and within social and environmental accounting, illustrating the potential for the integration of the two concepts. Finally, it concludes with a proposal for a new conceptualisation of accounting underpinned by these integrated feminist theories; to move from an accounting *for* care to accounting *as* care.

Chapter 8: Integrating feminist theories, methodologies and activism: the emancipatory potential of feminist accounting

The final chapter summarises the issues addressed by multiple feminisms, their theoretical position, application to accounting and their emancipatory potential, referring to accounting technologies and the accounting profession. It argues for the continuing relevance of feminism to accounting research and practice. The chapter then addresses some key principles of feminist methodologies for accounting research, such as reflexivity and ethics of care, together with notions of doing and writing feminist research differently. The central role of feminist activism in all its diverse forms for and within accounting is discussed. Feminist theories blend with feminist methodologies and feminist activism to form an integrative approach to feminist accounting which has emancipatory potential in generating new knowledge, practice and outcomes. Feminist accounting drives political intent to enhance solidarities between women, and between men, women and non-binary genders, to produce a more just world.

Conclusion

In summary, accounting is a powerful force in contemporary societies, arising from its construct as a calculative practice and technology of measurement and reporting, and from its status and role as a profession. Within contemporary global capitalism, it is implicated in creating and perpetuating inequalities related to gender. The role of a feminist approach to accounting is to highlight and overcome those gendered inequalities embedded in power relations, structures and cultures. Feminist theories can support an understanding of accounting in context, with attention to differences and solidarities between women, and with feminist emancipatory intent to promote freedom from sexism and oppression. This book, therefore, explores a wide range of feminist theories and their emancipatory implications for accounting.

Notes

1 Three sections in this chapter are reprinted from Haynes, K. (2017). Accounting as gendering and gendered: A review of 25 years of critical accounting research on gender. *Critical Perspectives on Accounting*, *43*, 110–124, with permission from Elsevier under license 5750290778424.
2 I use bell hooks' own spelling of her name in lower case letters, which she used to focus attention to her feminist message rather than herself.

References

Alawattage, C., Arjaliès, D.-L., Barrett, M., Bernard, J., Casa Nova, S. P. d. C., Cho, C. H., Cooper, C., Denedo, M., D'Astros, C. D., Evans, R., Ejiogu, A., Frieden, L., Ghio, A., McGuigan, N., Luo, Y., Pimentel, E., Powell, L., Pérez, P. A. N., Quattrone, P., Romi, A. M., Smyth, S., Sopt, J., & Sorola, M. (2021). Opening accounting: A manifesto. *Accounting Forum*, *45*(3), 227–246. https://doi.org/10.1080/01559982.2021.1952685

Anderson-Gough, F., Grey, C., & Robson, K. (2005). 'Helping them to forget..': The organizational embedding of gender relations in public audit firms. *Accounting, Organizations and Society*, *30*(5), 469–490. https://doi.org/10.1016/j.aos.2004.05.003

Bebbington, J., Österblom, H., Crona, B., Jouffray, J.-B., Larrinaga, C., Russell, S., & Scholtens, B. (2020). Accounting and accountability in the Anthropocene. *Accounting, Auditing & Accountability Journal*, *33*(1), 152–177. https://doi.org/10.1108/AAAJ-11-2018-3745

Broadbent, J., & Kirkham, L. (2008). Glass ceilings, glass cliffs or new worlds? *Accounting, Auditing & Accountability Journal*, *21*(4), 465–473. https://doi.org/10.1108/09513570810872888

Bryer, R. A. (2000). The history of accounting and the transition to capitalism in England. Part one: Theory. *Accounting, Organizations and Society*, *25*(2), 131–162. https://doi.org/10.1016/S0361-3682(99)00032-X

Butler, J. (2021, 07 September). We need to rethink the category of woman [Interview]. *The Guardian*. https://www.theguardian.com/lifeandstyle/2021/sep/07/judith-butler-interview-gender?CMP=Share_iOSApp_Other

Carmona, S., & Ezzamel, M. (2007). Accounting and accountability in ancient civilizations: Mesopotamia and ancient Egypt. *Accounting, Auditing & Accountability Journal*, *20*(2), 177–209. https://doi.org/10.1108/09513570710740993

Catchpowle, L., Cooper, C., & Wright, A. (2004). Capitalism, states and ac-counting. *Critical Perspectives on Accounting*, *15*(8), 1037–1058. https://doi.org/10.1016/S1045-2354(02)00214-9

Chiapello, E. (2007). Accounting and the birth of the notion of capitalism. *Critical Perspectives on Accounting*, *18*(3), 263–296. https://doi.org/10.1016/j.cpa.2005.11.012

Dambrin, C., & Lambert, C. (2012). Who is she and who are we? A reflexive journey in research into the rarity of women in the highest ranks of accounting. *Critical Perspectives on Accounting*, *23*(1), 1–16. https://doi.org/10.1016/j.cpa.2011.06.006

Dillard, J. (1991). Accounting as a critical social science. *Accounting, Auditing & Accountability Journal*, *4*(1), 8–28. https://doi.org/10.1108/09513579110143849

Edgley, C., Sharma, N., & Anderson-Gough, F. (2016). Diversity and professionalism in the Big Four firms: Expectation, celebration and weapon in the battle for talent. *Critical Perspectives on Accounting*, *35*, 13–34. https://doi.org/10.1016/j.cpa.2015.05.005

Gallhofer, S. (1998). The silences of mainstream feminist accounting research. *Critical Perspectives on Accounting*, *9*(3), 355–375. https://doi.org/10.1006/cpac.1997.0191

Gallhofer, S., & Haslam, J. (2003). *Accounting and Emancipation – Some Critical Interventions*. London: Routledge.

Gallhofer, S., & Haslam, J. (2019). Some reflections on the construct of emancipatory accounting: Shifting meaning and the possibilities of a new pragmatism. *Critical Perspectives on Accounting*, *63*, 101975. https://doi.org/10.1016/j.cpa.2017.01.004

Garbutt, D. (1984). The significance of ancient Mesopotamia in accounting history. *Accounting Historians Journal*, *11*(1), 83–101.

Guerriero, C., Haines, A., & Pagano, M. (2020). Health and sustainability in post-pandemic economic policies. *Nature Sustainability*, *3*(7), 494–496. https://doi.org/10.1038/s41893-020-0563-0

Hardies, K., & Khalifa, R. (2018). Gender is not "a dummy variable": A discussion of current gender research in accounting. *Qualitative Research in Accounting & Management*, *15*(3), 385–407. https://doi.org/10.1108/QRAM-08-2017-0083

Haynes, K. (2005). *(Sm)othering the Self: An Analysis of the Politics of Identity of Women Accountants in the UK* [Unpublished PhD thesis, University of St Andrews].

Haynes, K. (2008). Moving the gender agenda or stirring chicken's entrails?: Where next for feminist methodologies in accounting? *Accounting, Auditing & Accountability Journal*, *21*(4), 539–555. https://doi.org/10.1108/09513570810872914

Haynes, K. (2012). Body beautiful?: Gender, identity and the body in professional services firms. *Gender, Work & Organization*, *19*(5), 489–507. https://doi.org/10.1111/j.1468-0432.2011.00583.x

Haynes, K. (2017). Accounting as gendering and gendered: A review of 25 years of critical accounting research on gender. *Critical Perspectives on Accounting*, *43*, 110–124. https://doi.org/10.1016/j.cpa.2016.06.004

Haynes, K. (2025). The role of accounting in creating, perpetuating and overcoming inequalities: Going beyond discipline, borders and stasis towards accounting as activism. *Gender, Work & Organization*, *32*(2), 912–928. https://doi.org/10.1111/gwao.13191

Hines, R. D. (1988). Financial accounting: In communicating reality, we construct reality. *Accounting, Organizations and Society*, *13*(3), 251–261. https://doi.org/10.1016/0361-3682(88)90003-7
hooks, b. (2000). *Feminism Is for Everybody: Passionate Politics*. London: Pluto.
IPCC. (2007). *Fourth Assessment Report*. Geneva: WMO/Intergovernmental Panel on Climate Change.
IPCC. (2013). *Fifth Assessment Report*. Geneva: WMO/Intergovernmental Panel on Climate Change.
IPCC. (2023). *Climate Change 2023 – Synthesis Report*. Geneva: Intergovernmental Panel on Climate Change.
Jacobsen, L. E. (1983). Use of knotted string accounting records in old Hawaii and ancient China. *Accounting Historians Journal*, *10*(2), 53–61.
Jones, C., & Slater, J. (2020). The toilet debate: Stalling trans possibilities and defending 'women's protected spaces'. *The Sociological Review*, *68*(4), 834–851. https://doi.org/10.1177/0038026120934697
Kumra, S., & Vinnicombe, S. (2008). A study of the promotion to partner process in a professional services firm: How women are disadvantaged. *British Journal of Management*, *S1*(19), S65–S74. https://doi.org/10.1111/j.1467-8551.2008.00572.x
Laine, M., & Vinnari, E. (2017). The transformative potential of counter accounts: A case study of animal rights activism. *Accounting, Auditing & Accountability Journal*, *30*(7), 1481–1510. https://doi.org/10.1108/AAAJ-12-2015-2324
Lehman, C. R. (2012). We've come a long way! Maybe! Re-imagining gender and accounting. *Accounting, Auditing & Accountability Journal*, *25*(2), 256–294. https://doi.org/10.1108/09513571211198764
Lehman, C. R. (2019). Reflecting on now more than ever: Feminism in accounting. *Critical Perspectives on Accounting*, *65*, 102080. https://doi.org/10.1016/j.cpa.2019.04.001
Martinez, D., & Himick, D. (2023). Accounting in (direct) action: Prefiguring emancipation in accounting research. *Critical Perspectives on Accounting*, *93*, 102476. https://doi.org/10.1016/j.cpa.2022.102476
Meuwissen, R. (2014). The Auditing Profession. In D. Hay, R. W. Knechel, & M. Willekens (Eds.), *The Routledge Companion to Auditing* (pp. 13–22). Abingdon: Routledge.
Morales, J., Gendron, Y., & Guénin-Paracini, H. (2014). State privatization and the unrelenting expansion of neoliberalism: The case of the Greek financial crisis. *Critical Perspectives on Accounting*, *25*(6), 423–445. https://doi.org/10.1016/j.cpa.2013.08.007
Oldroyd, D. (1995). The role of accounting in public expenditure and monetary policy in the first century AD Roman Empire. *Accounting Historians Journal*, *22*(2), 117–129.
Pearce, R., Erikainen, S., & Vincent, B. (2020). TERF wars: An introduction. *The Sociological Review*, *68*(4), 677–698. https://doi.org/10.1177/0038026120934713
Rahman, M., & Jackson, S. (2010). *Gender & Sexuality. Sociological Approaches*. Cambridge: Polity Press.
Rumens, N. (2016). Sexualities and accounting: A queer theory perspective. *Critical Perspectives on Accounting*, *35*, 111–120. https://doi.org/10.1016/j.cpa.2015.05.003
Silva, I. C. B. d., Araújo, E. C. d., Santana, A. D. d . S., Moura, J. W. d. S., Ramalho, M. N. d. A., & Abreu, P. D. d. (2022). Gender violence perpetrated against

trans women. *Revista Brasileira de Enfermagem*, *75*, e20210173. https://doi.org/10.1590/0034-7167-2021-0173
Smith, L. M. (2022). Examining intersecting lives: Luca Pacioli, father of accounting, and his friend, Leonardo da Vinci. *Accounting History*, *27*(3), 343–369. https://doi.org/10.1177/10323732221084988
Stone, W. E. (1969). Antecedents of the accounting profession. *The Accounting Review*, *44*(2), 284–291.
Tanima, F. A., Brown, J., & Dillard, J. (2020). Surfacing the political: Women's empowerment, microfinance, critical dialogic accounting and accountability. *Accounting, Organizations and Society*, *85*, 101141. https://doi.org/10.1016/j.aos.2020.101141
United Nations Department of Economic and Social Affairs. (2010). *The World's Women 2010. Trends and Statistics*. New York. https://desapublications.un.org/publications/worlds-women-2010-trends-and-statistics
United Nations Department of Economic and Social Affairs. (2020). *The World's Women 2020. Trends and Statistics*. https://worlds-women-2020-data-undesa.hub.arcgis.com/
United Nations Department of Economic and Social Affairs. (2022). *The Sustainable Development Goals Report 2022*. https://unstats.un.org/sdgs/report/2022
United Nations Economic Commission for Africa. (2009). *Gender and Climate Change – Women Matter*. https://repository.uneca.org/handle/10855/15345
Walker, S. P. (2005). Accounting in history. *The Accounting Historians Journal*, *32*(2), 233–259.
Westbrook, L. (2023). The matrix of violence: Intersectionality and necropolitics in the murder of transgender people in the United States, 1990–2019. *Gender & Society*, *37*(3), 413–446. https://doi.org/10.1177/08912432231171172
Zanghellini, A. (2020). Philosophical problems with the gender-critical feminist argument against trans inclusion. *SAGE Open, 10*(2). https://doi.org/10.1177/2158244020927029

2

EARLY FEMINISMS, ACCOUNTING TECHNOLOGIES AND THE PROFESSIONALISATION OF ACCOUNTING

Introduction

This chapter expands on and contextualises the two key areas of focus that this book addresses to which the discussion of feminist theories is applied, namely, accounting technologies and the accounting profession. Explaining the development of the accounting profession in its historical and social context helps to understand why the application of feminist theory is necessary to address its contemporary challenges, ingrained structures and cultures, which the remainder of the book addresses. Understanding how accounting technologies can be gendered further addresses how accounting is not a neutral activity.

The chapter traces the history of early feminisms and their influence on the development of the accounting profession. Parallels with the women's rights movements for suffrage and economic rights of the late nineteenth and early twentieth century in Western contexts are explored. This is positioned in the context of the development of professions and the nature of social and professional closure which restricted entry. It draws attention to the dearth of women admitted to the accounting profession in its early years and gives accounts of some early women pioneers who gained entry. However, while many women globally shared similar challenges of gaining entry to the accounting profession, not all histories of women in accounting are shared; hence, I consider the professionalisation of accounting and the position of women accountants in both Western and non-Western contexts. The focus in this chapter is to trace how histories may influence the present, rather than on contemporary challenges and feminist theories which are addressed in subsequent chapters. I argue that the accounting profession, certainly in the West

DOI: 10.4324/9781032636603-2

with some non-Western exceptions, was conceptualised from its inception as a masculine practice. Finally, the chapter addresses wider structural and institutional male dominance over women in the form of patriarchy, which continues to have relevance to accounting.

Early feminisms in Western contexts

To understand the position of women in Western society requires an overview of the seventeenth and eighteenth centuries, and the Enlightenment period or 'Age of Reason'. Although this philosophical movement began in Europe, it was to have global influence on politics, culture and science. The fundamental paradigm of the Enlightenment, influenced by Isaac Newton's *Principia Mathematica* (1687 [2016])[1], was that the world was governed by a few simple, immutable mathematical laws, forming a world based on reason and irrefutable principles; 'anything that did not operate according to reason, was "other", that is secondary, not significant, less than real, not nameable' (Donovan, 2001, p. 19). These notions also dominated in the public and private spheres, so that women, whose primary role was in the domestic world, a world of qualitative judgements and assessments of value rather than mechanistic mathematical laws, were also relegated to the marginal 'other' world of the private sphere. Moreover, women had no legal rights under common law, so that they were subordinated to the father or husband of their family.

Hence, the early origins of modern Western feminism occurred in the nineteenth and early twentieth centuries, when what are sometimes known as the first wave of feminists fought for basic rights under the law, including the right to vote, own property, earn and have their own money. Particular emphasis was placed on women's right to suffrage, stemming from liberal political philosophy which asserted that 'all men should be equal under the law, and that no one should have special privileges or rights' (Lorber, 2012, p. 1). Campaigns for women's suffrage occurred in the late nineteenth century, but many countries in Europe were not to legalise suffrage for women until the early twentieth century, notably after the First World War (1914–1918) in which women had played a significant role in public work and in factories, needed by the absence of men. In the USA, women's suffrage was not granted in every state until 1920, but continued discrimination in voting laws against African American and other minority women persisted for many decades until the civil rights movement of the 1950s–1960s.

Donovan (2001) suggests that there is a tendency among feminists to write off this first wave of nineteenth-century feminism as a relative failure because it did not end women's subordinate status; yet, she argues, suffrage was a considerable success and other legislation began to protect women's property rights and economic status. For women with the means, access to higher levels of education began to be possible, which also opened up opportunities to join the many professions, such as accounting, which began to develop in the late nineteenth century. Nonetheless, women's access to the accounting profession was contested and highly problematic, requiring an understanding of the development of the profession or the professionalisation of accounting.

The professionalisation of accounting

There are two main rationales mooted around the development of traditional professions, such as accounting, medicine and law, in the early twentieth century (Haynes, 2013a). Classic texts suggest the first is as a body offering a public service, advancing the interests of the community and serving the dual goals of altruism towards the public good and a service ethic (Carr-Saunders & Wilson, 1933). Under this model, professionalism is underpinned by an ideology of service (Freidson, 2001), with professional competence affording members of professions public recognition and community sanction through a recognised code of ethics (Greenwood, 1957). However, the second rationale for the development of a profession is that professions are also a form of occupational labour market, where specialist qualifications and technical expertise act as mechanisms of occupational segregation and social closure, used to justify professions' often monopolistic provision of specific services offered (Abbott, 1988; Johnson, 1972). It is this ability of professions to exclude outsiders from the technical and legal basis of their practice, enabling skills to be both materially and symbolically rewarded, that maintains the power of professions (Larson, 1977). The two rationales are not mutually exclusive and modern professions combine an element of both.

The development of a professional body to control, organise and manage membership acts as a controlling mechanism to maintain exclusivity and expertise, meaning that the public service ethic is not sacrificed to loss of status. The accounting profession historically developed in the same way, being controlled and organised in ways similar to other groups deemed as professional in society, largely through self-regulation, stringent qualifications and professional standards of ethics and conduct (Haynes, 2013a). Sociologist Max Weber defined the term 'social closure' to identify the means by which elites maintained their status through monopoly power and restrictive access to power and resources (Weber, 1978). Social closure strategies, or in the case of professions – professional closure strategies – which are the exclusion of inferior outsiders to maintain monopolistic advantages, are based on membership eligibility secured through examinations and articles, and by apparent trust and respectability of members (MacDonald, 1995; O'Regan, 2008; Weber, 1978).

In the case of accounting, professional closure occurred through defence of members' interests from 'outsiders', such as women, the lower educated and the working class (Haynes, 2013a). As a result of these aspects of social closure, admission to the accounting profession for women occurred over many decades of struggle with significant barriers to entry and numerous gender conflicts. However, as admission to professions widens, with, for example, increased numbers of women entering, there is a potential shift from external closure mechanisms, which sanction access to the profession, to internal ones, which regulate career progression and control access to the most prestigious and rewarding positions (Ackroyd & Muzio, 2007). Chapters 3 and 4 offer much more detail on the nature of gender, class and race, which act as closure mechanisms in accounting, together with the feminisms that try to address them.

However, my focus in this chapter is to understand the gendered history of the development of the accounting profession, enabling us to trace the social and cultural norms which have influenced its formation and the gendered nature of accounting technologies and calculative practices. To address this, I next consider the explicit contribution of early feminism to understanding the professionalisation of accounting,

The interaction of feminism and the professionalisation of accounting in Western countries

There are three key areas of significance in the way accounting developed in Western countries in the nineteenth and early twentieth centuries into the modern, globalised phenomenon that it is today, which are addressed in this section. The first is the nature of accounting knowledge, and the logics underpinning accounting technologies, which can be argued as gendered. Accounting was conceptualised from the outset as a masculine practice and can be argued to have a masculinist underpinning logic. Second, this then influences who is a fit and proper person to hold this knowledge and apply it. The third area is the nature of legitimation as an accountant by being a member of a professional accounting body. The three areas interact as only those with suitable accounting knowledge, recognised by accredited qualifications, are enabled to be members of accounting bodies and to call themselves Chartered Accountants, Certified Accountants or Certified Public Accountants (CPAs). Women were considered some of those inferior outsiders who were not fit to join the profession of accounting. Their oppression within accountancy interacted with the development of power and influence in the profession itself and the constitution of its knowledge base in terms of gender (Kirkham, 1992). The profession reflected this through the application of social closure regimes, where knowledge, which could have been acquired by any person with the requisite intelligence, became socially confined to the masculine gender, to men with the requisite resources to undertake appropriate study. Or, as Larson (1977, p. 223) puts it, social closure occurs when 'theoretically inexhaustible knowledge resources become socially finite'. I will address each of these three areas in turn.

Accounting technologies and calculative practices as gendered

The first issue to consider in the development of modern accounting relates to the construction of the nature of accounting knowledge, its calculative practices and accounting technologies. Given accounting's emphasis on calculation and measurement, it is not surprising that it is influenced by mathematical and scientific logic. Some of these logics originated during the European so-called Scientific Revolution of the sixteenth and seventeenth centuries and the emergence of modern science. The philosopher Descartes divided human experience into two realms: the thinking or spiritual substance, *res cogitans* or mind; and the extended substance, *res extensa* or body (Grosz, 1994). This dualistic separation of subject and object has centred value, meaning and knowledge on the mind and largely dismissed the body as mere material, or a container for the mind or soul. The Cartesian view of the rational self separates emotion and passion from the mind by the control of reason, and divides off from the mind all that could be associated with the body through experience, growth or physical change; hence, the body functions according to the laws of nature and the mind has no place in the natural world (Haynes, 2005). In this lies the philosophical basis for understanding knowledge as being unconnected to the weakness of the body. Feminist scholars argue that the mind/body dualism has become representationally aligned and associated with another dualism: that which has been constructed between male and female. The two dualisms have become connected, since masculinity is linked with the mind, with knowledge and science, while femininity is connected with the body with nature and emotions. Herein lies the basis of more modern conceptualisations of masculinity and femininity. Gendered concepts of masculinity incorporate rationality, control, assertion, competitiveness, discipline and domination, whereas concepts of femininity include emotionality, irrationality, weakness and nurturing (Haynes, 2013b).

While these binary positions are reductionist and value-laden, placing them as either privileged or subservient by focusing on one set of attributes at the expense of the other, they persist in social norms and behaviours in our societies. Such binaries were strengthened by the further emphasis on mathematical reasoning during the Enlightenment period of the later seventeenth and eighteenth centuries. As accounting as a construct became solidified into modern forms of accounting, representing calculative practices and accounting technologies, it reflected the hard, supposedly objective, rationality of Western scientific logic. Accounting inherently privileges the masculine over the feminine through how its meanings are fixed in language and conceptualisation (Cooper, 1992). These issues will be developed further in Chapter 7.

In an innovative and influential article, Broadbent (1998) argued that 'accounting logic' is inherently gendered, representing the value set of the 'universal masculine' in binary opposition to the 'universal feminine', acknowledging that accounting as a construct is not value-free. She builds on Hines' (1992) argument that accounting reflects a Yang orientation without a balancing by the Yin, representing masculine and feminine in Oriental cultures. However, Broadbent goes further, with a feminist orientation and drawing from public sector accounting, to illustrate how accounting is pervaded by hard, rational decisions rather than softer values that allow for relationality, emotion and affect. Her concern is to support a more balanced, enabling, emancipatory form of accounting, which acknowledges subjectivities and allows for the inclusion of alternative or multiple value sets, in order to make financial decisions (Broadbent, 1998). Broadbent (1998) raises important and relevant issues about the gendered and singular nature of the values embedded in the 'accounting logic' underpinning conventional accounting (Haynes, 2017). Furthermore, Agyemang (2016) applies Broadbent's (1998) ideas to illustrate how 'accounting logic' leads to decisions based on financial inputs and expected outputs rather than humanitarian values in the treatment of migrants and refugees, with the effect of silencing other alternative logics and values. In Chapter 7, I will address my own argument for the inclusion of alternative values in accounting in making the case for accounting *as* care.

Women and accounting knowledge

By the nineteenth century, when the first accounting professional bodies were attempting to form, the question arises as to who is fit to acquire and utilise accounting knowledge. Gender relations were manifested in social-cultural norms and historical conditions, reflecting the social definitions of men and women of the period. Accounting is perceived as requiring reason, numeracy, logic and rationality to underpin its calculative practices, attributes that had come to be associated with men. Women were perceived as both physically and intellectually unfit for the role of accountant (Lehman, 1992), considered as being weak and emotionally laden or incapable of acquiring the requisite knowledge to be able to practise professional accounting. It is arguable that the very nature of the conceptualisation of accounting knowledge was so entrenched as masculine at the inception of the professionalisation of accounting that it has continued to influence the nature and culture of the contemporary profession, which gives an insight into the difficulties in shifting cultural norms.

Yet during the early professionalisation of accounting, many women were working in roles that could be associated with accounting work both inside and outside the home, including bookkeeping and clerical work, as most accounting work was defined. As accounting began to be professionalised, it began to take on a gendered construction and become value-laden in terms of its knowledge base. This process is powerfully illustrated by Kirkham and Loft's (1993) ground-breaking analysis of census records in England and Wales from 1870 to 1930, in which they illustrate the discursive construction of different types of work deemed suitable for the different sexes. Kirkham and Loft (1993) found that while accountants and clerks (doing bookkeeping) were broadly equivalent in the 1871 census, after the formation of the first professional accounting bodies in the later nineteenth century (e.g. the ICAEW [Institute of Chartered Accountants in England and Wales] in 1880), clerical work began to be transformed from 'men's work' to 'women's work'. The gendered discourse deployed by professional accountants not only served to legitimate the exclusion of women but was part of the process of constructing the meaning of professional accountancy and differentiating it from 'mere' bookkeeping. While professional accountancy might be perceived as rigorous, intellectual and studious, bookkeeping could be positioned as routine, more domestic and less cerebral. Hence, the masculine qualities of rationality, objectivity and competence required within the profession 'contrasted markedly with the image of the weak, dependent, emotional "married" woman of mid-Victorian Britain', which confined women to bookkeeping and clerical functions in late nineteenth-century Britain (Kirkham & Loft, 1993, p. 516). Walker (2003) similarly demonstrates that women tended to practice bookkeeping on the border of public and private domains such as in family businesses, hotels and retailing, reflecting the growth of women in the labour market as a source of cheap or unremunerated accounting labour, in work construed as suitable for women. This situation was mirrored in the USA, where there was substantial growth in the numbers of women in bookkeeping and cashier work, from 2.3% of the total in 1870 to 29.1% in 1900; in contrast by 1910, only 13 women were reported to be CPAs despite licencing opening up in 1896 (Guerra & Huset, 2008).

Women's admission to the accounting profession

The third area of significance in the development of accounting is the admission of women to the professional bodies, as professional status gives them legitimation and authority. Accounting or bookkeeping can be practised by anyone with the requisite knowledge, but to be Chartered or Certified as an accountant is a requirement in order to provide services of financial reporting, advice, audit and assurance to clients, whether in private practice or in a multinational professional services firm. By the early twentieth century, in Western contexts, the experience of the majority of women was of legal, socio-economic, constitutional and cultural opposition to their membership of the accounting profession. This resistance to the inclusion of women in the professionalisation of accounting became an issue of rights between men and women. Cooper K. (2010), for example, traces the campaign by women in Australia in the late nineteenth and early twentieth centuries to gain admission to accounting bodies, in a context where women were perceived as having neither the nature nor the intelligence for the commercial world and where many men feared that their rights would be compromised if women had equal rights to compete in the workforce. Professional and social closure mechanisms became entrenched, requiring significant resistance from aspirant women accountants. During the late nineteenth and early twentieth century in England and Wales, Walker (2011b) finds that the campaign for admission of women to the accounting profession comprised two sites of struggle: first, in civil society, where campaigns for equal rights were emphasised and tactics based on credentials, such as qualifications and experience, were deployed for admission of women; and, second, at the state level using legalistic tactics. Some detail of Walker's (2011b) study is helpful in understanding the nature of women's struggle to achieve the requisite knowledge of and admission to accounting. He explains that although credentialist tactics were successfully resisted by the professional elite, draft legislation in the UK, including the Professional Accountants Bill of 1909 that was intended to uphold the monopolistic power of the profession by admitting only qualified accountants, conceded the admission of women in principle. Until this point, despite the formation of the professional accounting bodies, an individual did not have to be a registered member to practise accounting. Ensuring only qualified accountants could be members of the professional bodies meant that qualified women *had* to be admitted. In practice, attitudes to women's membership of professional accounting bodies remained problematic, despite support from some male advocates (Walker, 2011b), and they were not admitted to the articled positions necessary to become qualified. It was only after legislation was passed, the Sex Disqualification (Removal) Act of 1919, did it become illegal for the profession to bar women from membership.

Campaigns to secure the admission of women to the accountancy profession in the UK drew upon the feminist movement of the nineteenth century that addressed women's rights. As the professionalisation of accounting progressed, it became linked with the wider feminist agendas of women's rights and suffrage. Walker's (2011b) powerful study emphasises the sustained nature of the campaign for the inclusion of women to the profession and its alignment with the campaign for suffrage, illustrated by the activities of Mary Harris Smith, a constitutional suffragist, accountant and auditor, with numerous women's organisations as clients. She was notable for her political activism and support of and involvement in the Parliamentary Committee for Women's Suffrage as well as multiple organisations that supported democratic reform and the advancement of women. Walker (2011b) argues that

Harris Smith actively pursued the admission of women to the accounting profession, drawing on support of contemporary leaders of the women's movement and the proxy support of sympathetic men. She was finally admitted to membership of the ICAEW in May 1920,[2] the first female Chartered Accountant in England and Wales.

Earlier, the militant suffragist Ethel Ayres Purdie had been admitted to the London Association of Accountants[3] in 1909, which did not have a royal charter, hence she could not be called a Chartered Accountant. Her close association with the militant suffragist movement was central to the development of her practice and specialist provision to women (Walker, 2011b), particularly in her campaign for taxation justice and equality for women (Walker, 2011a), and for her activism with the Women's Freedom League (WFL) and its agitation for the admission of women to the accountancy profession (Kirkham & Loft, 1993).

Women's actions in manufacturing, farming and commerce in the First World War had demonstrated their considerable contribution to society, meaning it was difficult to dismiss their capability for entering professions. However, Evans and Rumens' (2022) study of the professionalisation of accountancy in the UK suggests that a temporary increase in numbers of women in accountancy during wartime did not re-gender the accountancy profession as more accepting of femininity and women; indeed, it highlights the emergence and circulation of an ideal professional accountant constructed as male and masculine. Women's assimilation into the accounting profession continued to be problematic, such that in the UK census of 1931, women accountants were still barely visible and constituted less than 0.1% of all accountants (Kirkham & Loft, 1993). In other Western countries the position was similar. For example, although New Zealand was the first country within the Commonwealth to allow women to enter the profession of accountancy on a continuous basis, this did not result in a large number of women becoming professional accountants until the 1990s and the profession remained almost entirely male up to the 1960s (Emery, Hooks, & Stewart, 2002).

Despite this, there are several accounts of pioneering women in the accounting profession whose stories illustrate the struggle of women for admission to the profession in various contexts. For example, Mary Addison Hamilton (1893–1969) was the first woman to achieve membership of one of Australia's recognised professional accounting bodies in the early twentieth century, as early as 1915, achieving a permanent position in the public sector at a time when women were denied such positions (Cooper, 2008). In the USA, Jennie Palen (1891–1990) was one of the first women to become a CPA in New York State in 1923 and to work for a major accounting firm (Spruill & Wootton, 1995). Helen Lowe (1897–1996), one of Scotland's first female Chartered Accountants, established her own practice in 1928 (Jeacle, 2011). Harriett Amies (1907–2006) was the first female Bachelor of Commerce graduate of the University of Melbourne and the first female to qualify for membership of an accounting professional body in 1933 in Victoria, Australia, largely on the basis of tertiary qualifications (Hronsky, Burrows, & Cobbin, 2015). There are potentially many other women who similarly blazed a trail in becoming accountants.

Recognising the achievements of pioneering women overcoming obstacles to secure a professional position in the accounting profession through educational attainment, tenacity and perseverance is an important counterpoint to the majority of male histories of this period. Research on accounting history is prolific, but, as Bisman (2012, p. 7) notes, the 'hegemony of dead white males' is persistent, specifically women's histories are often marginalised or ignored and histories of non-Western contexts are underrepresented in the literature.

The development of the accounting profession in non-Western or developing contexts

Although much of the research on the development of the accounting profession or the experience of women accountants in entering the profession addresses Western contexts, there are also studies in non-Western contexts. I give a great deal more detailed discussion of accounting in non-Western contexts in Chapter 5 in which I address postcolonial, decolonial, transnational, Islamic and Muslim feminisms. Colonisation and accounting are invariably linked, with accounting technologies providing a foundational support for oppressive practices such as slavery (Jensen, Agyemang, & Lehman, 2021) or perpetuating Western influences in postcolonial periods (Hopper et al., 2009). However, in this chapter I am focusing on the historical development of the accounting profession as a masculine practice. Yapa (2022) provides a comprehensive review of the professionalisation of accounting in developing countries, noting the role of colonising countries in influencing its development in their former colonies, the broader influence of professional bodies such as the UK-based ACCA in operating at international levels and the operation of closure mechanisms, discrimination or marginalisation of accountants based on race or religion. However, he does not mention gender at all as a relevant factor in understanding the histories of professionalisation in developing countries. In contrast, Bohorquez and Sánchez (2023) provide an overarching historical review that covers many countries on the patriarchal obstacles affecting women in accounting between the eighteenth and twentieth centuries, as well as the means of entry to accounting which serviced to break stereotypes and gendered roles for women, but with less detail on the process of professionalisation. They are relatively in the minority of addressing accounting history as a feminist issue, also taking account of class perspectives.

Understanding contextual geographical, political, social and cultural issues in the development of the accounting profession enables a more nuanced approach to understanding women's early and current history in the profession. For instance, Rico-Bonilla's (2020) study of women's participation in the accounting history of Colombia, from colonial periods to the mid-twentieth century, charts the role of the Catholic convent in influencing women's roles in managing income and expenditure, as well as their resultant symbolic representation in society as 'office angel', which persisted long into modernity after the opening up of access to higher education in accounting and the expansion of the accounting labour market for women.

Moreover, in countries such as China and Japan, unlike in Western contexts, the state plays a key role in the professionalisation of accounting. In China, the state influenced the development of accounting through laws and regulations instead of the professionalisation process occurring independently (Yee, 2009). Xue and Zan's (2023) oral history research on the development of the profession in China finds that rather than being a professional elite, accountants before and during the Cultural Revolution up to 1976 had low status and professionalisation and certification was suspended. Accountants did not choose accounting as a personal preference but were assigned to the field in the planned economy system, with little choice of educational specialism or job role. In contrast to Western countries, the profession was not perceived as masculine from its inception, with both men and women being assigned accounting as a job (Xue & Zan, 2023). In Japan, Shinoto (2023) illustrates how Western style bookkeeping was introduced into schools, and originally taught to both boys and girls, by the Meiji government in the late nineteenth century. However, it soon became framed as an important part of women's household management, encompassing a critical role in the management of resources which was deemed to support the state (Shinoto, 2023). By the early twentieth century in Japan, in response to industrialisation, women were employed as bookkeepers outside the home, although this reverted to more of a household task after the First World War when the government emphasised the need for rigorous household accounting in response to austerity (Komori, 2007). The Japanese government supported the construction of a patriarchal family system through the notion of household accounting and the operationalisation of gendered roles 'as a social infrastructure to collect funding necessary for the country's business and military development' (Komori, 2007, p. 351).

These examples of the professionalisation of accounting in non-Western contexts give an insight into the need to consider specificities of context, rather than assuming a homogenous approach to professional development. It also reflects a need to consider accounts of the marginalised, specifically women, rather than the privileged, as what counts as valid or important history can also be gendered. However, historical accounts are not always feminist in approach, which can limit their scope in identifying and addressing wider ideological and structural problems facing women and focusing on those perceived as exceptional rather than the majority of women. Historians of accounting are afforded plenty of material in interrogating the development of the accounting profession, its gendered character and the largely ignored experiences of women, but according to Walker (2008) feminist and gender theorisations of accounting history remain the exception. He is right that few studies advance an explicitly feminist account of accounting history, with some notable exceptions such as Lehman's (1992) *herstory* of accounting, which contextualises the accounting profession's practices for restricting women's access within feminist theories of conflict that address cultural, educational, economic and political struggles and social practices.

In order to address ingrained structures and power relations in accounting, which are addressed through a feminist lens in the remainder of this text, I now turn to the concept of patriarchy and its application to professions such as accounting.

Patriarchy

To address feminist resistance to structural oppression and inequality, it is essential to examine patriarchy. The concept derives literally from the dominance of the father figure in familial relations, involving an ideology of protection and benevolence as well as power and control (Ortner, 2020). This concept of male dominance underpins gender inequality, as, under patriarchy, women are considered to be essentially inferior to men and therefore subject to control and domination or discrimination and exclusion.

Lerner's (1986) definition captures the duality of familial and societal dominance within patriarchy:

> The manifestation and institutionalization of male dominance over women and children in the family and the extension of male dominance over women in society in general. It implies that men hold power in all the important institutions of society and that women are deprived of access to such power. It does *not* imply that women are either totally powerless or totally deprived of rights, influence, and resources.
>
> *(Lerner, 1986, p. 239)*

While familial patriarchy may seem irrelevant to many contemporary women who exercise autonomy within relationships, it is important to recognise that not all women have such relative freedom of choice, and many are still subjected to domination and control through intimate partner violence and coercion. Despite high levels of female autonomy, the reinforcement or playing out of gender norms through gendered divisions of labour, expectations of gender roles and gender socialisation within family structures continue to persist as less overt examples of patriarchy. Beyond the family, in wider society, feminists conceptualise patriarchy as a 'system of power' (Ortner, 2020, p. 63) or 'an invisible but all pervasive, political and socially constructed system of male and masculinist domination' (Grant, 2016, p. 229).

Millett's (1971) classic radical feminist definition of patriarchy encapsulates the systematised and deeply embedded institutionalisation of patriarchy in the structures of everyday life:

> Our society… is a patriarchy. The fact is evident at once if one recalls that the military, industry, technology, universities, science, political offices, finances – in short, every avenue of power within the society, including the coercive force of the police, is entirely in male hands.
>
> *(Millett, 1971, p. 25)*

Although over 50 years old, this observation on patriarchy resonates with contemporary societies, where global data show that women continue to be underrepresented at all levels of political decision-making worldwide and that achieving gender parity in political life is a distant goal (Inter-Parliamentary Union [IPU] & UN Women, 2023). Leadership of organisations (Hideg & Shen, 2019; Knights, 2021) and other professions such as law (Batton & Wright, 2019) remain resolutely masculine and male-dominated. The military is endemically patriarchal in its organising (Ortner, 2022) and police forces are associated with misogyny, racism and homophobia (Baroness Casey of Blackstock, 2023), as well as involvement in the appalling sexual abuse and degradation of women (Hall, 2023; McNabb & Puddister,2022). The Covid-19 pandemic brought a surge in patriarchal repression and assault on women's rights around the globe (Brysk, 2023) and illustrated that women continue to bear the brunt of domestic care and organising (Boncori, 2020; McKinsey & Co., 2020).

Patriarchal relations may be based on essentialist characteristics (male over female) but they also relate to a hierarchy of relations between a patriarchal figure of some sort and other men (as, for example, found in the military or police or a charismatic CEO of a company); followed by homosocial relations between men themselves (where there may be a hierarchy between men which reflects race or class); and finally between men and women (Ortner, 2020). Although women may be at the bottom of this patriarchal hierarchy, the effects of its domination are much wider, as patriarchy intertwines with other structures of power aligned with racism, class or sexuality. It also reflects domination of non-binary, gay, queer or trans people due to its underlying heteronormativity and cis-gendered focus. The concept of heteropatriarchy reflects the structures, practices and processes through which binary gender relations, masculinity and heterosexuality become normalised and privileged within society (Catignani & Basham, 2021). Hence, patriarchy can be onsidered from a gendered perspective, but also where it is associated with White supremacy, normative heterosexuality and normative ablebodiedness (Ortner, 2022). In this sense, patriarchy and heteropatriarchy intertwine with structures of power under capitalism, colonialism, racism or imperialism, which are embedded in labour markets, economic relations and state systems (Ortner, 2020; Peterson, 2018; Walby, 1989).

This institutionalisation of male dominance also occurs in professions. Earlier in this chapter, I explored how the profession of accounting developed and how accounting technologies are imbued with gendered logics. Through the lens of feminist theorisation, these phenomena can be explained as underpinned by patriarchy. Indeed:

> the development of accounting and capitalism was made possible by the prior emergence of patriarchal societies, with their inherent violence, and this facilitated the normalisation of concepts such as accumulation, private property, exploitation, and domination.
>
> *(Gilbert, Everett, & Casa Nova, 2024, p. 2)*

Patriarchy entails 'a subconscious acquiescence and ritualized reproduction of the primacy of all things male and masculinist taking place both at the level of structure and of daily life' (Grant, 2016, p. 230). This is why Crompton (1987) observed that the male practices for excluding women from the higher levels of professions are so deeply ingrained they hardly give rise to comment, being regarded as 'natural'. Patriarchal institutions such as 'the all-male club, the single–sex prestige schools, the old-boy network', operated on the golf course or in the bar, represent the systematic exclusion of women from the acquisition of knowledge and networks necessary for development and progression within professional firms (Crompton, 1987, p. 108). They also reflect wider exclusions based often on class but also potentially race or sexuality. Under patriarchal conditions, organisations reproduce themselves through pressure for social conformity as lower-level managers are directed to present similar social, political and business behaviours to the majority in upper-level management, most of whom are men with a 'masculine ethic' (Kanter, 1977, p. 22), who consciously, or unconsciously, benefit from patriarchy. The deeply ingrained and embedded privileges and masculine domination arising from patriarchy and capitalism reflect why the liberal feminist reforms applied to the accounting profession, which I discuss next in Chapter 3, have failed to fully address and change professional culture.

Conclusion

This chapter has contextualised further the two key issues which are addressed in this book through the lens of various feminisms, namely, accounting technologies and the accounting profession. It examined early forms of feminism, linking the development of the accounting profession and its gendered nature to the early contemporary feminist movement for women's suffrage and economic independence of the late nineteenth and early twentieth centuries, which enables a broader understanding of the position of the professional accountant within society and the nature of accounting's gendered calculative practices. Although many accounting histories ignore gender and are not feminist in orientation, taking a feminist lens to the understanding of accounting professionalisation illustrates how it was gendered and imbued with power relations from its very inception, through mechanisms such as professional closure. The concept of patriarchy, as the normalisation of structures and power relations of gendered oppression, in society, institutions, organisations and the home, also applied to professions. Early feminisms, concerned with women's rights and suffrage, tended to focus on women with means and education, which was mirrored in the development of the early accounting profession that excluded the working class, ethnic minorities and many other women. These exclusions are addressed through feminist theorisations later in this text. A feminist account has the emancipatory potential to reveal the foundations of exclusion in accounting, its gendered character and the oppression and subordination of women. The next chapter addresses liberal feminism and equal opportunities which were designed to redress these inequalities.

Notes

1 Where the reference is to a text that has been republished from an earlier edition, the first year is the original year of publication and the second is the year of publication of the text which I used.
2 A timeline of the history of the ICAEW and other professional accounting bodies is provided at https://www.icaew.com/library/historical-resources/timeline
3 Through a process of several mergers, this body eventually became absorbed into what is now the ACCA [Association of Chartered Certified Accountants] https://www.icaew.com/library/historical-resources/timeline

References

Abbott, A. (1988). *The System of Professions: An essay on the Division of Expert Labour*. Chicago: Chicago University Press.

Ackroyd, S., & Muzio, D. (2007). The reconstructed professional firm: Explaining change in English legal practices. *Organization Studies*, *28*(5), 729–747. https://doi.org/10.1177/0170840607073077

Agyemang, G. (2016). Perilous Journeys across the Seas: The Accounting Logic in Europe's Agenda for Migration. In *Accounting in Conflict: Globalization, Gender, Race and Class* (Vol. 19, pp. 1–27). Emerald Group Publishing Limited. https://doi.org/10.1108/S1041-706020160000019002

Baroness Casey of Blackstock. (2023). *Final Report. An Independent Review into the Standards of Behaviour and Internal Culture of the Metropolitan Police Service.*

https://www.met.police.uk/police-forces/metropolitan-police/areas/about-us/about-the-met/bcr/baroness-casey-review/
Batton, C., & Wright, E. M. (2019). Patriarchy and the structure of employment in criminal justice: Differences in the experiences of men and women working in the legal profession, corrections, and law enforcement. *Feminist Criminology*, *14*(3), 287–306. https://doi.org/10.1177/1557085118769749
Bisman, J. E. (2012). Surveying the landscape: The first 15 years of Accounting History as an international journal. *Accounting History*, *17*(1), 5–34. https://doi.org/10.1177/1032373211424883
Bohorquez, M. V. U., & Sánchez, I. M. G. (2023). Women in accounting: A historical review of obstacles and drivers on a patriarchal and classist path. *Revista de Contabilidad-Spanish Accounting Review*, *26*(2), 241–254. https://doi.org/10.6018/RCSAR.480221
Boncori, I. (2020). The never-ending shift: A feminist reflection on living and organizing academic lives during the coronavirus pandemic. *Gender, Work & Organization*, *27*(5), 677–682. https://doi.org/10.1111/gwao.12451
Broadbent, J. (1998). The gendered nature of "accounting logic": Pointers to an accounting that encompasses multiple values. *Critical Perspectives on Accounting*, *9*(3), 267–297. https://doi.org/10.1006/cpac.1997.0158
Brysk, A. (2023). Pandemic Patriarchy: The Impact of a Global Health Crisis on Women's Rights. In S. Hertel & C. Buerger (Eds.), *Rights at Stake and the COVID-19 Pandemic* (pp. 168–188). London: Routledge. https://doi.org/10.4324/9781003270195
Carr-Saunders, A. M., & Wilson, P. A. (1933). *The Professions*. Oxford: Clarendon Press.
Catignani, S., & Basham, V. M. (2021). Reproducing the military and heteropatriarchal normal: Army Reserve service as serious leisure. *Security Dialogue*, *52*(2), 99–117. https://doi.org/10.1177/0967010620923969
Cooper, C. (1992). The non and nom of accounting for (M)other nature. *Accounting, Auditing & Accountability Journal*, *5*(3), 16–39. https://doi.org/10.1108/09513579210017361
Cooper, K. (2008). Mary Addison Hamilton, Australia's first lady of numbers. *Accounting History*, *13*(2), 135–161. https://doi.org/10.1177/1032373207088176
Cooper, K. (2010). Accounting by women: Fear, favour and the path to professional recognition for Australian women accountants. *Accounting History*, *15*(3), 309–336. https://doi.org/10.1177/1032373210368422
Crompton, R. (1987). Gender and accountancy: A response to Tinker and Neimark. *Accounting, Organizations and Society*, *12*(1), 103–110. https://doi.org/10.1016/0361-3682(87)90019-5
Donovan, J. (2001). *Feminist Theory: The Intellectual Traditions* (3rd ed.). New York: Continuum.
Emery, M., Hooks, J., & Stewart, R. (2002). Born at the wrong time? An oral history of women professional accountants in New Zealand. *Accounting History*, *7*(2), 7–34. https://doi.org/10.1177/103237320200700202
Evans, C., & Rumens, N. (2022). Gender inequality and the professionalisation of accountancy in the UK from 1870 to the interwar years. *Business History*, *64*(7), 1244–1259. https://doi.org/10.1080/00076791.2020.1763958
Freidson, E. (2001). *Professionalism: The Third Logic*. Cambridge: Polity Press.

Gilbert, C., Everett, J., & Casa Nova, S. P. d. C. (2024). Patriarchy, capitalism, and accounting: A herstory. *Critical Perspectives on Accounting*, *99*, 102733. https://doi.org/10.1016/j.cpa.2024.102733

Grant, J. (2016). Experience. In L. Disch & M. Hawkesworth (Eds.), *The Oxford Handbook of Feminist Theory* (pp. 227–246). Oxford: Oxford University Press. https://doi.org/10.1093/oxfordhb/9780199328581.013.12

Greenwood, E. (1957). Attributes of a profession. *Social Work*, *2*(July), 44–55.

Grosz, E. (1994). *Volatile Bodies: Towards a Corporeal Feminism*. Bloomington: Indiana University Press.

Guerra, B. B., & Huset, M. J. (2008). *AWSCPA History 75 Years*. Chicago, Illinois: American Women's Society of Certified Public Accountants (AWSCPA).

Hall, R. (2023, 14 March). More than 1,500 UK police officers accused of violence against women in six months. *The Guardian*. https://www.theguardian.com/uk-news/2023/mar/14/more-than-1500-uk-police-officers-accused-of-violence-against-women-in-six-months

Haynes, K. (2005). *(Sm)othering the Self: An Analysis of the Politics of Identity of Women Accountants in the UK* [Unpublished PhD thesis, University of St Andrews].

Haynes, K. (2013a). Gender and Diversity Challenges in Professional Services Firms. In K. Haynes & I. Grugulis (Eds.), *Managing Services: Challenges and Innovations* (pp. 66–82). Oxford: Oxford University Press.

Haynes, K. (2013b). Sexuality and sexual symbolism as processes of gendered identity formation: An autoethnography of an accounting firm. *Accounting, Auditing & Accountability Journal*, *26*(3), 374–398. https://doi.org/10.1108/09513571311311865

Haynes, K. (2017). Accounting as gendering and gendered: A review of 25 years of critical accounting research on gender. *Critical Perspectives on Accounting*, *43*, 110–124. https://doi.org/10.1016/j.cpa.2016.06.004

Hideg, I., & Shen, W. (2019). Why still so few? A theoretical model of the role of benevolent sexism and career support in the continued underrepresentation of women in leadership positions. *Journal of Leadership & Organizational Studies*, *26*(3), 287–303. https://doi.org/10.1177/1548051819849006

Hines, R. D. (1992). Accounting: Filling the negative space. *Accounting, Organizations and Society*, *17*(3/4), 313–341. https://doi.org/10.1016/0361-3682(92)90027-P

Hopper, T., Tsamenyi, M., Uddin, S., & Wickramasinghe, D. (2009). Management accounting in less developed countries: What is known and needs knowing. *Accounting, Auditing & Accountability Journal*, *22*(3), 469–514. https://doi.org/10.1108/09513570910945697

Hronsky, J. J., Burrows, G. H., & Cobbin, P. E. (2015). A fine education but no "bluestocking": Harriett Amies, pioneer female accounting professional. *Accounting History*, *20*(2), 118–137. https://doi.org/10.1177/1032373215574032

Inter-Parliamentary Union (IPU), & UN Women. (2023). *Women in Politics: 2023*. https://www.unwomen.org/en/digital-library/publications/2023/03/women-in-politics-map-2023

Jeacle, I. (2011). A practice of her own: Female career success beyond the accounting firm. *Critical Perspectives on Accounting*, *22*(3), 288–303. https://doi.org/10.1016/j.cpa.2010.12.002

Jensen, M. L., Agyemang, G., & Lehman, C. R. (2021). Accountabilities, invisibilities and silences in a Danish slave trading company on the Gold Coast in the early 18th century. *Critical Perspectives on Accounting*, *77*, 102181. https://doi.org/10.1016/j.cpa.2020.102181

Johnson, T. (1972). *Professions and Power*. London: Macmillan.

Kanter, R. (1977). *Men and Women of the Corporation*. New York: Basic Books.

Kirkham, L. (1992). Integrating herstory and history in accountancy. *Accounting, Organizations and Society*, *17*(3/4), 287–297. https://doi.org/10.1016/0361-3682(92)90025-N

Kirkham, L., & Loft, A. (1993). Gender and the construction of the professional accountant. *Accounting, Organizations and Society*, *18*(6), 507–558. https://doi.org/10.1016/0361-3682(93)90002-N

Knights, D. (2021). *Leadership, Gender and Ethics. Embodied Reason in Challenging Masculinities*. Abingdon: Routledge.

Komori, N. (2007). The "hidden" history of accounting in Japan: A historical examination of the relationship between Japanese women and accounting. *Accounting History*, *12*(3), 329–358. https://doi.org/10.1177/1032373207079037

Larson, M. (1977). *The Rise of Professionalism: A Sociological Analysis*. Berkeley: University of California Press.

Lehman, C. R. (1992). 'Herstory' in accounting: The first eighty years. *Accounting, Organizations and Society*, *17*(3–4), 261–285. https://doi.org/10.1016/0361-3682(92)90024-M

Lerner, G. (1986). *The Creation of Patriarchy*. New York: Oxford University Press.

Lorber, J. (2012). *Gender Inequality. Feminist Theories and Politics*. Oxford: Oxford University Press.

MacDonald, K. (1995). *The Sociology of the Professions*. London: Sage.

McKinsey & Co. (2020). *COVID-19 and Gender Equality: Countering the Regressive Effects*. https://www.mckinsey.com/featured-insights/future-of-work/covid-19-and-gender-equality-countering-the-regressive-effects/

McNabb, D., & Puddister, K. (2022). To serve and protect? An empirical study of police-involved sexual assault. *Women & Criminal Justice*, *34*(2), 149–170. https://doi.org/10.1080/08974454.2022.2126744

Millett, K. (1971). *Sexual Politics*. New York: Columbia University Press.

Newton, I. (1687 [2016]). *The Principia: The Authoritative Translation and Guide: Mathematical Principles of Natural Philosophy* (I. B. Cohen & A. Whitman, Trans.). Oakland, CA: University of California Press.

O'Regan, P. (2008). 'Elevating the profession': The Institute of Chartered Accountants in Ireland and the implementation of social closure strategies 1888–1909. *Accounting, Business & Financial History*, *18*(1), 35–59. https://doi.org/10.1080/09585200701824740

Ortner, S. B. (2020). Too Soon for Post-Feminism. The Ongoing Life of Patriarchy in Neo-Liberal America. In T. Oren & A. L. Press (Eds.), *The Routledge Handbook of Contemporary Feminism* (pp. 61–76). Abingdon: Routledge.

Ortner, S. B. (2022). Patriarchy. *Feminist Anthropology*, *3*(2), 307–314. https://doi.org/10.1002/fea2.12081

Peterson, V. S. (2018). Intimacy, informalization and intersecting inequalities: Tracing the linkages. *Labour and Industry*, *28*(2), 130–145. https://doi.org/10.1080/10301763.2018.1448966

Rico-Bonilla, C. O. (2020). Making women visible in the (accounting) history of Colombia. *Accounting History Review*, *30*(2), 207–232. https://doi.org/10.1080/21552851.2020.1763410

Shinoto, R. (2023). Good wives and wise mothers: Establishing the foundations of modern Japan through women's accounting education. *Accounting History*, *28*(3), 442–467. https://doi.org/10.1177/10323732231186219

Spruill, W. G., & Wootton, C. (1995). The struggle of women in accounting: The case of Jennie Palen, pioneer accountant, historian and poet. *Critical Perspectives on Accounting*, *6*(4), 371–389. https://doi.org/10.1006/cpac.1995.1033

Walby, S. (1989). Theorising patriarchy. *Sociology*, *23*(2), 213–234. https://doi.org/10.1177/0038038589023002004

Walker, S. P. (2003). Identifying the woman behind the "Railed-In Desk". *Accounting, Auditing & Accountability Journal*, *16*(4), 606–639. https://doi.org/10.1108/09513570310492326

Walker, S. P. (2008). Accounting histories of women: Beyond recovery? *Accounting, Auditing & Accountability Journal*, *21*(4), 580–610. https://doi.org/10.1108/09513570810872932

Walker, S. P. (2011a). Ethel Ayres Purdie: Critical practitioner and suffragist. *Critical Perspectives on Accounting*, *22*(1), 79–101. https://doi.org/10.1016/j.cpa.2010.09.001

Walker, S. P. (2011b). Professions and patriarchy revisited: Accountancy in England and Wales, 1887–1914. *Accounting History Review*, *21*(2), 185–225. https://doi.org/10.1080/21552851.2011.581840

Weber, M. (1978). *Economy and Society*. Berkeley: University of California Press.

Xue, Q., & Zan, L. (2023). The Chinese accounting profession in the People's Republic: A preliminary understanding from an oral history perspective. *Critical Perspectives on Accounting*, *94*, 102451. https://doi.org/10.1016/j.cpa.2022.102451

Yapa, P. W. S. (2022). Professionalisation of accounting in developing countries: 25 years of research. *Accounting, Auditing & Accountability Journal*, *35*(2), 439–462. https://doi.org/10.1108/AAAJ-04-2018-3455

Yee, H. (2009). The re-emergence of the public accounting profession in China: A hegemonic analysis. *Critical Perspectives on Accounting*, *20*(1), 71–92. http://dx.doi.org/10.1016/j.cpa.2007.03.008

3

LIBERAL FEMINISM AND EQUAL OPPORTUNITIES WITHIN THE ACCOUNTING PROFESSION

Introduction

The women's movements of the 1960s–1980s were influential in campaigning against the lack of equal opportunities given to women, in education, in the home and in their working lives. Following the development of professions and professional bodies in late nineteenth and earlier twentieth centuries, during the second half of the twentieth century the world of professional careers, such as accounting, opened up to women in much greater numbers. While greater access to equal opportunities in relation to men proved a major milestone in advancing women's career prospects, this was not without problems. Women continued to face multiple challenges and multiple burdens of responsibilities across domestic and working settings. The masculine culture of accounting, originating in the inception of modern professions under patriarchal conditions, changed little to accommodate women. This chapter outlines the influence and relevance of liberal feminism to understanding and challenging the position of women within the accounting profession.

Liberal feminism rejects concepts of essentialism between men and women, emphasising the need for equality of opportunity enacted through legislation and organisational policy. In doing so, it condemns discrimination and stands for personal freedom and autonomy. If women are empowered and given the opportunity, the notion is that they can overcome underrepresentation and exercise their progression in society. Liberal feminism represents an individualist sensibility rather than an argument for broader solidarities or collective organising for effective social change (see, for example, Grosser & Moon, 2019; Hughes, 2002; Lorber, 2012).

DOI: 10.4324/9781032636603-3

Liberal feminism is often associated with the period of feminism that came to be termed the 'second wave' of feminism which occurred predominantly in the 1960s–1980s, particularly in the USA, UK and parts of Europe. Yet this form of feminism was not the only feminism associated with this period; others included radical feminism and Marxist feminism amongst others (addressed in Chapter 4). All these different feminisms are not synonymous with this term 'second wave' and differ considerably in their remit and political orientation. I have avoided making too much use of the terms 'waves' of feminism because these are heavily contested and arguably exclusionary. So-called 'second wave' feminism has been critiqued as being far too focused on White, middle-class, usually US or Anglocentric, women, rather than the plethora of women globally and the distinct differences between them, which meant that it did not address the challenges faced by Black or minority ethnic groups or those from more working-class backgrounds. These are valid critiques of these feminisms, although Evans (2021, p. 27) argues that while the mainstream media often portrayed White and middle-class women as the face of women's liberation, feminist activism was simultaneously taking place amongst 'African American, Chicano, American Indian and Asian American movements', suggesting a different yet simultaneous struggle for emancipation.

In this chapter, I argue that liberal feminism, sometimes referred to as mainstream feminism, is the dominant, and even acceptable, form of feminism in the corporate world. With its emphasis on equality legislation and equal opportunities, it represents a means of reform from within the moderate structures of society and within the organisation. The chapter addresses the nature and impact of liberal feminism on the position of women within the accounting profession under neoliberal capitalism. The focus is on the accounting profession itself, rather than accounting as an oppressive or emancipatory technology, which is addressed further in Chapters 4–8.

While this form of liberal feminism within the profession can be said to focus on well-educated middle-class, and predominantly White, women, the accounting profession of the late twentieth century could also be critiqued for predominantly representing White, middle-class privilege. African Americans were actively excluded from full participation in the accounting profession in twentieth-century USA (Hammond & Streeter, 1994). It is only since 2017 that the Financial Reporting Council's annual reports on the state of the profession identify how many professional bodies in the UK have reported that they collect data on race and diversity issues other than gender. Moreover, this reveals only how many bodies collect data, not which bodies or the specific data itself, suggesting that the professional bodies' focus on data on race and other characteristics are in their infancy and have not been a priority. Additionally, only recently have the issues of the diversification of class and calls for more data on socio-economic backgrounds of accountants received attention within the profession (Austin, 2023; ICAEW Insights, 2022b). I address women's difference and the experiences of Black or minority ethnic women and working-class women, as well as intersectionality, in Chapter 4. Furthermore, postcolonial, transnational and Islamic/Muslim feminisms are addressed in Chapter 5. However, this chapter addresses where liberal feminism is relevant to the burgeoning diversity agendas of the professional services firms within accounting as they attempt to improve diversity through further reform initiatives.

After further explanation of the nature of liberal feminism, the chapter evaluates its influence on and potential for overcoming the challenges pertaining to women's careers in accounting. The chapter addresses essentialism, professional socialisation, feminisation and segmentation, stratification and career hierarchies, motherhood and work-life balance, choices and flexible working within the context of the accounting profession.

Liberal feminism and equal opportunities

Many feminist writers (see, for example, Lorber, 2012; Rahman & Jackson, 2010) trace the origins of challenging biological essentialism to the publication of Simone de Beauvoir's *The Second Sex* (de Beauvoir, 1949 [1972]). This argued that men's dominance and women's subordination, as the second sex, were socially, rather than biologically, constructed; hence, de Beauvoir's famous quote that 'One is not born, but rather becomes a woman' (de Beauvoir, 1949 [1972], p. 267). The construction of femininity became reified into an expected form and position for women as the 'Other' (de Beauvoir, 1949 [1972], p. 16), whereby women came to identify themselves through the views and position of the dominant group in society, men:

> The situation of woman is that she – a free and autonomous being like all human creatures – nevertheless finds herself living in a world where men compel her to assume the status of the Other.
>
> *(Simone de Beauvoir, 1949 [1972], p. 29)*

Although some of de Beauvoir's positioning, notably her negative view of women's bodies and insistence on women's complicity with their own oppression, are highly controversial, her argument that femininity and women's subordination to men are social constructs resonates with many feminists (Fraiman, 2019).

The premise of liberal feminism is also that gender is not based on biological essentialism, and therefore men and women are not entirely different. Any difference is caused by different social conditioning, through parenting or education, and cultural socialisation, which creates or perpetuates gendered difference. Inequalities between men and women are also caused by unequal access to opportunities, under the law or in the workplace. Thus, many liberal feminists of the 1960s–1980s worked to address women's social disadvantage in relation to men, particularly in relation to legal rights, political representation, entry into work and professions dominated by men, stratification into lower paid job roles, and inequality of unpaid labour and childcare in domestic settings. Such inequalities are perceived as structural and embedded in social constructs and hence require a structural solution. In this sense, liberal feminism is concerned with undoing the gendered effects of discrimination, ensuring that women have the same opportunities as men and the same rights under the law. It highlights the pervasiveness of discriminatory practices in domestic and organisational settings, working to overcome them. A key concept within liberal feminism and a strategy to overcome difference and discrimination is the notion of equal opportunities. Legislation to ensure equal opportunity in access to education, to outlaw sex discrimination and to ensure equal pay between the sexes was a central tenet in redressing inequality.

However, liberal feminism operates *within* the existing social system and within existing institutional structures, aiming for reform rather than radical overhaul. Hence it is what Lorber (2012) terms as Gender Reform Feminism, one which locates gender inequality in the structures of society rather than an outcome of psychology or individual behaviour. She gives two specific examples of political strategies to reform unequal social structures: first, the use of gender balance models, such as with women on boards, which aim to achieve parity in numbers of women and men in various institutional roles; and, second, the concept of gender mainstreaming, where governmental and organisational policies aim to put gender equality at the core of their decision-making, thereby eradicating any discriminatory effects for either women or men (Lorber, 2012).

Within the workplace, organisational policies and practices, underpinned by the wider legislative changes already in place, aim to promote equal opportunities and parity of treatment for men and women, eliminating discrimination and conscious or unconscious bias. Organisational reform involves voluntary organisational initiatives involving governance arrangements, employee training and adherence to various quality marks on equality, diversity and inclusion (EDI).

Liberal feminism, therefore, particularly in Western societies may have achieved a great deal in terms of supporting women's advancement within educational, domestic and organisational settings. Legislation against structural inequality is an important part of improving opportunity. Yet, our societies, organisations and professions are still a long way from gender equality, and notions of gender binarism strongly persist. Liberal feminism has enabled equal opportunities legislation, institutional and organisational reform, but has not necessarily overturned gendered essentialism, cultures, attitudes and behaviours, nor indeed some of the structural issues which it is designed to address.

In relation to the accounting profession, the dominant feminist position is that of liberalism. While many feminists critique liberal feminism as not representing the wide diversity of women and women's experiences, and not being radical enough in its activism to address change, it has been widely influential in society in addressing equality of opportunity. It is the dominant position within the corporate world. While accounting researchers may critique the profession from numerous perspectives, which are addressed in this text, the profession itself adheres to the prevailing mainstream view that equality of opportunity and internal reform is the means of ensuring professional careers for all accounting professionals. The following sections illustrate the multiple challenges for women in the accounting profession situated within this theoretical paradigm of liberal feminism.

Multiple challenges for women in accounting

From barriers to entry to increasing numbers of women

Chapter 2 explored women's access to the accounting profession during the process of its professionalisation, where a lack of access to admission caused by professional closure processes caused major barriers to entry for women. These were overcome by the persistence of women who were prepared to challenge the structural inequalities of professional membership and access to accounting qualifications during a period of emancipation coinciding with the fight for women's suffrage. This subsequent chapter, following the advent of liberal feminist ideals and legislative change, illustrates the more contemporary position of women in accounting and the multiple challenges they continue to face, albeit on different grounds.

Recent decades have seen significant increases each year in the numbers of women attracted to the accounting professions, and the professional service firms within them.

As Table 3.1 shows, in 2003, females represented only 27% of the worldwide membership of the six members of the Consultative Committee of Accountancy Bodies (CCAB) originating in the UK and Ireland.[1] By 2022, females represented 38% of the worldwide members of the same six bodies with the addition of the Association of International Accountants (AIA) (with 10,699 members in 2022) (Professional Oversight Board for Accountancy, 2023). In 20 years, the overall growth of worldwide members of these bodies had increased from 329,108 to 606,640, an 84.32% rise. Although women still represent only 38% of the total members, their rate of growth over 20 years was 159%, representing their steady influx into the growing profession.

TABLE 3.1 Total members and percentage of female members in accountancy professional bodies worldwide since 2003

Year		*ACCA*	*CIMA*	*CIPFA*	*ICAEW*	*CAI*	*ICAS*	*AIA*	*TOTAL*
2022	Members	243,302	117,183	13,872	166,397	31,683	23,504	10,699	606,640
	Women %	48	36	33	31	43	35	37	38
2021	Members	236,827	116,302	13,991	161,411	30,622	23,252	10,061	592,466
	Women %	48	36	33	30	42	35	37	37
2020	Members	228,771	114,492	13,207	157,812	29,596	23,062	9,541	576,481
	Women %	48	36	33	30	42	35	37	37
2019	Members	223,454	112,617	13,362	154,531	28,479	22,495	8,718	563,656
	Women %	47	36	33	29	42	34	36	37
2018	Members	214,319	110,493	13,358	151,761	27,367	22,028	8,164	547,490
	Women %	47	35	33	29	42	34	36	37
2017	Members	204,336	109,415	13,735	149,298	26,562	21,503	7,166	532,015
	Women %	46	35	32	28	41	34	34	36
2016	Members	193,976	106,095	14,266	147,538	25,496	21,152	6,786	515,309
	Women %	46	35	32	28	41	33	32	35
2015	Members	183,386	102,942	13,640	145,746	24,496	20,709	6,755	497,674
	Women %	46	34	33	28	40	33	30	35
2014	Members	174,227	99,942	13,327	144,167	23,778	20,401	9,250	485,092
	Women %	46	34	32	27	40	33	33	35
2013	Members	165,625	95,925	13,328	142,334	22,828	20,109	8,545	468,694
	Women %	45	33	32	26	39	32	32	35
2012	Members	158,574	91,744	13,541	140,573	21,844	19,739	7,983	453,998
	Women %	45	33	31	26	38	31	30	35
2011	Members	151,283	87,316	13,544	138,464	20,905	19,334	7,300	438,146
	Women %	44	32	31	25	37	31	29	34
2010	Members	144,397	83,487	13,668	136,615	20,010	18,780	7,046	424,003
	Women %	44	31	30	25	36	30	28	34
2009	Members	137,233	79,757	13,790	134,698	18,802	18,278	6,566	409,124
	Women %	43	30	30	24	35	29	26	33
2008	Members	131,398	76,368	13,697	132,411	17,843	17,671	6,064	395,452
	Women %	42	30	29	24	33	28	27	32
2007	Members	122,426	73,356	13,689	130,243	16,691	17,083	5,689	379,177
	Women %	41	29	28	23	31	27	25	31
2006	Members	115,345	70,016	13,661	128,416	15,791	16,710	5,973	365,912
	Women %	40	28	27	23	31	26	24	30
2005	Members	109,588	67,670	13,565	127,826	14,973	16,388	-	350,010
	Women %	40	27	26	22	29	25	-	29
2004	Members	104,613	65,053	13,499	126,597	14,193	15,931	-	339,886
	Women %	39	26	26	21	28	24	-	27
2003	Members	98,293	62,361	13,510	125,643	13,551	15,479	-	329,108
	Women %	38	24	25	21	27	23	-	27

Source: Key Facts and Trends in the Accountancy Profession, Professional Oversight Board for Accountancy, Financial Reporting Council annual reports (analysis author's own).

Table 3.2 shows student members[2] of the six members of the CCAB over a 20-year period. When student members are considered, as seen in Table 3.2, the last two decades have seen virtual parity between male and females registering as students with the professional bodies. However, not all students successfully pass the exam entry requirements, securing a position in an accounting firm or in industry. Moreover, even allowing for a time lapse between student entry as a member of a professional body and accreditation as a full member, the gap between female student entry and female membership is striking. It is clear that professional closure has been significantly eroded over time and women are entering the profession in large numbers, but their lack of retention suggests the existence of a gendered 'leaky pipeline', the phenomenon originally attributed to STEM[3] disciplines but now applied widely, whereby women do not continue on their chosen career path for numerous reasons (Rauhaus & Schuchs Carr, 2022).

As the next sections illustrate, the position of women in the contemporary accounting profession is not straightforward. I therefore evaluate the contribution of liberal feminism to addressing gender neutrality, essentialism and professional socialisation; segregation; stratification and gendered career hierarchies, all of which may contribute to that leaky pipeline.

Gender neutrality, essentialism and professional socialisation

Liberal feminism is based on the premise that socialisation in society causes differences between genders but that there is no essential difference between men and women. Yet, our societies are not yet equal and societal socialisation continues to occur. This is evident in the way children are socialised within the family to take on particular roles and behaviours, to aspire to futures or jobs, which are stereotypically associated with a particular gender. While it is important to acknowledge that behaviours and attitudes to gender and its inculcation are shifting within many societies, progress towards gender neutrality, or a state where gender is irrelevant, is negligible. Institutions and organisations such as the law, the police, or higher education remain gendered even within a rhetoric of gender neutrality (Batton & Wright, 2019; Lo & Lim, 2023; Verge, Ferrer-Fons, & González, 2018). Gender neutrality, Korvajärvi (2011) argues, can be a way of masking gender conflicts, by the non-reflective practice of gender that is intended to create or sustain harmony in organisations but which fails to challenge internalised views or gendered structures.

Socialisation also occurs within the accounting profession where organisations such as accounting firms, like elsewhere in society, are not gender-neutral but draw on and socialise ingrained gendered, behavioural and cultural attributes and attitudes. Professional service firms such as the Big Four[4] are important sites where 'professional identities are mediated, formed

TABLE 3.2 Total students and percentage of female students in accountancy professional bodies worldwide since 2003

Year		*ACCA*	*CIMA*	*CIPFA*	*ICAEW*	*CAI*	*ICAS*	*AIA*	*TOTAL*
2022	Students	437,952	87,573	6,199	36,084	7,776	4,103	5,431	585,118
	Women %	60	47	51	46	48	43	56	50
2021	Students	446,232	93,696	5,842	33,958	7,668	4,154	5,556	597,106
	Women %	60	48	51	46	48	43	56	50
2020	Students	435,088	98,833	5,280	31,656	7,352	3,851	5,381	587,441
	Women %	60	49	49	46	48	42	57	50
2019	Students	445,186	107,049	5,001	30,241	7,011	3,872	5,624	603,984
	Women %	60	49	49	45	48	41	58	50
2018	Students	431,821	117,817	4,749	28,700	6,792	3,488	5,458	598,825
	Women %	58	49	48	44	47	40	58	49
2017	Students	414,562	127,241	4,401	27,866	6,662	3,849	5,365	589,946
	Women %	57	48	48	43	47	44	58	49
2016	Students	405,376	125,380	4,254	25,822	6,334	3,735	5,244	576,145
	Women %	54	47	49	42	48	43	58	49
2015	Students	388,636	125,763	3,779	24,149	6,627	3,366	7,474	559,794
	Women %	54	46	49	42	48	41	61	49
2014	Students	373,668	127,813	3,362	22,001	6,548	3,071	9,064	545,527
	Women %	53	44	48	40	49	41	62	48
2013	Students	365,488	122,394	2,550	20,121	6,440	2,989	9,607	529,589
	Women %	51	44	48	39	49	43	63	49
2012	Students	353,589	112,727	2,336	20,037	6,276	3,083	8,952	507,000
	Women %	49	44	49	38	50	43	63	48
2011	Students	349,325	106,612	2,550	19,073	6,361	3,024	8,431	495,376
	Women %	50	44	48	38	51	44	63	48
2010	Students	357,952	99,264	2,764	17,653	5,771	3,004	7,813	494,221
	Women %	49	44	50	40	52	45	64	49
2009	Students	334,423	92,909	2,978	16,517	6,171	3,119	7,157	463,274
	Women %	50	44	50	41	53	47	63	49
2008	Students	307,457	91,524	2,885	16,165	5,958	3,466	6,514	433,969
	Women %	50	45	48	41	53	47	–	49
2007	Students	276,057	89,272	2,993	14,422	6,653	3,460	–	393,857
	Women %	50	45	49	40	52	46	–	48
2006	Students	252,767	88,256	3,071	13,551	4,525	3,154	–	365,324
	Women %	50	44	50	41	54	46	–	48
2005	Students	260,644	86,565	3,194	10,406	3,880	2,636	–	367,325
	Women %	50	44	49	41	54	44	–	48
2004	Students	240,741	84,868	2,954	8,910	3,167	2,497	–	343,137
	Women %	50	43	50	44	54	44	–	48
2003	Students	221,261	81,590	2,707	8,694	3,000	2,431	–	319,683
	Women %	51	43	49	45	54	43	–	49

Source: Key Facts and Trends in the Accountancy Profession, Professional Oversight Board for Accountancy, Financial Reporting Council annual reports (analysis author's own).

and transformed, and where important conceptions of personal, professional and corporate governance and management are transmitted' (Cooper & Robson, 2006, p. 415). There is a body of literature on professional socialisation in accounting but much of it does not address gender *per se*; rather, it explores how an accountant is moulded into an archetypal professional, such that he or she possesses the technical and behavioural attributes required. For example, early work by Anderson-Gough, Grey, and Robson (1998a) finds that professional and organisational discourses within accounting exercise a significant degree of institutional power in the socialisation of the individual. They find a number of issues are central to this socialisation process, including the client service ethic, which prioritises client needs over personal relationships (Anderson-Gough, Grey, & Robson, 2000), the learning of appropriate professional appearance and conduct (Anderson-Gough, Grey, & Robson, 2002) and the sacrifice of personal time to corporate socialising and study (Anderson-Gough, Grey, & Robson, 2001). In Haynes (2005), I recollected some of my own socialisation as a professional accountant on residential training courses with a large firm where compulsory socialising, stamina and commitment was tested and inculcated, and where poor behaviour – 'boys will be boys' – was acceptable as long as it signified commitment to the firm's needs and potentially hardened one up or built resilience for future client relations. This resonates with the use of cliched discourse through which trainees learn the important of teamwork and the expected 'work hard, play hard' culture that signals their relationship to the firm (Anderson-Gough, Grey, & Robson, 1998b). Recent research, however, indicates that socialisation within accounting firms may be a two-way process where the values and demands of young millennials for more flexibility, variety of work and use of technology are influencing the communication from firms to manage their legitimacy in the eyes of prospective employees in the competition for talented workers (Durocher, Bujaki, & Brouard, 2016). It is less clear whether this two-way process will influence the durability of long working hours and client focus.

However, professional identity as an accountant is not just defined within social interaction between the members of the firm or between firm and client, but within the institutional structures of the profession itself. Given the challenging inception of the profession and exclusionary environment for women as discussed in Chapter 2, it is not surprising that some residual cultural norms persist within professional socialisation even into the twenty-first century. Recruitment and socialisation are a form of social reproduction (Carrington et al., 2023). Socialisation is normative such that those who do not fit the norm are marginalised and excluded. For example, Duff and Ferguson's (2011) study of disabled accountants in the UK accounting industry found that aspects of professional socialisation, such as the image and appearance of staff, the discourse of the client, the rigidity of accounting practice and importance of temporal commitment, impact on their employment. Moreover, socialisation is not gender-neutral, nor are the cultures of the firms. Temporal norms of being available and working long hours affect all accounting professionals, but may disproportionately affect those with family commitments, who are often women as discussed further below. The presentation of the self, in terms of appearance and embodiment, may reflect a masculine archetype, which I address in more detail in Chapter 6. Despite the passing of laws such as the Equality Act, 2010, and subsequent legislation which consolidated and extended UK law on discrimination, the struggles between concepts of merit and diversity in professional evaluation processes remain intractable (Anderson-Gough et al., 2022). Moreover, in a global context, diversity and professionalism in the Big Four is associated with attachment to traditional, commercial, professional discourses and motifs rather than any deep change in professional logics (Edgley, Sharma, & Anderson-Gough, 2016)

Therefore, although the modern global accounting profession is beginning to be much more aware of gender and other characteristics, the continued masculine culture of the accounting profession and firms within it gives rise to some particular outcomes and challenges, which have not been solved by the reforms of liberal feminism.

Gender segregation

As feminisation occurs within professions, they have become increasingly segmented on gendered lines, which can have the effect of marginalising and downgrading women's work (Bolton & Muzio, 2008). Gender segregation occurs where men and women tend to cluster into certain types of work, men working with men and women working with women, in masculinised or feminised sectors. To some degree, this may reflect assumptions about the natural attributes of males and females, for example, men being more suited to abstract and scientific work, and women being more nurturing. Horizontal segregation occurs within organisations, where, as in accounting, it may reflect the structural and cultural positioning of gender.

Accounting tends to have relatively formal spheres of professional work, such as tax, audit and management consultancy, but although women have entered the profession in unprecedented numbers, they are not evenly distributed across those specialisms (Khalifa, 2013). Khalifa's (2013) study found that gendered discourses, around working long hours and socialising with clients and peers, framed the attributes of the different specialisms, causing segregation to occur, where the more 'public' the ideology of a specialism, the more masculine it was perceived to be. Similarly, Joyce and Walker (2015) found that advances towards egalitarianism in professional recruitment of insolvency practitioners were offset by processes of horizontal segregation underpinned by gender essentialism, which pervade the distribution of roles and the allocation of work tasks. Their study suggests that physical essentialism, such as assumption of male strength and ability to deal with conflict or threats of violence, explains why insolvency practice has been traditionally gendered as male. In addition, essentialist assumptions around nurturing, emotionality and interaction with others including the management of work-life balance result in the subfields of corporate and personal insolvency being defined as masculine and feminine, respectively, indicating the continuing potency of gender in everyday professional life (Joyce & Walker, 2015). This also reflects the early divisions of labour during the inception of the profession with women being more focused towards household accounting, as discussed in Chapter 2.

My own study (Haynes, 2005) from the UK found that women often selected specialisms based on their perceptions and experience of areas of professional work where they could combine career and family life more readily. Taxation, for example, was perceived as being more office based, which could be advantageous if they had children, as one of my study participants commented:

> There are a lot of women in tax. I don't quite know why they end up there but definitely you are in the office a lot more if you are in tax, you are not out and about for weeks, months, all over the country, so I suppose if these people have thought ahead that they want kids or have got kids there would be advantages.
>
> *(Haynes, 2005, p. 127)*

The specialism of tax is perceived as more feminised in Western contexts because of a lack of client contact, lack of need for travel and potential for reduced hours (Dambrin & Lambert, 2008; Tiron-Tudor & Faragalla, 2018). However, local context is important as evidenced by Al-Asfahani, Hebson and Bresnen's (2024) study of professional specialisms in professional services firms in Kuwait, where proportionally women were more likely to work in consulting, which is more flexible, than audit, and especially tax, which requires long office hours. Potentially this is because in the Kuwait context there is no legal right to request flexible working. They found that the Covid pandemic offered some lasting shifts in post-Covid working patterns within the audit specialism, where remote working became more acceptable, but entrenched gender norms within tax were soon returned to and reinforced, which meant it remains a highly masculine specialism in that context.

Gender stratification and gendered career hierarchies

Gender stratification, or vertical segregation, occurs where males and females tend to be positioned at different levels of the organisational hierarchy; for example, men dominating senior management positions. Figure 3.1 illustrates women's representation at the upper echelons of senior management in the largest audit firms with Public Interest Entity (PIE)[5] clients. These audit firms tend to represent the Big Four and the larger audit firms, auditing clients in, for example, the FTSE 250 (Professional Oversight Board for Accountancy, 2023). A list of these firms who responded to the Financial Reporting Council's annual survey (Professional Oversight Board for Accountancy, 2023), from which the data in Figure 3.1 derives, is shown in Appendix 1.

Women's representation at the manager level was approximately equal to men's in 2019 and 2020. However, more recently, it has slipped back to just over 40%, perhaps speculatively due to the effects of the Covid pandemic on households, which disproportionately increased the burden of care falling on women and exacerbated existing gender inequalities (McKinsey & Co., 2020; PWC, 2021). The global pandemic of 2020–2022 is known to have been a destabilising event for women auditors, exacerbating tensions in work and home life, and highlighting women's fragile positions in balancing multiple demands (Ghio, Moulang, & Gendron, 2023), perhaps leading some who had reached manager level to take a step back or leave in a potential example of a leaky pipeline. Promotion beyond manager requires a new set of learned practices needed to navigate the complex network of a large firm (Kornberger, Justesen, & Mouritsen, 2011). At the higher levels of director, and especially at the highest level of partner where it is less than 20%, women's representation remains much lower.

Despite the influx of women, the professional hierarchies of accounting remain resolutely gendered, with a preponderance of men at senior levels,

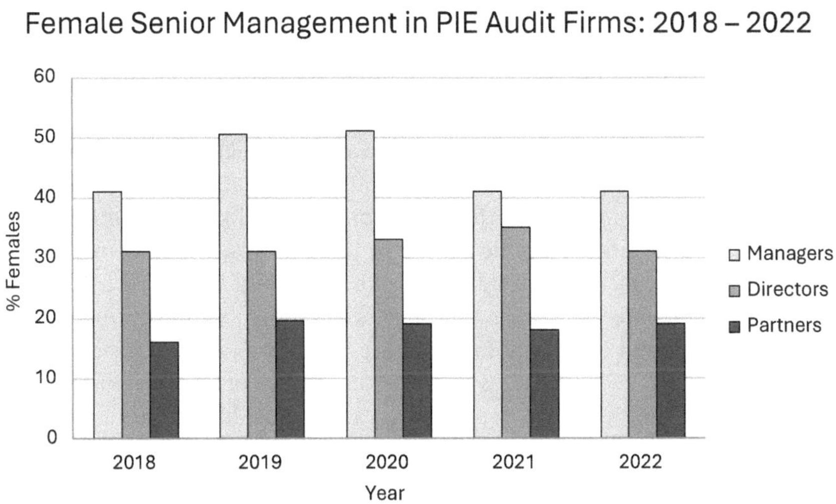

FIGURE 3.1 Female senior management in audit firms with PIE clients 2018–2022.

Source: Key Facts and Trends in the Accountancy Profession, Professional Oversight Board for Accountancy, Financial Reporting Council annual reports 2018-2022 (analysis author's own).

despite the efforts of the accounting firms to target policies towards supporting women (Broadbent & Kirkham, 2008). Dambrin and Lambert's (2012) review of the lack of women in the higher echelons of accounting suggests that until stereotypes are challenged gender inequality will remain. They link the need to perform critical and reflective research on gender with an ongoing struggle to improve the position of women's representation in the accounting profession.

Given the masculine history of the profession, stereotypes may be difficult to shift, one rationale for this being male organisational homo-sociality in the profession, or the tendency for male partners to recruit those from similar backgrounds to themselves (Anderson-Gough, Grey, & Robson, 2005; Kanter, 1977). In addition, the evaluation of career promotion opportunities involves not only technical and perceived managerial skills of leadership and team working, but also integration into norms of temporal commitment and a firm-approved social life, which erodes the boundaries between firm and private time that systematically disadvantage female auditors with family commitments (Anderson-Gough et al., 2005). Therefore, as Anderson-Gough et al. (2005) point out, research on gendering processes in the accounting profession needs combined consideration of both the *formal* mechanisms of organisational structuration, such as recruitment, appraisal and training, and the *informal* processes in terms of cultural norms, values and beliefs that play through how the formal processes are enacted and reproduced.

Career advancement necessitates self-management to demonstrate individual contribution and the need to 'fit' a prevailing model of success within the firm which is arguably a masculine model and hence more problematic for women (Kumra & Vinnicombe, 2008). In addition, the need to develop strong social networks for career advancement is well-established in professional services firms (Anderson-Gough et al., 2005; Grey, 1998). Various strategies are utilised to achieve this development of social networks and social capital. Kokot's (2014) comparative study of Germany and UK finds that in Germany, career advancement is often negotiated through personal relationships of trust in smaller firms and professional relationships that are maintained largely in the public sphere in larger firms, whereas in the UK, head hunters and recruitment agents are an important tool used by women to navigate their careers because such agents can more neutrally point out the skills of women and disrupt homo-sociality. Kumra and Vinnicombe (2010, p. 521) argue that career success necessitates the use of impression management to ensure one is always perceived as 'ambitious, likable and available'; these are key organisational norms that women need to actively accumulate in order to dispel the negative stereotypes of lack of ambition and unavailability for long hours of work that attach to them because of their gender. In a similar vein, Mueller, Carter, and Ross-Smith (2010) find that women's career advancement in Big Four accounting firms is shaped by their real and perceived willingness to be 'bothered to be playing the game' in addition to providing a good client service and participating in the ongoing rationalisation of professional practices. They go further to examine the effects on women in the performance of gender, finding that on the one hand women have to be perceived as ambitious, committed and loyal to the firm and to the notion of performing. On the other hand, they experience disenchantment with existing organisational practices and the reluctant acknowledgement that the reality of their career progression is characterised by a culture of visibility and exposure, the need to network, play politics and be 'playing the game', none of which are gender-neutral.

Moreover, despite the policies and practices of accounting firms to encourage women's career progression, and increasing numbers of women reaching manager status, the higher echelons of the accounting profession, particularly partner level, continue to be dominated by men. The so-called glass ceiling, or the phenomenon of an invisible barrier that prevents women from attaining leadership or higher management positions in organisations (see, for example, Barretto, Ryan, & Schmitt, 2009; Powell & Butterfield, 2015; Wirth, 2001), retains some resonance in professions some 30 years after it became a widely known concept (Adapa, Rindfleish, & Sheridan, 2016; Dambrin & Lambert, 2012; Tiron-Tudor & Faragalla, 2018). A recent study of career progression in accounting found that the continued existence of and perceptions of the existence of a glass ceiling relate to biased-centred, structural and cultural effects, such as bias against females for top-level roles, a lack of mentoring and networking opportunities and a lack of social support from male leaders within the organisation (Cohen et al., 2020). However, the ceiling does not necessarily relate to all women. Some do reach seniority, but this is not necessarily representative of the numbers who enter the profession, suggesting that the leaky pipeline is also occurring.

Hence, despite the influence and importance of liberal feminism in enabling equal (or at least somewhat more equal) opportunities for women in society and in the professions, socialisation is not gender-neutral, discrimination and bias still exist against women and structures and cultures continue to relate to a masculine model of behaviour. Research illustrates that career structures and career hierarchies continue to be gendered in the accounting profession, particularly in the large professional service firms.

Liberal feminism and motherhood

In Western societies, liberal feminism may have achieved a great deal in supporting women's advancement within education, domestic and organisational settings, and may have broken down many barriers to entry into jobs and professions which have been traditionally dominated by men. However, there are particular areas where liberal feminism has not achieved equalities.

One key area is parenting and caring for children, where gender differences and perceptions of essentialism persist in the predominant organisation of child rearing in society, which places the primary responsibility on mothers. A second area is the socialisation of gender through consumerism and the mass media where gender inequalities are embedded into socialisation processes of masculinity and femininity. These two facets interrelate since the way both women and men choose to, or are constrained in, behaving as parents relates to socialised cultures and ingrained structures.

Motherhood is a contested area within feminist theory. Motherhood encapsulates not just the experience of looking after and caring for a child but being ascribed or taking on an identity as mother (Haynes, 2005). It illustrates tension between essentialism, making assumptions that all women share mothering characteristics (whether mothers or not), and non-essentialism, which focuses on differences between women. Liberal feminism, emerging from the 1960s and 1970s, challenged biologically determinist assumptions about women's position within the family and about motherhood in particular (Woodward, 1997). The role of 'mother' itself is a social creation, which ensures that women become mothers and practise motherhood (Campbell, 2003). Some feminist critiques expose the tension between motherhood as an institution of social control over women (Millett, 1971), on the one hand, and as a celebration of essential womanhood, on the other (Rich, 1977). While Rich, for example, believes that a unique and powerful bond exists between mothers and their children that she refers to as an 'invisible strand' (Rich, 1977, p. 36), she is angered by the institution of motherhood which 'ensures that all women shall remain under male control' (Rich, 1977, p. 13). Rich (1977) suggests that motherhood is taken for granted as an identity for women, and as such is constructed within naturalistic discourse as a biological role where being a mother is seen as the distinguishing female characteristic. The dominant view of society remains that it is the primary responsibility of women to mother, and, whether mothers themselves or not women are defined in relation to this role (Letherby, 1994).

Some decades on, young women (and men) continue to be socialised by mass consumerist media that encourages them to take on attributes of an 'ideal' mother, providing healthy, nutritious food, being active and taking care of themselves, putting the needs of others above themselves, all while striving for self-fulfilment outside the home, in an impossible and unattainable position. Meanings about motherhood are produced discursively though practices, ideas and representations of what it is to be a mother, and through knowledge, whether this is expert knowledge or that which informs daily practice and routine. In other words, whether women do or do not become mothers, or mother in ways that veer away from the dominant mothering norms, cultural images of motherhood, and what it is to be a woman, provide coercive prescriptions of gender behaviour that influence most women's lives. All mothers, however, find themselves being subjected to the unsolicited advice, judgements and moral values of others (Haynes, 2005). Moreover, this type of moral judgement on women as mothers also pertains to those who cannot, or choose not to, become mothers.

In recent decades, parenting has become a more shared phenomenon. It is important to acknowledge that not all parents are made up of a father and a mother figure, and may be two mothers, two fathers, single mothers or fathers, another carer or various forms of blended step-parenting family. Generally, fathers are, rightly, more active and engaged with children's day-to-day upbringing and care. More fathers are taking paternity leave and undertaking part-time working to play a fuller and shared role in childcare and such actions are becoming more culturally acceptable (Brooks & Hodkinson, 2021; Fatherhood Institute, 2022). Yet, as was widely found during the Covid-19 pandemic, women's responsibilities for caring roles in the home tended to considerably outweigh men's, resulting in widened gender gaps and deepened gender inequalities (Collins et al., 2020; Ghio et al., 2023; Parlak, Cakiroglu, & Gul, 2021). In addition, economic conditions in many developed countries require two parents to contribute income to the family in order not only to thrive as a family unit but to survive. In the UK context, for example, decades of austerity and lack of state investment, inflationary pressures and high interest rates after the Covid-19 pandemic have resulted in high housing costs and a rising cost of living, which has also exacerbated a shortage of affordable and flexible childcare. Many parenting couples find they both need to work to afford a reasonable standard of living, and the pressure on single parents is inevitably increased. Yet childcare costs in the UK are increasingly rising, paradoxically causing many parents, particularly women, to leave the workforce or reduce hours because being in work is unaffordable (Pregnant Then Screwed, 2023).

Moreover, there are severe inequalities in the way our societies organise paid work, care work and parenting. Professional women and men with skills and qualifications may have the ability to utilise opportunities that provide flexibility for caring, while also accessing other paid labour from nurseries, childminders or other care workers, which are less well remunerated. Other non-professional workers with caring responsibilities may not be able to afford such opportunities and may experience more marginal, precarious or part-time positioning in the workforce. There is a paradox in the continued affirmation of women's commitment to mothering and caring, while such commitments are socially undervalued in many societies.

Motherhood and accounting

The experience of motherhood within the accounting profession demonstrates an area of social life where private, domestic and personal experiences intersect with professional and public-facing working life (Haynes, 2008). My desire to understand my own experiences of working as a professional Chartered Accountant while also bearing and raising children was the impetus behind my own early academic research (Haynes, 2005, 2006). Trying to be both a 'good' mother and a 'professional' accountant with all the connotations of social and moral pressure involved was trying, invoking both pleasure and guilt. Addressing the social, structural and power relations behind personal, organisational and societal responses to becoming a mother while working as a professional accountant became a feminist endeavour. My research on new mothers who had recently returned to professional work as accountants addressed how they made sense of these different social identities and how institutional and cultural factors shaped and restricted the ways in which they experienced their identity, illustrating the process of redefining and transforming the self (Haynes, 2008). The women had clear expectations of themselves as mothers derived from idealised perspectives on motherhood or personal experience of being mothered, but they also subscribed to the liberal feminist ideal that as professional, highly educated women it was the norm that they should want to work and be given the same opportunities as men to do so. However, the interaction of motherhood and professional work was difficult in the long-hours and client-focused culture prevalent within accounting, causing a need to renegotiate not only their professional work and mothering practices but their two identities of mother and accountant. While the women in this study had reached senior manager or partner status, and had received some degree of accommodation by the firms to their new status as mothers, they were still subject to varying degrees of inequality, manifested in the lack of role models, derogatory comments, institutional long-hours culture, lack of understanding of childcare constraints and, in one case, apparent virtual constructive dismissal, demonstrating a continued reproduction of inequalities in the accounting profession (Haynes, 2008).

Motherhood, therefore, is an example of where women are subjected to gendered and gendering processes in both accounting and wider society. They face the societal and cultural norms associated with mothering, and the stereotypical assumptions surrounding mothers in firms, leading to difficult personal choices in relation to working life and juxtapositions between personal and professional identities (Haynes, 2008). Although parenting is acknowledged to be a joint responsibility, mothers retain the primary caregiving role in most countries and economies. Whiting and Wright (2001) find that while the New Zealand accounting profession has a scarcity of female personnel in the top echelons, it accommodates working mothers to a larger extent than in Ireland, but requires mothers to undertake a balancing act between career and family responsibilities that often takes the form of part-time working, whereas male accountants work longer hours and suffer less discrimination. In France, auditor mothers are faced with societal and organisational expectations which conflict, leading to their being excluded or excluding themselves from the group 'who may become partners' (Dambrin & Lambert, 2008). As a result, women who try to manage the dilemmas caused by motherhood attempt to shape their working practices by implementing tactics to adapt their work-life balance, through specialisation or moving into staff positions, leading to individual trajectories that do not conform to the organisational model and thus account for the scarcity of women in the upper management levels in audit firms (Dambrin & Lambert, 2008). It is hard to separate motherhood from other aspects of career advancement (or limitation), as it is clearly intertwined with society's expectations of mothers, particularly working mothers, in terms of stereotyped ability to commit to work and the organisation and the ability to work the required hours. This leads to tensions and choices in managing the interface between 'work' and 'life', as if they are two separate spaces and relations, whereas they are incommensurably intertwined in modern family life and organisation.

Work-life balance, choice and career pathways

Work-life constraints, choices and difficulties occur in many working contexts, for both women and men, but in accounting they are exacerbated by the requirement for long working hours reflecting perceived levels of commitment (Anderson-Gough et al., 2005). Ladva and Andrew's (2014) study of young accounting professionals finds that time budgeting controls and the dominant discourses of 'efficiency' and 'career' form a web of control within accounting firms that sustain this long-hours culture, which is actively produced by junior accountants to secure their identity. Career progression to manager requires the destabilisation of previous identities and the taking on of new practices shaping the identity of managers in the Big Four (Kornberger et al., 2011). It is not surprising, then, that when accountants become mothers their identities go through further transition and transformation, as they negotiate their identity roles (Haynes, 2008), and some of them then decide to work part-time or opt for flexible working. Windsor and Auyeung's (2006) study of career progression in Australia and Singapore finds that dependent children significantly affect the management advancement of mothers, whereas the careers of fathers advance more quickly than their female counterparts, causing the authors to conclude that international accounting firms should have formal policies such as flexible working arrangements and appropriate job designs to encourage more mothers into senior management.

However, the consequences of flexible or part-time working are contested. Gammie and Whiting (2013) suggest that the primary reason women leave professional accountancy firms is to seek more interesting work as opposed to obtaining more flexibility in their working lives, whereas Dambrin and

Lambert (2008, p. 502) conclude that audit firms will not jeopardise the business model by proposing true flexibility to parents, and by failing to allow flexible working 'suffer from resource wastage because they cannot, or will not manage flexibility'. Part-time work in accounting is perceived as career limiting despite the fact that when accountants work part-time they are likely to work longer hours than contracted (Crompton & Lyonette, 2011). Moreover, Kornberger, Carter, and Ross-Smith's (2010) study finds that when Big Four firms initiate flexible working policies with the intended aim of enhancing the progression and retention of professional women at senior levels, the practice is subverted and undermined by three issues: the redefinition of flexibility to mean serving clients flexibly rather than organising family life flexibly, the link between visibility and perceived increased work performance and the notion that flexibility caused an inability to service large client's needs adequately. Such flexible working perceptions also act as a gendering process (Kornberger et al. 2010) as it is women, the object of the policies they are designed to support, who are more likely to be affected negatively by their implementation. The myth of 'choice' in flexible working patterns is exposed as a construct which is subjected to organisational constraints. Women in professional firms do not feel that they have genuine choice in their career development due to structural constraints such as masculine models of success (Kumra, 2010). In fact, Storm and Muhr (2023) equate the work-life balance initiatives taken up by the female accountants in their study as gas-lighting, a process of epistemic control that distorts their realities and persuades them to work less than male counterparts, feminises them and constructs them as fragile, which ultimately directs their careers sideways instead of upwards to partnership level. The end result is that women are often directed into so-called 'mommy tracks' or career pathways that will never result in promotion to partner. Lupu (2012) identifies early voluntary exit from the path to partnership as one of several alternative paths, also including part-time work, narrow specialisation and support jobs, that women may choose to follow in order to balance their professional and family aspirations, which lack the legitimacy of 'approved' routes and derail women's careers in accounting firms. It is also worth noting that aside from women's careers being affected by perceptions and constraints of motherhood, they are also more likely than men to be other forms of carers (Seedat & Rondon, 2021), such as for older or sick relatives, which has similar effects.

The accounting profession reflects some wider societal norms about the role and position of women and men in society; but it also shapes and influences that society through the employment of large numbers of professionals in increasingly powerful global firms. Women's career and work-lifestyle choices are limited by structural constraints, both organisational and societal. In a postfeminist climate, where there is a pervasive belief that equalities have been met and feminism is no longer relevant (McRobbie, 2004, 2009), especially amongst young professionals (Kelan, 2014), there is all the more need to explore the subtle inequalities inherent in global employment practices, where despite the recognition that in some cases individual needs may be met, structural issues remain. For example, women may exercise 'choice' in flexible or part-time working, especially related temporally to raising children, but if they want to return to full-time work or progress their career they are still subjected to stereotyping, gender pay gaps, gendered hierarchies and discrimination. A more politically informed feminist perspective is therefore still relevant to identify and understand gendered power relations in accounting, and also to understand where 'choice' is constituted by social relations. It is also important to relate the institutions of accounting to other societal and cultural regimes such as the economy, where employment patterns have become more precarious, and family, whereby traditional heterosexual, two-parent, permanent family structures have shifted in significance.

Problematising liberal feminism and accounting

Liberal feminism has made an important contribution to enabling access for women to areas traditionally perceived as men's spheres within employment. The professions, including accounting, are a key example where barriers to entry have been largely removed and theoretically the profession is open to people of any gender. The focus of liberal feminism on equality of opportunity and organisational reform makes it the dominant model in addressing gender equality in professions such as accounting. Its reformist, individualist and mainstream approach appeals to corporate agendas under free-market neoliberalism, where individual responsibility is uppermost. However, despite entry structures being ostensibly equal, organisational cultures, career structures and hierarchies persist in being gendered. A further complicating and contributory factor in the gendering of career structures is whether women have, or are perceived potentially to have, children. Although liberal feminism argues against essentialism, and that parenting is a social rather than biological phenomenon, societal and organisational expectations continue to assume that women have the primary responsibility for childcare, resulting in increased intensity of physical and emotion work. Women also tend to disproportionally experience the 'second shift' of employment and domestic caring responsibilities. There are therefore several problems with liberal feminism, which leave some challenges intact.

First, although liberal feminism ostensibly eschews essentialism, it still tends to privilege a masculine binary position by adopting some of the positions derived from post-Enlightenment thought (as discussed in Chapter 2) as the prevailing norm. Hence, characteristics such as rationality, competitiveness and stamina, which are privileged in Western masculinity, tend to represent the required attributes for success in business or professional careers.

Within the accounting profession, for example, and particularly within the global professional services firms, socialisation continues to reference a masculine model of career, where typically success requires long working hours, availability to clients, the possibility of travel in some sectors, generation of billable hours and hence profits, and a perception of commitment.

Second, the emphasis on structural reforms can place the responsibility for career success back on the individual. Professional services firms have responded to continued inequalities with equality and diversity initiatives designed to enable women to complete on equal terms with men or to work on different terms on alternative career paths. However, there is a risk that such initiatives result in sidelining women or result in initiatives to 'fix the women', without shifting or overturning the underlying gendered cultures. Ashley and Empson (2016), for example, find that the business case for diversity has made a limited contribution to transformational change in accountancy firms because it is based on the retention of talent, when instead perceived competitive advantage and career progression depend on an extended commitment to work. Moreover, as these liberal feminist reforms tend to work on an individualistic, competitive basis, it puts the onus of achieving professional 'success' back on to women rather than challenging underlying gendered assumptions. Women are encouraged to network harder, be more assertive or be more confident to progress their careers.

Third, there are some unanticipated outcomes of liberal feminism for women in organisational and professional fields such as accounting. The focus on overcoming the barriers and structures which create the glass-ceiling effect and inhibit women's careers assumes a model where everyone aspires to working at the higher echelons. Women, and indeed men, who try to work in a countercultural way or take up an alternative identification or position can be perceived as problematic, a 'failure' or an outsider. Given the normative pressures on women to achieve success in career and family life, while bearing the brunt of care work, even those who do achieve 'success' in the conventional sense of career and family life may experience crippling self-doubt, guilt and imposter syndrome. The performance of gender in a constrained environment such as accounting causes considerable tensions in identity formation and execution (Haynes, 2006, 2008, 2011).

Lastly, liberal feminism fails to reflect several areas of human experience, especially in the way in which it has been embedded in the corporate environment. It has tended to ignore differences between women, in women's subjectivities, in women's embodiment or in women's class or race. As the mainstream, dominant feminism it actually reflects the position of White, middle-class women rather than working-class or Black and minority ethnic women. In the way in which liberal feminism is applied to professions, it reflects a normative identity of a professional as White, middle-class and likely to be male, with their counterpoint being a White, middle-class female. Liberal feminism tends not to address race and other characteristics. It can also be critiqued as heteronormative as it does not address the rights and experiences of non-heterosexual, non-binary or non-cis people. Feminisms which address these issues, within the context of accounting, are addressed in subsequent chapters.

Conclusion

This chapter has addressed the influence of liberal feminism on the position of women in the accounting profession. While equal opportunities legislation and structural reform have been influential in supporting access to higher education, the workplace and indeed professional work, where barriers to entry may have been overcome, there are still significant challenges for women in the accounting context. Despite liberal feminism's rebuttal of essentialism, the socialisation processes, cultures, structures and career hierarchies of professional work remain gendered. For accountants who are mothers, liberal feminist ideals have failed to dismantle the problematic expectations placed on women in society and in the workplace, resulting in individualised responses and constrained choices rather than cultural shifts. Yet liberal feminism has become the dominant and acceptable face of feminism in the professional domain by reflecting a neoliberal, individualised responsibility under capitalist conditions, which deflects attention away from more radical feminist transformation.

Notes

1 The profession in the UK and Republic of Ireland is largely represented by the six members of the CCAB which comprises: the Institute of Chartered Accountants in England and Wales (ICAEW); the Institute of Chartered Accountants of Scotland (ICAS); Chartered Accountants Ireland (CAI); the Association of Chartered Certified Accountants (ACCA); the Chartered Institute of Management Accountants (CIMA) and the Chartered Institute of Public Finance and Accountancy (CIPFA).

2 Students are those who are registered as a student member of a professional body and training for their qualifications before admission to membership, not necessarily university students of accounting and/or finance. An undergraduate degree in accounting, or even a degree at all, is not a prerequisite for entry into the profession, as each professional body runs its own set of qualifications.

3 Science, Technology, Engineering and Medicine (STEM).

4 'The Big Four' refers to the largest global accounting firms, which are PricewaterhouseCoopers (PwC), Ernst & Young (EY), Klynveld Peat Marwick Goerdeler (KPMG) and Deloitte. They offer numerous professional services including audit, accounting, management consulting, tax, risk management and advisory functions.

5 Public Interest Entity – currently defined as large firms whose shares are traded on a UK regulated market, or a credit institution, or an insurer. However, the definition is set to be expanded under proposed legislative changes and the UK government's audit reform agenda.

ICAEW Insights. (2022a, 27 July). *The new definition of PIE*. ICAEW. Retrieved 30 October 2023 from https://www.icaew.com/insights/viewpoints-on-the-news/2022/jul-2022/the-new-definition-of-pie

References

Adapa, S., Rindfleish, J., & Sheridan, A. (2016). 'Doing gender' in a regional context: Explaining women's absence from senior roles in regional accounting firms in Australia. *Critical Perspectives on Accounting*, *35*, 100–110. https://doi.org/10.1016/j.cpa.2015.05.004

Al-Asfahani, L., Hebson, G., & Bresnen, M. (2024). Reinforced or disrupted ideal worker norms in the pandemic? Analyzing the gendered impact of the pandemic on professional specialisms in a professional services firm in Kuwait. *Gender, Work & Organization*, *31*(2), 644–665. https://doi.org/10.1111/gwao.12932

Anderson-Gough, F., Edgley, C., Robson, K., & Sharma, N. (2022). Organizational responses to multiple logics: Diversity, identity and the professional service firm. *Accounting, Organizations and Society*, 101336. https://doi.org/10.1016/j.aos.2022.101336

Anderson-Gough, F., Grey, C., & Robson, K. (1998a). *Making Up Accountants: The Organisational and Professional Socialisation of Trainee Chartered Accountants*. Farnham, Surrey: Ashgate Publishing Company.

Anderson-Gough, F., Grey, C., & Robson, K. (1998b). 'Work Hard, Play Hard': An analysis of cliché in two accountancy practices. *Organization*, *5*(4), 565–592. https://doi.org/10.1177/135050849854007

Anderson-Gough, F., Grey, C., & Robson, K. (2000). In the name of the client: The service ethic in two professional service firms. *Human Relations*, *53*(9), 1151–1174. https://doi.org/10.1177/0018726700539003

Anderson-Gough, F., Grey, C., & Robson, K. (2001). 'Tests of Time': Organisational time reckoning and the making of accountants in two multi-national accounting firms. *Accounting, Organizations and Society*, *26*(2), 99–122. https://doi.org/10.1016/S0361-3682(00)00019-2

Anderson-Gough, F., Grey, C., & Robson, K. (2002). Accounting professionals and the accounting profession: Linking conduct and context. *Accounting and Business Research*, *32*(1), 41–56. https://doi.org/10.1080/00014788.2002.9728953

Anderson-Gough, F., Grey, C., & Robson, K. (2005). 'Helping them to forget..': The organizational embedding of gender relations in public audit firms. *Accounting, Organizations and Society*, *30*(5), 469–490. https://doi.org/10.1016/j.aos.2004.05.003

Ashley, L., & Empson, L. (2016). Convenient fictions and inconvenient truths: Dilemmas of diversity at three leading accountancy firms. *Critical Perspectives on Accounting*, *35*, 76–87. https://doi.org/10.1016/j.cpa.2015.05.002

Austin, M. (2023). Class prevents young people from accountancy jobs. *Accountancy Daily*. https://www.accountancydaily.co/class-prevents-young-people-accountancy-jobs

Barretto, M., Ryan, M. K., & Schmitt, M. T. (Eds.) (2009). *The Glass Ceiling in the 21st Century: Understanding Barriers to Gender Equality*. Washington: American Psychological Association.

Batton, C., & Wright, E. M. (2019). Patriarchy and the structure of employment in criminal justice: Differences in the experiences of men and women working in the legal profession, corrections, and law enforcement. *Feminist Criminology*, *14*(3), 287–306. https://doi.org/10.1177/1557085118769749

Bolton, S., & Muzio, D. (2008). The paradoxical process of feminization in the professions: The case of established, aspiring and semi-professions. *Work, Employment and Society*, *22*(2), 281–299. https://doi.org/10.1177/0950017008089105

Broadbent, J., & Kirkham, L. (2008). Glass ceilings, glass cliffs or new worlds? *Accounting, Auditing & Accountability Journal*, *21*(4), 465–473. https://doi.org/10.1108/09513570810872888
Brooks, R., & Hodkinson, P. (2021). *Sharing Care. Equal and Primary Carer Fathers and Early Years Parenting*. Bristol: Bristol University Press.
Campbell, A. (2003). Cutting Out Motherhood: Childfree Sterilised Women. In S. Earle & G. Letherby (Eds.), *Gender, Identity and Reproduction* (pp. 191–204). New York: Macmillan.
Carrington, T., Johansson-Berg, T., Johed, G., & Öhman, P. (2023). The Average Professional: On the Selection and Socialisation of Auditors. In J. Marton, F. Nilsson, & P. Öhman (Eds.), *Auditing Transformation: Regulation, Digitalisation and Sustainability* (pp. 275–293). Abingdon: Routledge.
Cohen, J. R., Dalton, D. W., Holder-Webb, L. L., & McMillan, J. J. (2020). An analysis of glass ceiling perceptions in the accounting profession. *Journal of Business Ethics*, *164*(1), 17–38. https://doi.org/10.1007/s10551-018-4054-4
Collins, C., Landivar, L. C., Ruppanner, L., & Scarborough, W. J. (2020). COVID-19 and the gender gap in work hours. *Gender, Work & Organization*, *28*(S1), 101–112. https://doi.org/10.1111/gwao.12506
Cooper, D. J., & Robson, K. (2006). Accounting, professional and regulation: Locating the sites of professionalization. *Accounting, Organizations and Society*, *21*, 415–444. https://doi.org/10.1016/j.aos.2006.03.003
Crompton, R., & Lyonette, C. (2011). Women's career success and work–life adaptations in the accountancy and medical professions in Britain. Gender, Work and Organization, 18(2), 231–254. http://dx.doi.org/10.1111/j.1468-0432.2009.00511.x
Dambrin, C., & Lambert, C. (2008). Mothering or auditing? The case of two Big Four in France. *Accounting, Auditing & Accountability Journal*, *21*(4), 474–506. https://doi.org/10.1108/09513570810872897
Dambrin, C., & Lambert, C. (2012). Who is she and who are we? A reflexive journey in research into the rarity of women in the highest ranks of accounting. *Critical Perspectives on Accounting*, *23*(1), 1–16. https://doi.org/10.1016/j.cpa.2011.06.006
de Beauvoir, S. (1949/1972). *The Second Sex*. London: Penguin.
Duff, A., & Ferguson, J. (2011). Disability and the socialization of accounting professionals. *Critical Perspectives on Accounting*, *22*(4), 351–364. https://doi.org/10.1016/j.cpa.2010.12.009
Durocher, S., Bujaki, M., & Brouard, F. (2016). Attracting Millennials: Legitimacy management and bottom-up socialization processes within accounting firms. *Critical Perspectives on Accounting*, *39*, 1–24. https://doi.org/10.1016/j.cpa.2016.02.002
Edgley, C., Sharma, N., & Anderson-Gough, F. (2016). Diversity and professionalism in the Big Four firms: Expectation, celebration and weapon in the battle for talent. *Critical Perspectives on Accounting*, *35*, 13–34. https://doi.org/10.1016/j.cpa.2015.05.005
Evans, S. M. (2021). Women's Liberation. Seeing the Revolution Clearly. In C. R. McCann, S.-k. Kim, & E. Ergun (Eds.), *Feminist Theory Reader. Local and Global Perspectives* (5th ed., pp. 26–31). New York and London: Routledge.
Fatherhood Institute. (2022). *Closing the Gap: UK Working Fathers' and Mothers' Use of Time 2014–22*. https://www.fatherhoodinstitute.org/2022/closing-the-gap-uk-fathers-doing-18-more-childcare-since-pre-pandemic/
Fraiman, S. (2019). Everyday Life Studies and Feminism. In T. Oren & A. L. Press (Eds.), *The Routledge Handbook of Contemporary Feminism* (pp. 113–126). London and New York: Routledge.

Gammie, E., & Whiting, R. (2013). Women accountants: Is the grass greener outside the profession? *British Accounting Review*, *45*(2), 83–98. https://doi.org/10.1016/j.bar.2013.03.005

Ghio, A., Moulang, C., & Gendron, Y. (2023). Always feeling behind: Women auditors' experiences during COVID-19. *Auditing*, *42*(3), 137–154. https://doi.org/10.2308/AJPT-2021-139

Grey, C. (1998). On being a professional in a Big 6 firm. *Accounting, Organizations and Society*, *23*(5/6), 569–587. https://doi.org/10.1016/S0361-3682(97)00003-2

Grosser, K., & Moon, J. (2019). CSR and feminist Organization Studies: Towards an integrated theorization for the analysis of gender issues. *Journal of Business Ethics*, *155*(2), 321–342. https://doi.org/10.1007/s10551-017-3510-x

Hammond, T., & Streeter, D. (1994). Overcoming barriers: Early African-American certified public accountants. *Accounting, Organizations and Society*, *19*(3), 271–288. https://doi.org/10.1016/0361-3682(94)90035-3

Haynes, K. (2005). *(Sm)othering the Self: An Analysis of the Politics of Identity of Women Accountants in the UK* [Unpublished PhD thesis, University of St Andrews].

Haynes, K. (2006). Linking narrative and identity construction: Using autobiography in accounting research. *Critical Perspectives on Accounting*, *17*(4), 399–418. https://doi.org/10.1016/j.cpa.2004.08.005

Haynes, K. (2008). Transforming identities: Accounting professionals and the transition to motherhood. *Critical Perspectives on Accounting*, *19*(5), 620–642. https://doi.org/10.1016/j.cpa.2006.10.003

Haynes, K. (2011). Tensions in (re)presenting the self in reflexive autoethnographical research. *Qualitative Research in Organizations and Management*, *6*(2), 134–149. https://doi.org/10.1108/17465641111159125

Hughes, C. (2002). *Key Concepts in Feminist Theory and Research*. London: Sage.

ICAEW Insights. (2022a, 27 July). *The New Definition of PIE*. ICAEW. Retrieved 30 October 2023 from https://www.icaew.com/insights/viewpoints-on-the-news/2022/jul-2022/the-new-definition-of-pie

ICAEW Insights. (2022b). *Socioeconomic Taskforce Calls Out Working Class Bias*. London. https://www.icaew.com/insights/viewpoints-on-the-news/2022/nov-2022/socioeconomic-taskforce-calls-out-working-class-bias

Joyce, Y., & Walker, S. P. (2015). Gender essentialism and occupational segregation in insolvency practice. *Accounting, Organizations and Society*, *40*(0), 41–60. https://dx. doi.org/10.1016/j.aos.2014.12.001

Kanter, R. (1977). *Men and Women of the Corporation*. New York: Basic Books.

Kelan, E. K. (2014). From biological clocks to unspeakable inequalities: The intersectional positioning of young professionals. *British Journal of Management*, *25*(4), 790–804. https://doi.org/10.1111/1467-8551.12062

Khalifa, R. (2013). Intra-professional hierarchies: The gendering of accounting specialisms in UK accountancy. *Accounting, Auditing & Accountability Journal*, *26*(8), 1212–1245. https://doi.org/10.1108/AAAJ-05-2013-1358

Kokot, P. (2014). Structures and relationships: Women partners' careers in Germany and the UK. *Accounting, Auditing & Accountability Journal*, 27(1), 48–72. https://doi.org/10.1108/AAAJ-04-2013-1321

Kornberger, M., Carter, C., & Ross-Smith, A. (2010). Changing gender domination in a Big Four accounting firm: Flexibility, performance and client service in practice

Accounting, Organizations and Society, *35*(8), 775–791. https://doi.org/10.1016/j.aos.2010.09.005

Kornberger, M., Justesen, L., & Mouritsen, J. (2011). 'When you make manager, we put a big mountain in front of you': An ethnography of managers in a Big 4 accounting firm. *Accounting, Organizations and Society*, *36*(8), 514–533. https://doi.org/10.1016/j.aos.2011.07.007

Korvajärvi, P. (2011). Practicing Gender Neutrality in Organization. In E. Jeanes, D. Knights, & P. Yancey Martin (Eds.), *Handbook of Gender, Work and Organization* (1st ed. pp. 231–244). Chichester: Wiley.

Kumra, S. (2010). Exploring career "choices" of work-centred women in a professional service firm. *Gender in Management: An International Journal*, *25*(3), 227–243. https://doi.org/10.1108/17542411011036428

Kumra, S., & Vinnicombe, S. (2008). A study of the promotion to partner process in a professional services firm: How women are disadvantaged. *British Journal of Management*, *S1*(19), S65- S74. https://doi.org/10.1111/j.1467-8551.2008.00572.x

Kumra, S., & Vinnicombe, S. (2010). Impressing for success: A gendered analysis of a key social capital accumulation strategy. *Gender, Work & Organization*, *17*(5), 521–546. https://doi.org/10.1111/j.1468-0432.2010.00521.x

Ladva, P., & Andrew, J. (2014). Weaving a web of control: "The Promise of Opportunity" and work-life balance in multinational accounting firms. *Accounting, Auditing & Accountability Journal*, *27*(4), 634–654. https://doi.org/10.1108/AAAJ-02-2012-00955

Letherby, G. (1994). Mother or not, mother or what? Problems of definition and identity. *Women's Studies International Forum*, *17*, 525–532. https://doi.org/10.1016/0277-5395(94)00038-7

Lo, J., & Lim, A. (2023). Sexism without sexists: Gender-blind frames in police work. *Gender, Work & Organization*, *30*(6), 1885–1902. https://doi.org/10.1111/gwao.13020

Lorber, J. (2012). *Gender Inequality. Feminist Theories and Politics*. Oxford: Oxford University Press.

Lupu, I. (2012). Approved routes and alternative paths: The construction of women's careers in large accounting firms. Evidence from the French Big Four. *Critical Perspectives on Accounting*, *23*(4–5), 351–369. https://doi.org/10.1016/j.cpa.2012.01.003

McKinsey & Co. (2020). *COVID-19 and Gender Equality: Countering the Regressive Effects*. https://www.mckinsey.com/featured-insights/future-of-work/covid-19-and-gender-equality-countering-the-regressive-effects/

McRobbie, A. (2004). Post-feminism and popular culture. *Feminist Media Studies*, *4*(3), 255–264. https://doi.org/10.1080/1468077042000309937

McRobbie, A. (2009). *The Aftermath of Feminism: Gender, Culture and Social Change*. Los Angeles and London: Sage.

Millett, K. (1971). *Sexual Politics*. London: Rupert Hart-Davis.

Mueller, F., Carter, C., & Ross-Smith, A. (2010). Making sense of career in a Big Four accounting firm. *Current Sociology*, *59*(4), 551–567. https://doi.org/10.1177/0011392111402734

Parlak, S., Cakiroglu, O. C., & Gul, F. O. (2021). Gender roles during COVID-19 pandemic: The experiences of Turkish female academics. *Gender, Work & Organization*, *28*(S2), 461–483. https://doi.org/10.1111/gwao.12655

Powell, G. N., & Butterfield, D. A. (2015). The glass ceiling: What have we learned 20 years on? *Journal of Organizational Effectiveness: People and Performance*, *2*(4), 306–326. https://doi.org/10.1108/JOEPP-09-2015-0032
Pregnant Then Screwed. (2023). *The '£50k parent penalty'*. https://pregnantthenscrewed.com/the-50k-parent-penalty-one-in-five-parents-in-households-earning-under-50k-leave-the-workforce-due-to-childcare-costs/
Professional Oversight Board for Accountancy. (2023). *Key Facts and Trends in the Accounting Profession*. London: Financial Reporting Council. https://www.frc.org.uk/library/supervision/professional-bodies-supervision/key-facts-and-trends-in-the-accountancy-profession/
PWC. (2021). *COVID-19 Is Reversing the Important Gains Made over the Last Decade for Women in the Workforce – PwC Women in Work Index*. https://www.pwc.com/gx/en/news-room/press-releases/2021/women-in-work-index-2021.html
Rahman, M., & Jackson, S. (2010). *Gender & Sexuality. Sociological Approaches*. Cambridge: Polity Press.
Rauhaus, B. M., & Schuchs Carr, I. A. (2022). Chapter 25: The Leaky Pipeline: Gender and Public Administration Professional Education. In P. M. Shields & N. M. Elias (Eds.), *Handbook on Gender and Public Administration*. Cheltenham: Edward Elgar Publishing. https://doi.org/10.4337/9781789904734.00035
Rich, A. (1977). *Of Woman Born: Motherhood as Experience and Institution*. London: Virago.
Seedat, S., & Rondon, M. (2021). Women's wellbeing and the burden of unpaid work. *BMJ*, *374*, n1972. https://doi.org/10.1136/bmj.n1972
Storm, K. I. L., & Muhr, S. L. (2023). Work-life balance as gaslighting: Exploring repressive care in female accountants' careers. *Critical Perspectives on Accounting*, *95*, 102484. https://doi.org/10.1016/j.cpa.2022.102484
Tiron-Tudor, A., & Faragalla, W. A. (2018). Women career paths in accounting organizations: Big4 scenario. *Administrative Sciences*, *8*(4), 62. https://doi.org/10.3390/admsci8040062
Verge, T., Ferrer-Fons, M., & González, M. J. (2018). Resistance to mainstreaming gender into the higher education curriculum. *European Journal of Women's Studies*, *25*(1), 86–101. https://doi.org/10.1177/1350506816688237
Whiting, R., & Wright, C. (2001). Explaining gender inequity in the New Zealand accounting profession. *British Accounting Review*, *33*(2), 191–222. https://doi.org/10.1006/bare.2001.0161
Windsor, C., & Auyeung, P. (2006). The effect of gender and dependent children on professional accountants' career progression. *Critical Perspectives on Accounting*, *17*(6), 828–844. https://doi.org/10.1016/j.cpa.2004.11.007
Wirth, L. (2001). *Breaking Through the Glass Ceiling: Women in Management*. Geneva: International Labour Office.
Woodward, K. (1997). Motherhood: Identities, Meaning and Myths. In K. Woodward (Ed.), *Identity and Difference* (pp. 240–297). Milton Keynes: Open University.

4

FEMINIST DIFFERENCE AND RESISTANCE

Class, race, and intersectionality within accounting

Introduction

Chapter 4 focuses on feminist resistance to embedded structures of inequality and forms of oppression, based on theories of difference. It addresses the constitution of class and race, and considers their implications for accounting as a profession and as a technology. The role of accounting in perpetuating such structures and power relations is also examined. As was discussed in Chapter 3, liberal feminism provided some important legislation and structural reform which has supported women's opportunities in society, as well as the accounting profession. Yet, it has not yet fully overcome many of the challenges facing women. Moreover, with its origins in Western US and Anglocentrism and focus on White, middle-class women, liberal feminism failed to address the experience of working-class and Black or minority ethnic women. Chapter 4, therefore, considers theories of difference between women, based, for example, on class or race, and more radical approaches to feminism which shift away from an individualised responsibility for representation to a more collective response based on shared oppressions and shared solidarities of resistance.

The chapter addresses radical feminism, and classed-based feminisms, such as Marxist feminism. Although these feminisms came to the fore in the women's movements of the 1960s–1970s, I illustrate that there is still a contemporary relevance to accounting in terms of the nature of masculine dominance, class and social mobility in the accounting profession. I then discuss race and resistance to oppression that originates in Black feminisms, and explore the relevance of these feminisms to the contemporary accounting profession and accounting technologies. Class and race-based feminisms

DOI: 10.4324/9781032636603-4

elucidate the structural dimensions of oppression and inequality which both require and generate resistance from oppressed groups. The concept of intersectionality, which highlights the multiple disadvantages at the intersection of difference (Crenshaw, 1994), such as gender, race and class, is addressed in this chapter as highlighting structural and political resistance. However, I also return briefly to the relevance of intersectionality in the discussion of identity and sexuality in Chapter 6.

I therefore turn to other feminisms, resistance feminisms that go beyond reform, to evaluate their potential for accounting.

Radical feminism

What is often termed 'Radical Feminism' as a movement emerged from the so-called second wave of feminism in the 1960s and 1970s and referred to a particular conceptualisation of feminism, which resists the nature of patriarchy and a male-dominated social order. To resist this gendered ideology, radical feminists confronted the existing social order by overturning its values, arguing for a feminism based on women's perspectives and experiences (Lorber, 2012). As a movement:

> Radical feminism... turned the reality of sexual inequality on its head by arguing for the essential superiority of women's nature, identifying their generally less violent behaviour, historic lack of support for war, and often noted greater selflessness, compassion and concern for the welfare of others.
>
> *(Oren & Press, 2020, p. 3)*

As a result, radical feminism faces critiques about gendered essentialism and whether women and men can be reduced to particular essentialist attributes and characteristics such as these. However, radical feminism goes beyond essentialism between men and women, to incorporate an expanding definition of patriarchy (see Chapter 2) as a global system of subordination of women, legitimised by social institutions such as the church, medicine, science and professions, which enable men to have patriarchal privileges using sexual and emotional exploitation as a key means of control (Lorber, 2012).

Radical feminism highlights the sexual objectification of women and the offences of rape, abuse, sexual harassment and violence against women (Donovan, 2001; Lorber, 2012). Radical feminists also addressed the autonomy of women's bodies, to escape the prospect of continual pregnancy and reproduction, through the right to contraception and abortion (Bordo, 1993; Willis, 1984). Firestone (2015 [1971]) argued that women's oppression lay in childbearing and reproduction and appeared to advocate artificial reproduction. Others critiqued the institution of motherhood while valorising women's role in nurturing and caring as mothers (Rich, 1977). Some US radical feminists, notably MacKinnon (1987) and Dworkin (1981), highlighted the exploitative nature of the pornography industry which they argued encouraged and legitimised violence against women.

The radical feminist movement of the 1970s also included a stream of lesbian feminism which is exemplified in the work of Rich (1980) on *Compulsory Heterosexuality and Lesbian Existence*, arguing for cultural separatism and the essentially different experience of women. Lesbian feminism argues that the dominance of heterosexuality places women in potentially coercive and violent positions, which are rebutted by lesbianism as a sexuality and as a political positioning, separate from male dominance (Lorber, 2012). However, lesbian feminism as a theoretical position has had little or no direct influence on accounting and separatist lesbian feminism has largely been displaced in contemporary society, with awareness of intersecting power differentials with other characteristics, diverse sexualities and queer solidarities, as I discuss further in Chapter 6.

As a movement, radical feminism of the 'second wave' was highly important in focusing on women's experiences of living under patriarchy, raising consciousness with reflection on that experience, and thereby resisting patriarchal norms. Moreover, it highlighted the inherent violence underpinning the sexual, physical, political and economic oppression of women, in their position as women collectively under patriarchy. However, a critique of radical feminism concentrated on its origins in and focus on White American women, its exclusion of Black women and the tendency to ignore differences arising from race, class or ethnicity, which meant that only a particular form and experience of patriarchy was addressed. Lorber (2012) also argues that radical feminism's focus on condemning men's violence and unequal power relations in heterosexual relationships can alienate women in heterosexual relationships with men, and its idealisation of women as mothers can ostracise childfree women. It can also be argued that contemporary forms of trans exclusionary radical feminism emerged from some of the ideas of earlier radical feminism as an offshoot of the theory. The focus by radical feminists on binary essentialism and male violence, requiring the need for sex-segregated spaces for women, seems to underpin some of the main points of the gender-critical argument against trans inclusion and the misidentification of trans women (Hines, 2020; Pearce, Erikainen, & Vincent, 2020; Zanghellini, 2020). It is important to recognise, however, that this position does not wholly represent radical feminism, as a theory or a movement. Research and activism around trans experiences and rights can, and to my mind should, be much more inclusive (McFadden et al., 2024).

Despite these problems with radical feminism, a form of feminism that is radical, as opposed to radical feminism as a social movement of the 'second wave', is still sorely needed, as the challenges raised are global and persistent.

Violence against women is 'devastatingly pervasive' according to the World Health Organisation's (WHO's) (2021) report which estimates that globally about one in three (30%) women worldwide have been subjected to physical and/or sexual intimate partner violence or non-partner sexual violence in their lifetime. Among the factors associated with intimate and sexual violence are ideologies of sexual entitlement and control and weak legal and social sanctions (WHO, 2021), which may be consequences of patriarchy. As well as personal and health issues, this results in significant social and economic consequences, where women may suffer isolation, inability to work, loss of wages, lack of participation in regular activities and limited ability to care for themselves and their children (WHO, 2021). New intimidations and harassment from trolling and rape threats on social media, revenge porn perpetrated by intimate partners and deep-fake pornography supported by AI reflect continuing misogyny in our societies. Women's health is known to be disproportionality affected by the incidence of pandemics due to long-existing inequalities and social disparities (Simba & Ngcobo, 2020). The way that reproduction, abortion and fertility technologies are controlled largely by men under patriarchal conditions echoes Firestone's (2015 [1971]) predictions and remains relevant to contemporary life, especially in ways that biological norms and nuclear families dominate reproductive ideals (Margree, 2018).

A radical feminist approach to accounting

There are critical areas where some of the impetus behind, and insights from, radical feminism can be applied to accounting. A feminism which is radical is needed to tackle grave societal challenges, power relations and inequalities. One such area is sexual and gendered violence which can be addressed at three levels. Sexual violence can be understood as a social and cultural phenomenon, not only as a private phenomenon, that reveals and constructs gender and sexuality in many ways: at the state level through the use of rape as a tool of war or through perpetuation by lack of state intervention and appropriate access to justice; at the community and organisational level, through human trafficking, prostitution and sexual commodification; and at the individual level through experience of rape and domestic violence. These issues may seem to be far removed from the confines and remit of accounting and accounting scholars, and no doubt they are difficult to research. However, as outlined earlier in Chapter 1, accounting is both a tool and a political construct implicated in globalised capitalism through the pursuit of profit which underpins social and economic relationships. One might rightly ask, therefore, what is the role of accounting in perpetuating sexual violence? This relates to both accounting as a calculative practice or technology and accounting as a profession.

There are a small number of studies addressing some of the issues raised by radical feminism in association with the calculative practices of accounting, although few actually identify as feminist. For example, Chwastiak (1999, 2001; Funnell & Chwastiak, 2015) presents a powerful body of work illustrating the role of accounting in supporting war and armed conflict, where, rather than being value-free, accounting controls and resource allocation are used to exercise significant power and legitimise the use of force, even in nuclear terms. Although not explicitly feminist in nature, Chwastiak and Lehman's (2008) article illustrates how accounting is rationalistic and normalises violence. Such a critique of conflict and accounting could be expanded to incorporate more radical feminist perspectives on the institutionalisation of violence and its effects under patriarchal conditions. Similarly, although not explicitly feminist, Killian (2015) offers a damning account of how a lack of formal accounting and accountability in Ireland's infamous Magdalen laundries, where women and girls were incarcerated, devalued their labour and absolved the state of their responsibility. Subordination of stigmatised, 'fallen' or 'weak-minded' women (Killian, 2015) undoubtedly relates to the patriarchal conditions and institutions occurring in the mid-twentieth century.

An exception, which is explicitly feminist, is Lehman's (2016) study of calculative techniques intersecting with gender, race and class in US prisons, where accounting discourse supports the justification for and normalisation of surveillance, dominance and injustice. Structural systems of gender, race and class within state-controlled prisons can be interrogated as manifestations of patriarchy, although Lehman does not frame them as such; rather, she considers the experience of prisoners as an interaction of neoliberalism, race and gender. She argues for counter accounts or shadow accounts as an alternative way of providing narratives of lived experience rather than 'sterile apolitical accounts cast in calculative techniques' (Lehman, 2016, p. 103). Shadow accounts are alternative representations of organisations, industries or governance, which originated in the social and environmental or sustainability accounting field, to provide enhanced transparency about sustainability performance or accountability (Rodrigue & Laine, 2022). Given that accounting measurement renders things governable, and legitimates knowledge and power, shadow accounts can create alternative representations of oppressed social groups, exposing silenced voices and creating new visibilities (Dey, Russell, & Thomson, 2010). As such, they can take a number of forms, such as alternative reporting, use of social media, whistleblowing or activism (Rodrigue & Laine, 2022). Twyford, Tanima, and George (2022, p. 330), for example, argue for the emancipatory potential of what they call 'counter-stories' in retelling the narratives of asylum seekers, to hold to account the Australian government for their policy of offshore immigration detention, and to 'make visible oppressive forces and the hidden practices of racialized social practices and norms'. Feminist shadow accounts could include the role of accounting's calculative practices in any arena where women are oppressed, including trafficking or modern slavery. Shadow accounts could potentially include alternative accounts or narratives of experience and emotion that provide a counterpoint to the normative behaviours and experiences of those subjected to such accounting practices, since shadow accounts intend to be transformative and emancipatory (Rodrigue & Laine, 2022). The #MeToo movement, in which women around the world spoke out about their experiences of sexual assault, acted as a form of shadow account to counter unspoken or hidden violence often perpetrated by powerful people in organisations. The debate reached the environs of accounting by challenging NGO accountability for sexual misconduct (Goncharenko, 2023a) and by influencing perceptions of organisational accountability for sexual wrongdoing and harassment through engagement and activism (Goncharenko, 2023b). Thus, in all the above, there is the potential to bring a more radical feminist account to challenge and resist the use of accounting technologies to uphold gendered, raced, classed or patriarchal norms; to challenge the culture of the accounting profession; and to give shadow accounts of experiences that counter or critique the discourses of equality, which were discussed in Chapter 3.

While radical feminism resists sexual oppression on the grounds of being women under patriarchy, other feminisms address and resist forms of oppression based on labour and class, as well as gender.

Class-based feminisms

Class-based approaches to feminism are often associated with Marxist ideologies and approaches to class. Marxism is concerned with the 'relations of production' between those who own or control the means of production (the capitalists or bourgeoisie) and those who do not (the workers or proletariat), 'giving rise to class relations' (Rahman & Jackson, 2010, p. 67). Marxism tended to 'develop a theory of class oppression rather than gender or sexual oppression' (Rahman & Jackson, 2010, p. 64). In relation to women, the goal of early Marxism was to bring women into public production alongside men which would overturn the sexual division of labour between men and women and within the private and the public domains (Hartmann, 2021). Hence some of the caring work traditionally associated with women, such as care for children, was conceived as more of a public, collective responsibility rather private, with the expected result that once this domestic oppression of women was removed, they could overcome the oppressions of capitalism collectively with men (Alsop, Fitzsimons, & Lennon, 2002).

Unlike liberal feminists who tend to work within the existing social system, feminists who associate with Marxism take a more revolutionary approach to overturning social structures, and consider the subordination of women to be associated with the labour process (Rahman & Jackson, 2010). Marxist feminisms address resistance, by focusing on inequalities associated with capitalist economies that exploit or subordinate workers, but their approach to difference varies depending on the degree of focus on the interaction of class and gender. Marxist feminist Hartmann (2021) gives an overview of the interaction of Marxism and feminism which outlines some of the challenges between the perspectives. She contests the argument of early Marxists that women's liberation required women to become wage earners and join the revolutionary struggle, because it failed to focus on the differences between women's and men's experiences under capitalism and the vested interests that men retained in women's subordination. She argues that society is organised both in capitalist and in patriarchal terms, in which the accumulation of capital underpins and perpetuates the patriarchal social order (Hartmann, 2021). This interaction of patriarchy and the labour process is fundamental to understanding feminist critiques of power relations (Oren & Press, 2020) and the means by which social relations are organised to exploit women's labour in domestic modes of production (Rahman & Jackson, 2010).

Hence, some of the Marxist feminist debates of the 1970s and 1980s focused on the issue of women's difference not only in class terms, but also in the difference in their social position and social identity in relation to men. For example, despite Marxist orientations towards public responsibility by the state for caring for children, the sick, and the elderly, reproduction and maternity remains the primary responsibility of women, meaning that their subjective experience of their own bodies and their experience of themselves as gendered is constructed as different to men (Alsop et al., 2002). In structural analyses of material oppressions, the social relations of *re*production were central to women's oppression, as much as production. This might constitute literal reproduction, through childbirth, or the supporting role of women's unpaid labour and housework, that facilitated their own ability, or more significantly the ability of men, to play a productive role in the labour process. Hence, some Marxist feminists, notably Federici (2021), argued for wages for the domestic labour that effectively contributed to the continuing supply of waged labour under capitalism, in a powerful critique that recognises the reproduction of labour is created within the family as well as markets. Moreover, although tangential to Marxism with its focus on the working classes, these debates did little to address the difference between women of different classes, which is arguably relevant to consciousness raising in feminism. Women of upper classes may have considerable privilege and are not subject to forms of domestic labour (having working-class women to undertake that for them) but are still subjected to patriarchal norms and material reproduction of the landed classes under capitalism that renders them potentially exploited under different terms.

However, these debates did not succeed in challenging the dominance of patriarchy. Hartmann's Marxist analysis of the partnership between patriarchy and capital suggests that capitalist societies are systematically patriarchal, because:

> patriarchy, by establishing and legitimating hierarchy among men (by allowing men of all groups to control at least some women), reinforces capitalist control, and capitalist values shape the definition of the patriarchal good.
>
> *(Hartmann, 2021, p. 137)*

By this she suggests that a form of sexist ideology exists that reifies capitalist values (associated with male characteristics) and negates social need (associated with female characteristics), each of which are underpinned by the patriarchal sexual division of labour which places women in lower paid, lower status and supposedly appropriate roles, thus maintaining male dominance (Hartmann, 2021).

There is an assumption here of patriarchal capitalism being underpinned by essentialist masculine characteristics, such as competition, dominance and rationality, which may give rise to critiques of Marxist feminism being essentialist (Carbin, 2021), although it is actually this form of capitalism that it seeks to overthrow. However, as was discussed in Chapter 1, essentialist gendered characteristics are widely accepted to be socially constructed; in the case of patriarchy, they form a system of gendered social relations. The emphasis within Marxist feminism on women's role in *re*production in the labour process, whether literal childbearing or women's role in domestic labour which makes it possible for men to take part in productive labour, also lays claim to essentialism, reducing women's oppression to their reproductive capacities (Rahman & Jackson, 2010). Moreover, the family unit inherent in Marxist analysis, which defines women's sexuality and role, is a heterosexual monogamous form that may exclude non-heterosexual or non-monogamous relations. Marxist feminism appears to have done little to contend this, leaving lesbian feminists and gay men marginalised by the normative assumptions (see, for example, MacKinnon, 1982; Rich, 1980; Weeks, 2018 [1980]). As discussed earlier in this chapter, heteropatriarchy under capitalism tends to be intertwined with structures of power.

While Marxist feminism is less often embraced beyond academia in recent years, its resurgence is being urged as a counter to neoliberalism and neoconservatism to challenge the multifaceted structures of oppression perpetuated by capitalism (Lin & Wang, 2023). It can support an analysis of class division within our societies and the dominance of the capital accumulation process under capitalism, which perpetuate power relations and inequalities. When capitalism and patriarchy are intertwined, the challenges addressed are highly relevant to the role of accounting in perpetuating the exploitation of labour (particularly relating to poorer women), the sexual division of labour and the perpetuation of power differentials and class difference. While other feminisms, such as postcolonialism feminism or transnational feminism, addressed in Chapter 5, may have more fruitful or nuanced insights into exploitative globalised capitalism, a contemporary approach to class-based feminism, or Marxist feminism, could play a significant role in understanding feminist resistance to class-based inequalities. The next section addresses such class inequalities within accounting.

Class, social mobility and the accounting profession

There is some early critical accounting research that addresses the political economy of accounting with its origins in neo-classical economics and capitalist regimes (Cooper, 1980; Tinker, 1980), and some that has taken a Marxist or socialist approach to the analysis of class and power relations (Bryer, 2013; Oldroyd, Tyson, & Fleischman, 2015). Catchpowle and Smyth (2016, p. 220), for example, provide a Marxist analysis of what they term the 'class belongingness' of accounting information in a trade union dispute, arguing for alternative uses of accounting information in the struggles for an emancipated world. A Marxist approach to accounting is argued to support an understanding of accounting's role in the 2008 financial crisis (Cooper, 2015) and enable emancipation to be contextualised within the material realities of global capitalism, particularly inequality and exploitation (Andrew & Baker, 2020). Nonetheless, although tracing the origins of what they term 'emancipatory accounting' to a Marxist-inspired revolutionary transformation, Gallhofer and Haslam (2019) argue for a post-Marxist pragmatist perspective that broadens critique of accounting and widens its emancipatory potential. The main focus of this body of work is to illustrate the role of accounting technologies in underpinning capitalism, rather than to address the interaction of class with gender (or any other) identities.

Yet, class remains a restrictive and potentially oppressive feature of the accounting profession and is relatively underexplored compared to gender. Jacobs' (2003) study of class in controlling entry to the profession in the early 2000s examined the role of graduate application forms in emphasising charismatic qualities, leadership and transferable skills, which he argues favours applicants from the middle-class and fee-paying schools. Duff (2017) found that despite UK Labour Government initiatives to widen access to the professions (see Panel of Fair Access to the Professions, 2009), Big Four and mid-tier accountancy firms remained relatively socially exclusive, largely due to the requirement for high educational entry standards, which again favour those from elite schools, and a discourse of hiring 'the brightest and the best' to satisfy perceived client demand. Working-class graduates need to consciously and continuously modify their class-specific dispositions so that they can fully engage with higher education and elite placement experiences to achieve social mobility (Crawford & Wang, 2019).

The accounting profession itself is beginning to be aware of the issue of class amongst its membership in privileging or inhibiting progress. However, for the year 2022, only two of the seven UK professional accounting bodies reported that they collect data on the socio-economic backgrounds of their members and students (Professional Oversight Board for Accountancy, 2023). Diversity information indicative of class, such as school type attended, first generation to attend university and socio-economic background, is amongst the lowest reported as being collected by the 30 audit firms with PIE clients who responded to the survey[1] (Professional Oversight Board for Accountancy, 2023), as illustrated in Figure 4.1. This low indication on class represents their relatively recent interest in this diversity characteristic.

Nonetheless, class status acting as a mode of professional or social closure remains highly relevant to accountancy. Research by KPMG found that social class and nepotism play a major role when accessing the work experience necessary for entry to the largest, most prestigious professional

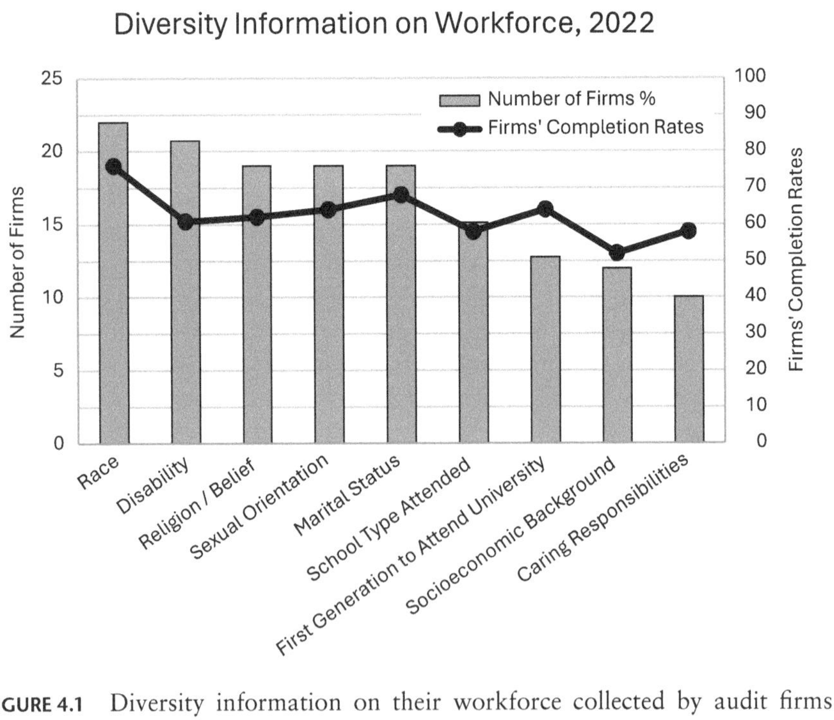

FIGURE 4.1 Diversity information on their workforce collected by audit firms with PIE clients, 2022.

Source: Key Facts and Trends in the Accountancy Profession, Professional Oversight Board for Accountancy, Financial Reporting Council annual report 2023, reproduced by the author.

services firms and PIE audit firms, making access more difficult for those from lower socio-economic backgrounds (Austin, 2023). When people from working-class backgrounds attain a professional career in finance and accounting, they face a 'class pay gap' or earnings penalty of 17% less each year compared to colleagues from more affluent backgrounds, potentially due to having poorer access to networks, being more reluctant to ask for pay rises, excluding themselves from promotion for fear of not 'fitting in' or conscious or unconscious discrimination (Friedman, Laurison, & Macmillan, 2017). Accountants tend to come from more privileged backgrounds, and this is particularly marked in the Big Four firms (Paisey et al., 2020). KPMG found that class is the biggest barrier to career progression in the firm, taking account of gender, ethnicity, disability, sexual orientation and socio-economic background, and finding that those from lower socio-economic backgrounds took an average of 19% longer to progress through grades compared to those from higher socio-economic backgrounds (KPMG, 2022). The report also found what it terms 'a recurring "hierarchy of progression" based on combined characteristics', where the intersection of low socio-economic background with female gender identity and/or ethnic minority background is associated with the slowest rate of career progression (KPMG, 2022, p. 9).

It is rare for studies relating to class and accountancy to address intersection with other characteristics, although the relevance of intersectionality to accounting is discussed in more detail below. None of the studies in this section uses an explicitly feminist analysis, whether Marxist or not. However, there is a rich possibility in the feminist analysis of class and gender (amongst other characteristics) that interrogates the interaction of these oppressions. There is a strong link between patriarchy and capitalism because capitalism creates a hierarchy of workers and patriarchy determines which particular workers are deemed suitable for certain roles. These issues relate to the challenges affecting women in the accounting profession evaluated in Chapter 3. For example, they pertain to horizontal segregation into masculinised or feminised specialisms, and vertical segregation that prevents many women from achieving the higher echelons of professional work. A Marxist feminist analysis of the professional services labour market which addresses the interaction of patriarchy and the labour process could explain why liberal feminism has failed fully to address these challenges for women. Analysis of class in diversity research can ground the critique of diversity in the critique of capitalism (Romani, Zanoni, & Holck, 2021).

Nonetheless, there are other feminist approaches and theoretical lenses, other than Marxist feminism, highly relevant to understanding class and gender in the accounting profession. My research in professional services firms utilised a Bourdieusian theoretical lens to explore the interaction of women accountants' social and physical capital on their bodies and identities (Haynes, 2008). Bourdieu suggests that the body bears an imprint of an individual's social class, because of the class-based *social location* they occupy and their *habitus* or ingrained dispositions, which can then clash with the cultural capital required in the *field* they occupy, such as accounting. This is exemplified by a quote from one participant in my research project who stated:

> I think the London office was very much geared towards public school and Oxbridge graduates and very Home Counties focused really, so the fact that I had a Yorkshire accent and I don't have a posh accent, I felt, it made me feel, the only way I can explain it is as if I have got dirty fingernails…I felt sort of scruffy and working class and felt I was being looked down on.
> *(Haynes, 2008, p. 335)*

Although Bourdieu is not associated with analysis of gender, except in the domestic setting in his later work *Masculine Domination* (Bourdieu, 2001), he did recognise that where a culture, such as accounting, has been historically highly masculine, its socialised embodied forms become synonymous with masculine attributes (Haynes, 2012), for example, 'typically masculine and bourgeois virtues… character, manliness, leadership' (Bourdieu, 1996, p. 118 cited in Haynes, 2012, p. 502). Applying a feminist approach to Bourdieu's concepts of field and capital enables an analysis of gender and class grounded in power and domination (Adkins & Skeggs, 2004). I address the embodiment elements of this study in more detail in Chapter 6.

Race-based feminisms and intersectionality

In this next section, I give an overview of some feminist theorists who address race and racism, albeit I acknowledge that there are many others not able to be covered in this book. In those represented, race is central to their feminism, grounded in their own identity, history and experience of race and racism, to which resistance is essential. For them, analysis of race may be more to the fore as a means of oppression and difference than gender, although they intersect. As a White Western woman, it is difficult to comprehend what it feels like to be subjected to racism, in everyday or institutional forms, as my society reflects the privilege of Whiteness. Yet, there is an onus on scholars such as me to 'unlearn Whiteness' (Liu, 2022) and to understand the salience of race in organisations to undo the effects of racism (Nkomo, 2021). Hence, in the next section, I discuss some key thinkers in Black and anti-racist feminism, relevant to the later discussion of race and intersectionality in accounting. Most scholars in this section are from the US context, where the civil rights movement sparked significant resistance to racism. However, it is fully acknowledged that race is relevant to other feminisms and further discussion of colonialism, transnational feminism, Muslim and Islamic feminism takes place in Chapter 5.

Patricia Hill Collins' book *Black Feminist Thought* was originally published in 1990 and yet retains a relevance more than 30 years on. Focusing on

African American women in the USA, Collins was influential in deliberately placing Black women's experiences and ideas at the centre of her analysis, in stark contrast to the women's movement of the 1960s and 1970s, which were more White, middle class focused. Moreover, because she intended to capture the 'interconnections of race, gender, and social class in Black women's lives' (Collins, 2022 [1990], p. xi), she did not place her analysis in any particular theoretical tradition. Rather, she discusses Black women's experiences within a series of 'intersecting oppressions' or a 'matrix of domination' which has resonance with Crenshaw's (1989, 1994) concept of intersectionality. While Crenshaw's perspective is informed by an understanding of prejudice against Black women under the legal system, Collins provides a more sweeping analysis on the position of Black women under slavery, in the civil rights movement and in relation to contemporary culture in the USA, addressing sexuality and sexualisation, motherhood, relationships and working lives. Collins' Black feminism has an overarching aim to foster 'both Black women's empowerment *and* conditions of social justice' (Collins, 2022 [1990], p. xv). Yet, Collins is careful to articulate that empowerment is not something that can be done *to* or *for* Black women. She argues it must be grounded in Black women's own resistance and activism to challenge how the matrix of domination operates though 'interconnected domains of power – structural, interpersonal, disciplinary and hegemonic' (Collins, 2022 [1990], p. 365). Empowerment, for Collins (2022 [1990]), is twofold, comprising, first, 'critical consciousness to unpack hegemonic ideologies' (p. 362) and, second, construction of new knowledge that rejects 'objectification, commodification, and exploitation' (p. 366).

For Audre Lorde, the 'Black lesbian feminist' (Lorde, 2018, p. 14), poet, essayist and activist, empowerment for women comes from feelings and experience which then translate into action. In *Poetry Is Not a Luxury* (Lorde, 2018, p. 2), she defines poetry as 'the revelation or distillation of experience', which enables Black women to hope and dream for survival, revealing 'those hidden sources of our power from where true knowledge and, therefore, lasting action comes'. She argues in *Uses of the Erotic* that what she terms the 'erotic' is a sense of self, depth of feeling, self-respect and creative energy, which is a 'source of power and information in our lives' (Lorde, 2018, p. 6).

Interestingly, there is an element of Lorde's work that is prescient of the role of accounting in capitalist systems, although she is not explicitly anti-capitalist but more focused on endemic racist structures and systems. In *Poetry Is Not a Luxury,* she argues:

> For within living structures defined by profit, by linear power, by institutional dehumanisation, our feelings were not meant to survive... They surface in our dreams and it is our dreams that point the way to freedom.
> *(Lorde, 2018, p. 5)*

In *Uses of the Erotic*:

> The principal horror of any system which defines the good in terms of profit rather than in terms of human need, or which defines human need to the exclusion of the psychic and emotional components of that need… robs our work of its erotic value, its erotic power and life appeal and fulfilment.
>
> *(Lorde, 2018, pp. 8–9)*

She is speaking of the struggle, particularly of poorer Black women, simply to survive economically and socially, where work may be a means to an end. *In Uses of Anger: Women Responding to Racism* she acknowledges that:

> We operate in the teeth of a system for which racism and sexism are primary, established, and necessary props of profit.
>
> *(Lorde, 2018, p. 27)*

In doing so, she gives examples of Black women's work often servicing the needs of White women. Her anger against racism is:

> The anger of exclusion, of unquestioned privilege, of racial distortions, of silence, ill-use, stereotyping, defensiveness, misnaming, betrayal and co-option.
>
> *(Lorde, 2018, p. 22)*

In what is perhaps her most well-known essay, *The Master's Tools Will Never Dismantle the Master's House*, Lorde explicitly addresses differences of race, sexuality, class and age between feminists, arguing that:

> difference must be not merely tolerated, but seen as a fund of necessary polarities between which our creativity can spark like a dialectic.
>
> *(Lorde, 2018, p. 18)*

She argues that understanding differences and working together as a community can be a strength and can support lasting change, but requires going beyond narrow existing knowledge and action:

> What does it mean when the tools of a racist patriarchy are used to examine the fruits of that same patriarchy? It means that only the most narrow perimeters of change are possible and allowable.
>
> *(Lorde, 2018, p. 17)*

The phrase 'for the master's tools will never dismantle the master's house' is taken as a term to mean that working in commonality with others outside established structures can support an opportunity to flourish, whereas, continuing in a racist, patriarchal system will not necessarily change that system from within. Lorde's work, thus, captures the strong element of resistance inherent in much Black feminist writing and activism.

The feminist theorist and cultural critic bell hooks argues in *Feminist Theory from Margin to Center* that:

> ...feminism is the struggle to end sexist oppression. Its aim is not to benefit solely any specific group of women, any particular race or class of women. It does not privilege women over men. It has the power to transform in a meaningful way all our lives.
>
> *(hooks, 2000, p. 28)*

However, in making this argument, she centres it in a searing critique of White, middle-class mainstream feminism that fails to address the experiences of Black and poor women and aim for a more fundamental transformation of society. Her earlier work, *Ain't I a Woman? Black Women and Feminism*, outlines the convergence of sexism and racism under slavery that she argues lingers in the 'devaluation of black womanhood' in modern society (hooks, 1982, p. 13), inherent in attitudes to their bodies, sexuality, imagery, identity and work. Hooks argues that 'privileged feminists have largely been unable to speak to, with, and for diverse groups of women because they either do not understand fully the interrelatedness of sex, race, and class oppression or refuse to take this interrelatedness seriously' (hooks, 2000, p. 15). In saying this, she makes a fair point that could be upheld against much research on gender and accounting, something that I reflect on further below.

These issues of the interconnectedness of various oppressions based on gender, race or class, amongst others, resonate with concepts of intersectionality. This influential term was first coined and developed by Kimberle Crenshaw in two articles *Demarginalizing the Intersection of Race and Sex: A Black Feminist Critique of Antidiscrimination Doctrine, Feminist Theory and Antiracist Politics* (Crenshaw, 1989) and *Mapping the Margins: Intersectionality, Identity Politics, and Violence against Women of Color* (Crenshaw, 1991). However, Cooper's (2016) extensive analysis of intersectionality argues that Crenshaw drew from earlier feminist theorising on 'proto-intersectionality' that advanced understanding of systems of oppression. Crenshaw's analysis drew from her experience as a legal scholar observing the US criminal justice system where she observed that in terms of male violence against women, the experiences of Black women were the 'product of intersecting patterns of racism and sexism... that tend not to be represented within the discourse of either feminism or antiracism' (Crenshaw, 1991, pp. 1243–1244). In other words, intersectionality takes into account an understanding of how gender, race and class are implicated in political and social systems of oppression, which are entirely different for White and Black women, or for Black men and Black women, and which go beyond 'double discrimination' to a deeper, interconnected level of oppression. Understanding the intersection of racism and sexism means going beyond raced and gendered experiences separately (Crenshaw, 1989). Crenshaw argues:

> Because women of color experience racism in ways not always the same as those experienced by men of color, and sexism in ways not always parallel to experiences of white women, dominant conceptions of antiracism and feminism are limited, even on their own terms.
>
> *(Crenshaw, 1991, p. 1252)*

Crenshaw (1991) outlines two forms of intersectionality, which together expose systems of power that marginalise Black and Latina women. First political intersectionality 'highlights the fact that women of color are situated within at least two subordinated groups that frequently pursue conflicting political agendas' (Crenshaw, 1991, pp. 1251–1252). This can result in even more disempowerment because political energies have to be split between potentially opposing subordinated groups (Muñoz-Puig, 2023). Second, Crenshaw (1991) illustrates how structural intersectionality, based on race, gender and class, constitutes the experience of women who have suffered from domestic violence and rape, resulting from a multiplicity of structural challenges. The concept of intersectionality, therefore, forms a framework for understanding the subordination of Black women under mutually constitutive systems of power. This is why I have included it in this discussion of race-based feminisms which address social justice and forms of resistance to racism.

However, intersectionality has also been taken up by feminists, and indeed by non-feminists in organisational diversity debates, to signal a framing of identity that aims to capture the complexities of multiple forms of identity. These categorisations might include, for example, 'sex, gender, race, sexuality, class, age, ability, and the like' (Westbrook, 2023, p. 415), 'gender, marital status, motherhood, race and other factors' (Tiron-Tudor & Faragalla, 2022, p. 28) or 'the intersectionality of gender, class, race, caste and religion, and sexuality when portraying non-Western women' (Al-wazedi, 2020, p. 170). To some degree, the concept of intersectionality is being mainstreamed in diversity discourses as an organisational buzzword referring to multiple identity characteristics that potentially weakens its original intention, which Crenshaw intended to address overlapping forms of oppression, representing systemic inequalities, for Black women. I discuss identity and its relation to accounting in more detail in Chapter 6. Of course, understanding the lived experience of persons feeling and facing these identity categories can be done in such a way that links to the structures and systems of power that underlie them. Yet, Crenshaw herself did not favour intersectionality embracing identity politics, and explicitly states it is not 'some new, totalizing theory of identity' (Crenshaw, 1991, p. 1244), because she felt that it ignores intra-group differences, which lead to tensions within groups, and thwarts attempts to politicise (and therefore resist) oppressions. Her argument is that 'Through an awareness of intersectionality, we can better acknowledge and ground the differences among us and negotiate the means by which these differences will find expression in constructing group politics' (Crenshaw, 1991, p. 1299). It is worth reflecting that intersectionality is essentially a political insight into gendered racism and its effects.

Race, intersectionality and the accounting profession

In the discipline of accounting, as I go on to elaborate in this section, there are a small number of powerful studies addressing race, and sometimes its interaction with gender, race and class, but few are explicitly feminist, and none specifically invoke Black or anti-racist feminism. This is not dissimilar to other areas of business and management; for example, Fotaki and Pullen's (2024) recent review of feminist articles in *Organization Studies* laments the lack of articles drawing on anti-racist feminism, as they found only one such article in a 20-year period. The issue of race is rarely addressed in relation to the professionalisation of accounting, unlike gender, as was discussed in Chapter 2. Annisette and Prasad (2017) forcefully argue that the paucity of accounting research on race is of critical concern and its tendency to focus on historical matters tends to inadvertently reinforce the fallacy that race does not persist in contemporary institutional and societal structures. And yet, this is clearly not the case, as Nkomo (2021, p. 212) asserts:

> The confluence of resurgent white supremacy, the stark global racial inequalities revealed by the COVID-19 pandemic and calls to end anti-Blackness and systemic racism by the Black Lives Matter Movement underscore the immense importance of race in every aspect of society including organizations.

Nonetheless, historical research is important in illuminating racial struggles within the accounting profession and the barriers to entry, using forms of professional social closure, that sustained the power and income of its White elite members. As professions, including accounting, opened up to women, it was largely White women who benefitted. Black women, and Black men, continued to be denied access. For example, the work of Theresa Hammond has been influential in exploring the histories of African American accountants in the USA including their admission to and experience in the profession. With unprecedented access to the National Association of Black Accountants in the USA, Hammond carried out oral history interviews with nearly half of the first 100 Blacks to pass the Certified Public Accountant (CPA) examination in the USA, finding that despite the growth and professionalisation of the accounting profession generally, few White-owned firms were prepared to employ Black accountants, claiming that this would be unacceptable to their White clients (Hammond, 2002). Given qualifying as a CPA required an experience element to become certified, this effectively prevented the inclusion of Black CPAs until a few pioneers gained the relevant experience and began to set up their own practices, which in turn supported other Black CPAs to meet the experience requirements. Although Hammond centres her work on the issue of race and racism, rather than any other attribute such as gender, she makes links with other historical research on gender and accounting being carried out on a similar period (see, for example, Kirkham & Loft, 1993; Lehman, 1992), which demonstrated that particular types of work are deemed suitable for particular categories of person. In the case of African American accountants, whose ancestors were likely to be people who were forcibly kidnapped and enslaved, this legacy informed an institutionalised racism that maintained the privilege of dominant Whites and deemed Blacks not fit for professional work in business (Hammond & Streeter, 1994). Only after the Civil Rights Act in 1964 did Black accountants in the USA begin to gain more prolific admission to the public accounting profession, aided by specific programmes to increase their representation but then only to 1% CPAs as opposed to their 12% representation in the population, and these interventions did not persist and proliferate in the 1980s (Hammond, 1997).

In other contexts, Annisette (2003) examined the situation of people of African and East Indian descent in Trinidad and Tobago, where despite being the majority population, they were subject to racist attitudes that deemed them unfit to practise accountancy, reinforced by exclusionary practices which excluded the local population, such as the need to undertake articles in Britain, suggesting that the colonial social order remained a powerful force. Similarly, Poullaos' (2009) study of accountants from the former British colonies in the 1920s found racist attitudes pervading the centre of the British profession that restricted access to non-Whites.

These studies are powerful stories of historical exclusion based on race but there are few studies that address the contemporary accounting profession. Indeed, it is difficult to ascertain the racial composition of the profession in countries such as the UK, where data is limited. Some audit firms with PIE clients report on collecting diversity information in respect of their workforce. Figure 4.1 shows that of the 30 PIE audit firms responding to the Financial Reporting Council's (Professional Oversight Board for Accountancy, 2023) annual survey,[2] between 20 and 25 indicated they collect data on the race of their employees, the highest of all the diversity characteristics in Figure 4.1. However, it is not possible to ascertain the actual composition of that data.

In addition, PIE audit firms report on the diversity of their senior management at the three levels of seniority of manager, director and partner, across categories relating to gender, race, disability and LGBTQI+[3] identity (Professional Oversight Board for Accountancy, 2023). Figure 4.2 shows this senior management diversity, where percentages of non-White senior management are much lower than female.

It appears that the proportion of senior management from Black, Asian and Minority Ethnic (BAME) backgrounds is well under 10% at director and partner levels, indicating that the senior levels of UK accountancy remain significantly White. Moreover, it is impossible to ascertain any intersectionality within this data, such as proportions of Black women in senior management in these PIE audit firms, or the interaction with class, as discussed earlier. Significantly, in 2022, 83% of the 30 PIE audit firms who responded to the Financial Reporting Council's annual survey had a diversity policy, compared to 77% of the 25 firms who had diversity policies in 2021 (Professional Oversight Board for Accountancy, 2023). Given these audit firms are those which provide assurance on financial position and risk to their public interest entity clients, it is indeed surprising that they do not all take diversity issues more seriously.

Studies which specifically address race in the contemporary accounting profession in Western contexts such the UK and the USA are few, although those which do occur in these contexts point to continued exclusion and racist challenges. For example, Lewis (2016) argues that an apparent belief in colourblindness and neutrality within the profession actually masks continued processes of racist homogeneity based on the White, middle-class archetype

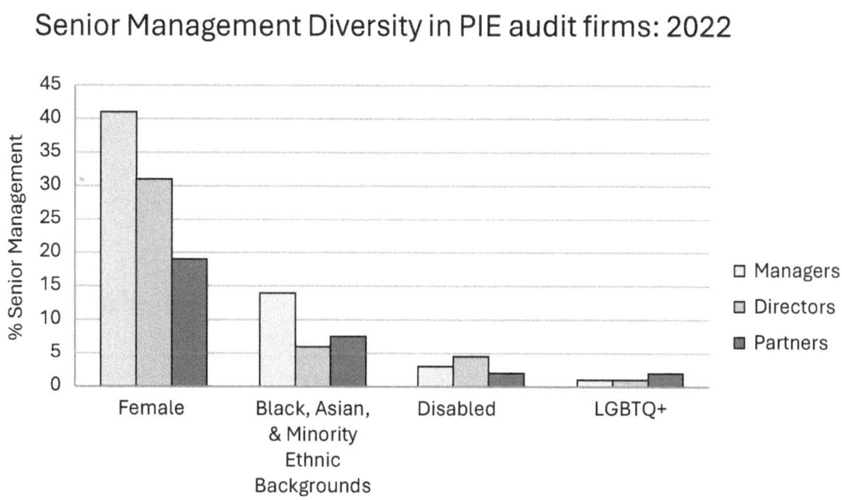

FIGURE 4.2 Senior management diversity in audit firms with PIE clients, 2022.

Source: Key Facts and Trends in the Accountancy Profession, Professional Oversight Board for Accountancy, Financial Reporting Council annual report 2023, reproduced by the author.

accountant, which makes critical discussion about race highly problematic. The lack of racial diversity inherent in the figures discussed above are testament to a profession which has not addressed its racial composition, even when it makes claims of diversity.

Moreover, intersectionality as a means of understanding interconnected oppressions offers further insight into exclusion and inclusion within accounting. Although intersectionality can support an analysis of the structural oppressions faced by Black or other minority ethnic women in the accounting context, it remains important not to reduce them to their race, and/or gender, which of itself forms a type of essentialism. Black women may experience some shared dimensions of racism but the way this is experienced can differ according to other factors pertaining to gender norms, class or other characteristics, which underpin difference between themselves. This point is seen clearly in Ogharanduku, William and Paterson's (2020) study on the development of the Society of Women Accountants in Nigeria (SWAN), where contextual factors are important in understanding how ethnicity, relation, class and age shape the engagement of women leaders within the profession that determines whether they transform or reinforce inequality. The authors argue that despite the success of particular women in achieving the upper echelons of the professional body and reducing stigma towards women accountants in the profession, the main beneficiaries were those from the Yoruba ethnic groups of upper-class status. The longer-term outcome did little to transform the profession for women from the Islamic North, as well as younger women with children, as socio-cultural norms around women's status as primary caregivers was reproduced by SWAN's own actions which continued to marginalise women at the margins (Ogharanduku et al., 2020). Hence, forms of resistance and emancipatory intentions may not benefit all women.

Ethnicity also played a part in the multiple oppressions experienced by women accountants in Malaysia in Adapa and Sheridan's (2021) study, forming part of the complex intersections of class, ethnicity, religion and gender, which influenced how they were perceived by employers and clients alike.

> The male principals and partners were aware of the particular cultural and ethnic constraints that see working Malaysian-Chinese women as 'too proactive'; Malay women as 'religious' and Malaysian-Indian women as possessing many 'cultural inhibitions' as deterrents to firm performance.
>
> *(Adapa & Sheridan, 2021, p. 2431)*

Stereotypical attitudes towards women accountants' ethnicity were perceived as impediments to the growth and success of the business, limiting women's career opportunities (Adapa & Sheridan, 2021). Similar racialised discourses combine with gender and class to form discriminatory attitudes towards Chinese women accountants in New Zealand (Kim, 2004).

Accounting technologies, race and class

Moreover, as I have already identified in Chapter 1, accounting as a technology is underpinned by ideological assumptions regarding neoliberal capitalism. Accounting logic is based on a set of values evaluated in financial terms that are then used to communicate and convince of courses of action despite the possibility of it being underpinned by alternative values (Broadbent, 1998). Hence, accounting technologies are implicated in the perpetuation of inequalities through their use in decision-making. These inequalities pertain heavily to race and class and as well as gender.

Agyemang (2016), for example, draws from Broadbent's critique of accounting logic to examine the EU policy response to the perilous journey taken by migrants and refugees across seas that leads to a financial decision-making mentality which leads to solutions that may mean a loss of humanity and humanitarianism. Notably, these migrants are usually Black, brown or minority ethnic, and sometimes Islamic; therefore, they are racialised as 'other' in the predominantly White countries of Eastern Europe to which they hope to migrate. According to Lehman, Hammond, and Agyemang (2018), accounting claims objectivity but has undeniable discriminatory impacts; for example, they argue it normalises responses to crime, based on race and class within the US criminal justice system, that are underpinned with prejudice. The role of accounting in controlling the racial organisation of work is illustrated in Ramírez-Henao and Sánchez-Guevara's (2023) study of a sugar plantation in Colombia. Accounting is used to control the labour of salaried and non-racialised employees by focusing on its role in generating efficiency and profitability in governing the people and workspaces. However, when exercised over racialised people, predominantly the Black, female workers on the plantation, the calculative practices of accounting serve to reproduce the racialised power relations underpinning their exploitation, thus maintaining an unequal and racist social order. Hence accounting is never neutral in its effects on gender, race and class.

Annisette and Prasad (2017) go much further to critique the role of accounting under neoliberalism to fuel racism by dehumanising people, perceiving them as numbers and rendering them invisible as people. They give the example of how the current accounting model naturalises and legitimises the trend of low wages and economic marginalisation of Black people, and how lending reflects patterns of racial discrimination, as racialised groups are also more likely to be targeted by loan companies. Moreover, they call for more research that problematises the social and political construction of race and challenges contemporary systems and practices of inequality based on race, although they acknowledge that claims of racism are counter to neoliberal ideologies that suggest a colourblind world, meaning confronting racial exclusion is difficult (Annisette & Prasad, 2017).

These are powerful arguments, often reflecting the role of accounting in multiple oppressions of race, gender and class, although not feminist in theoretical orientation. One of the few accounting studies on race and class that explicitly defines as feminist is Clavijo, Perry-Redslob and Mandalaki's (2024) powerful account of a community of Black, Senegalese, relatively poor and precarious women living in France who devise an alternative accounting scheme between themselves to work towards their 'situated emancipation', thereby alleviating their economic and racialised vulnerability and marginalisation. The authors use Lorde's essay *The Master's Tools Will Never Dismantle the Master's House* (Lorde, 2018) to illustrate a type of counter account where a new, yet simple, form of accounting technology built on terms of shared sisterhood outside of established systems can support the women's survival despite their precarity and difference (Clavijo et al., 2024). In this case, accounting technology embraces alternative principles based on care and trust, rather than profit, that counters neoliberal ideologies.

Yet, despite the evidence of a lack of racial and class diversity in accounting, research on race in particular is minimal, and very little is feminist, although I further address the role of race and racism in the relationships between postcolonial and transnational feminisms and accounting in Chapter 5. However, given the clear interaction between oppressions due to gender and race, it is surprising that not more focus is given to feminisms based on race in the accounting context. Considering the relevance of race-based feminisms to contemporary society and the accounting profession, a strong theme is how Black women are defined as being different to White women, by what they appear *not* to be rather than what they *are*. Thus, understanding the institutions and structures of racism which underpin this difference is sorely needed. Feminist accounting research generally fails to engage with racial injustice or to address resistance to racism. It points to the continuing mainstreaming of White feminism and White class privilege. White feminist researchers, such as myself, need continually and reflexively to interrogate our assumptions, alliances and privilege within academia and wider society if we are not, advertently or inadvertently, to perpetuate or ignore issues of race (Haynes, 2023).

Conclusion

This chapter has focused on feminist resistance to embedded structures of inequality and forms of oppression based on difference, primarily arising from gender, class and race. It argued for more radical approaches to feminism which shift away from an individualised responsibility for representation to a more collective response based on shared oppressions and shared solidarities of resistance. The chapter illustrated continuing and significant issues within the accounting profession arising from assumptions based on class or race. The role of accounting technologies in perpetuating the current constitution of gender, class and race was examined. Marxist feminism, feminist research that addresses class and Black feminism can highlight embedded and institutionalised inequalities and support resistance to existing structures which privilege the wealthy, the landed classes over the waged or the White privileged over the non-White. Intersectional approaches can support a more integrated analysis of structures and power relations. However, the final call is for much more expansive feminist research that addresses racial injustice, in relation to the accounting profession and the use of accounting technologies, where there is currently much less focus than on gender injustice.

Notes

1 A list of the 30 audit firms with PIE clients who responded to the Financial Reporting Council's annual survey is provided in Appendix 1.
2 A list of the 30 PIE audit firms who responded to the Financial Reporting Council's annual survey is provided in Appendix 1.
3 I have used the term LGBTQI+ throughout this book, which is commonly used to reflect the diverse non-heterosexual community, meaning Lesbian, Gay, Bi-sexual, Trans, Queer, Intersex and others, who might include Questioning, Pansexual, Non-binary, A-sexual or Two-spirits people, among other self-identifications. I have been consistent with the use of this term, even when authors may have used other versions or similar acronyms, e.g. LGBT, unless I am quoting directly.

References

Adapa, S., & Sheridan, A. (2021). A case of multiple oppressions: Women's career opportunities in Malaysian SME accounting firms. *The International Journal of Human Resource Management*, *32*(11), 2416–2442. https://doi.org/10.1080/09585192.2019.1583269

Adkins, L., & Skeggs, B. (Eds.) (2004). *Feminism after Bourdieu*. Oxford: Blackwell.

Agyemang, G. (2016). Perilous Journeys across the Seas: The Accounting Logic in Europe's Agenda for Migration. In *Accounting in Conflict: Globalization, Gender, Race and Class* (Vol. 19, pp. 1–27). Emerald Group Publishing Limited. https://doi.org/10.1108/S1041-706020160000019002

Al-wazedi, U. (2020). Postcolonial Feminism. In N. A. Naples (Ed.), *Companion to Feminist Studies* (pp. 155–173). Chichester: John Wiley & Sons.

Alsop, R., Fitzsimons, A., & Lennon, K. (2002). *Theorizing Gender: An Introduction*. Cambridge: Polity.

Andrew, J., & Baker, M. (2020). For emancipation: A Marxist critique of structure within critical realism. *Accounting, Auditing & Accountability Journal*, *33*(3), 641–653. https://doi.org/10.1108/AAAJ-11-2019-4251

Annisette, M. (2003). The colour of accountancy: Examining the salience of race in a professionalisation project. *Accounting, Organizations and Society*, *28*(7–8), 639–674. https://doi.org/10.1016/S0361-3682(02)00030-2

Annisette, M., & Prasad, A. (2017). Critical accounting research in hyper-racial times. *Critical Perspectives on Accounting*, *43*, 5–19. https://doi.org/10.1016/j.cpa.2016.06.002

Austin, M. (2023). Class prevents young people from accountancy jobs. *Accountancy Daily*. https://www.accountancydaily.co/class-prevents-young-people-accountancy-jobs

Bordo, S. (1993). *Unbearable Weight: Feminism, Western Culture and the Body*. Berkeley: University of California Press.

Bourdieu, P. (1996). *The State Nobility*. Cambridge: Polity.

Bourdieu, P. (2001). *Masculine Domination*. Cambridge: Polity Press.

Broadbent, J. (1998). The gendered nature of "accounting logic": Pointers to an accounting that encompasses multiple values. *Critical Perspectives on Accounting*, *9*(3), 267–297. https://doi.org/10.1006/cpac.1997.0158

Bryer, R. (2013). Americanism and financial accounting theory – Part 3: Adam Smith, the rise and fall of socialism, and Irving Fisher's theory of accounting. *Critical Perspectives on Accounting*, *24*(7), 572–615. https://doi.org/10.1016/j.cpa.2012.09.004

Carbin, M. (2021). Feminist struggles as anti-capitalist struggles: Rediscovering Marxist feminism. *International Feminist Journal of Politics*, *23*(3), 508–512. https://doi.org/10.1080/14616742.2021.1927133

Catchpowle, L., & Smyth, S. (2016). Accounting and social movements: An exploration of critical accounting praxis. *Accounting Forum*, *40*(3), 220–234. https://doi.org/10.1016/j.accfor.2016.05.001

Chwastiak, M. (1999). Accounting and the Cold War: The transformation of waste into riches. *Critical Perspectives on Accounting*, *10*(6), 747–771. https://doi.org/10.1006/cpac.1998.0276

Chwastiak, M. (2001). Taming the untamable: Planning, programming and budgeting and the normalization of war. *Accounting, Organizations and Society*, *26*(6), 501–519. https://doi.org/10.1016/S0361-3682(01)00010-1

Chwastiak, M., & Lehman, G. (2008). Accounting for war. *Accounting Forum*, *32*(4), 313–326. https://doi.org/10.1016/j.accfor.2008.09.001

Clavijo, N., Perray-Redslob, L., & Mandalaki, E. (2024). Cracking a brick in the master's house: Counter practices as counter-accounts of difference and survival. *Accounting, Auditing & Accountability Journal*, *37*(4), 1153–1177. https://doi.org/10.1108/AAAJ-07-2022-5936

Collins, P. H. (2022 (1990)). *Black Feminist Thought. Knowledge, Consciousness, and the Politics of Empowerment* (30th Anniversary Edition ed.). Abingdon: Routledge.

Cooper, B. (2016). Intersectionality. In L. Disch & M. Hawkesworth (Eds.), *The Oxford Handbook of Feminist Theory* (pp. 385–406). Oxford University Press. https://doi.org/10.1093/oxfordhb/9780199328581.013.20

Cooper, C. (2015). Accounting for the fictitious: A Marxist contribution to understanding accounting's roles in the financial crisis. *Critical Perspectives on Accounting*, *30*, 63–82. https://doi.org/10.1016/j.cpa.2014.08.002

Cooper, D. (1980). Discussion of towards a political economy of accounting. *Accounting, Organizations and Society*, *5*(1), 161–166. https://doi.org/10.1016/0361-3682(80)90032-X

Crawford, I., & Wang, Z. (2019). Social mobility via elite placements: Working class graduates in elite accounting and banking firms. *Accounting Education*, *28*(5), 508–531. https://doi.org/10.1080/09639284.2019.1661857

Crenshaw, K. W. (1989). Demarginalizing the intersection of race and sex: A Black feminist critique of antidiscrimination doctrine, feminist theory and antiracist politics. *University of Chicago Legal Forum*, *1*(8), 139–167. https://doi.org/10.4324/9780429500480

Crenshaw, K. W. (1991). Mapping the margins: Intersectionality, identity politics, and violence against women of color. *Stanford Law Review*, *43*(6), 1241–1299.

Crenshaw, K. W. (1994). Mapping the Margins: Intersectionality, Identity Politics, and Violence against Women of Color. In M. A. Fineman & R. Mykitiuk (Eds.), *The Public Nature of Private Violence* (pp. 93–118). Abingdon: Routledge.

Dey, C., Russell, S., & Thomson, I. (2010). Exploring the Potential of Shadow Accounts in Problematising Institutional Conduct. In S. Osbourne & A. Ball (Eds.), *Social Accounting and Public Management: Accountability for the Public Good* (pp. 64–75). Abingdon: Routledge.

Donovan, J. (2001). *Feminist Theory: The Intellectual Traditions* (3rd ed.). New York: Continuum.

Duff, A. (2017). Social mobility and fair access to the accountancy profession in the UK. *Accounting, Auditing & Accountability Journal*, *30*(5), 1082–1110. https://doi.org/10.1108/AAAJ-10-2012-1133

Dworkin, A. (1981). *Pornography: Men Possessing Women*. New York: Putnam.

Federici, S. (2021). *Patriarchy of the Wage: Notes on Marx, Gender, and Feminism*. San Francisco, CA: PM Press.

Firestone, S. (2015 [1971]). *The Dialectic of Sex. The Case for Feminist Revolution*. London and New York City: Verso.

Fotaki, M., & Pullen, A. (2024). Feminist theories and activist practices in organization studies. *Organization Studies*, *45*(4), 593–616. https://doi.org/10.1177/01708406231209861

Friedman, A., Laurison, D., & Macmillan, L. (2017). *Social Mobility, the Class Pay Gap and Intergenerational Worklessness: New Insights from the Labour Force Survey*. London. https://www.lse.ac.uk/business/consulting/reports/social-mobility-the-class-pay-gap-and-intergenerational-worklessness

Funnell, W., & Chwastiak, M. (2015). *Accounting at War: The Politics of Military Finance*. Abingdon: Routledge.

Gallhofer, S., & Haslam, J. (2019). Some reflections on the construct of emancipatory accounting: Shifting meaning and the possibilities of a new pragmatism. *Critical Perspectives on Accounting*, *63*, 101975. https://doi.org/10.1016/j.cpa.2017.01.004

Goncharenko, G. (2023a). In the spotlight: Rethinking NGO accountability in the #MeToo era. *Critical Perspectives on Accounting*, *92*, 102308. https://doi.org/10.1016/j.cpa.2021.102308

Goncharenko, G. (2023b). The #MeToo legacy and "the Collective Us": Conceptualising accountability for sexual misconduct at work. *Accounting, Auditing & Accountability Journal*, *36*(7/8), 1814–1838. https://doi.org/10.1108/AAAJ-01-2022-5642

Hammond, T. (1997). From complete exclusion to minimal inclusion: African Americans and the public accounting industry, 1965–1988. *Accounting, Organizations and Society*, *22*(1), 29–53. https://doi.org/10.1016/0361-3682(95)00047-X

Hammond, T. (2002). *A White-Collar Profession: African American Certified Public Accountants since 1921*. Chapel Hill and London: The University of North Carolina Press.

Hammond, T., & Streeter, D. (1994). Overcoming barriers: Early African-American certified public accountants. *Accounting, Organizations and Society*, *19*(3), 271–288. https://doi.org/10.1016/0361-3682(94)90035-3
Hartmann, H. (2021). The Unhappy Marriage of Marxism and Feminism: Towards a More Progressive Union. In C. R. McCann, S.-K. Kim, & E. Ergun (Eds.), *Feminist Theory Reader. Local and Global Perspectives* (5th ed., pp. 131–140). Abingdon: Routledge.
Haynes, K. (2008). (Re)figuring accounting and maternal bodies: The gendered embodiment of accounting professionals. *Accounting, Organizations and Society*, *33*(4–5), 328–348. https://doi.org/10.1016/j.aos.2007.04.003
Haynes, K. (2012). Body beautiful?: Gender, identity and the body in professional services firms. *Gender, Work & Organization*, *19*(5), 489–507. https://doi.org/10.1111/j.1468-0432.2011.00583.x
Haynes, K. (2023). Reflexivity and academic identity in accounting: Intersubjective reflexive identity work as a feminist academic. *Accounting, Auditing & Accountability Journal*, *36*(5), 1379–1395. https://doi.org/10.1108/AAAJ-10-2022-6099
Hines, S. (2020). Sex wars and (trans) gender panics: Identity and body politics in contemporary UK feminism. *The Sociological Review*, *68*(4), 699–717. https://doi.org/10.1177/0038026120934684
hooks, b. (1982). *Ain't I a Woman? Black Women and Feminism*. London: Pluto Press.
hooks, b. (2000). *Feminist Theory from Margin to Center*. London: Pluto Press.
Jacobs, K. (2003). Class reproduction in professional recruitment: Examining the accounting profession. *Critical Perspectives on Accounting*, *14*(5), 569–596. https://doi.org/10.1016/S1045-2354(02)00140-5
Killian, S. (2015). "For lack of accountability": The logic of the price in Ireland's Magdalen Laundries. *Accounting, Organizations and Society*, *43*, 17–32. https://doi.org/10.1016/j.aos.2015.03.006
Kim, S. N. (2004). Racialized gendering of the accountancy profession: Toward an understanding of Chinese women's experiences in accountancy in New Zealand. *Critical Perspectives on Accounting*, *15*(3), 400–427. https://doi.org/10.1016/S1045-2354(02)00208-3
Kirkham, L., & Loft, A. (1993). Gender and the construction of the professional accountant. *Accounting, Organizations and Society*, *18*(6), 507–558. https://doi.org/10.1016/0361-3682(93)90002-N
KPMG. (2022). *Social Mobility Progression Report 2022: Mind the Gap*.
Lehman, C. R. (1992). 'Herstory' in accounting: The first eighty years. *Accounting, Organizations and Society*, *17*(3–4), 261–285. https://doi.org/10.1016/0361-3682(92)90024-M
Lehman, C. R. (2016). Unshackling Accounting in Prisons: Race, Gender, and Class. In *Accounting in Conflict: Globalization, Gender, Race and Class* (Vol. 19, pp. 89–112). Leeds: Emerald Group Publishing Limited. https://doi.org/10.1108/S1041-706020160000019006
Lehman, C. R., Hammond, T., & Agyemang, G. (2018). Accounting for crime in the US: Race, class and the spectacle of fear. *Critical Perspectives on Accounting*, *56*, 63–75. https://doi.org/10.1016/j.cpa.2018.01.002
Lewis, A. (2016). A Critical Race Theory Discussion of Neutrality and Colorblindness in Accounting. In *Accounting in Conflict: Globalization, Gender, Race and Class* (Vol. 19, pp. 113–134). Leeds: Emerald Group Publishing Limited. https://doi.org/10.1108/S1041-706020160000019005

Lin, J., & Wang, Y. (2023). Back to Marx: Reflections on the feminist crisis at the crossroads of neoliberalism and neoconservatism. *Humanities and Social Sciences Communications*, *10*(954), 1–10. https://doi.org/10.1057/s41599-023-02341-2

Liu, H. (2022). How we learn Whiteness: Disciplining and resisting management knowledge. *Management Learning*, *53*(5), 776–796. https://doi.org/10.1177/13505076211061622

Lorber, J. (2012). *Gender Inequality. Feminist Theories and Politics*. Oxford: Oxford University Press.

Lorde, A. (2018). *The Master's Tools Will Never Dismantle the Master's House*. London : Penguin.

MacKinnon, C. A. (1982). Feminism, Marxism, method, and the state: An agenda for theory. *Signs: Journal of Women in Culture and Society*, 7(3), 515–544. https://doi.org/10.1086/493898

MacKinnon, C. A. (1987). *Feminism Unmodified. Discourses on Life and Law*. Cambridge: Harvard University Press.

Margree, V. (2018). *Neglected or Misunderstood: The Radical Feminism of Shulamith Firestone* Alresford, Hampshire: John Hunt Publishing.

McFadden, C., Crowley-Henry, M., Rumens, N., Rocco, T. S., & Collins, J. C. (2024). Doing transgender: Gender minorities in the organization. *Gender, Work & Organization*, *31*(5), 1754–1765. https://doi.org/10.1111/gwao.13165

Muñoz-Puig, M. (2023). Intersectional power struggles in feminist movements: An analysis of resistance and counter-resistance to intersectionality. *Gender, Work & Organization*, *31*(3), 1133–1147. https://doi.org/10.1111/gwao.12995

Nkomo, S. M. (2021). Reflections on the continuing denial of the centrality of "race" in management and organization studies. *Equality, Diversity and Inclusion: An International Journal*, *40*(2), 212–224. https://doi.org/10.1108/EDI-01-2021-0011

Ogharanduku, B. E., William, J. J., & Paterson, A. S. (2020). Beautiful SWAN, or ugly duckling? The attempt to reduce gender inequality by the society of women accountants of Nigeria. *Critical Perspectives on Accounting*, 102245. https://doi.org/10.1016/j.cpa.2020.102245

Oldroyd, D., Tyson, T. N., & Fleischman, R. K. (2015). American ideology, socialism and financial accounting theory: A counter view. *Critical Perspectives on Accounting*, *27*, 209–218. https://doi.org/10.1016/j.cpa.2014.03.001

Oren, T., & Press, A. L. (Eds.) (2020). *The Routledge Handbook of Contemporary Feminism*. Abingdon: Routledge.

Paisey, C., Paisey, N., Tarbert, H., & Wu, B. (2020). Deprivation, social class and social mobility at Big Four and non-Big Four firms. *Accounting and Business Research*, *50*(1), 61–109. https://doi.org/10.1080/00014788.2019.1647127

Panel of Fair Access to the Professions. (2009). *Unleashing Aspiration: Summary and Recommendations of the Full Report*. London. https://dera.ioe.ac.uk/9496/7/fair-access_Redacted.pdf

Pearce, R., Erikainen, S., & Vincent, B. (2020). TERF wars: An introduction. *The Sociological Review*, *68*(4), 677–698. https://doi.org/10.1177/0038026120934713

Poullaos, C. (2009). Profession, race and Empire: Keeping the centre pure, 1921–1927. *Accounting, Auditing & Accountability Journal*, *22*(3), 429–468. https://doi.org/10.1108/09513570910945688

Professional Oversight Board for Accountancy. (2023). *Key Facts and Trends in the Accounting Profession*. London: Financial Reporting Council. https://www.frc.

org.uk/library/supervision/professional-bodies-supervision/key-facts-and-trends-in-the-accountancy-profession/

Rahman, M., & Jackson, S. (2010). *Gender & Sexuality. Sociological Approaches.* Cambridge: Polity Press.

Ramírez-Henao, D. F., & Sánchez-Guevara, A. (2023). The roles of accounting in the racial organization of work. *Critical Perspectives on Accounting*, *98*, 102661. https://doi.org/10.1016/j.cpa.2023.102661

Rich, A. (1977). *Of Woman Born: Motherhood as Experience and Institution.* London: Virago.

Rich, A. (1980). Compulsory heterosexuality and lesbian existence. *Signs: Journal of Women in Culture and Society*, *5*(4), 631. https://doi.org/10.1086/493756

Rodrigue, M., & Laine, M. (2022). Shadow Accounts and Alternative Portrayals. In C. A. Adams (Ed.), *Handbook of Accounting and Sustainability* (pp. 157–172). Cheltenham: Edward Elgar.

Romani, L., Zanoni, P., & Holck, L. (2021). Radicalizing diversity (research): Time to resume talking about class. *Gender, Work & Organization*, *28*(1), 8–23. https://doi.org/10.1111/gwao.12593

Simba, H., & Ngcobo, S. (2020). Are pandemics gender neutral? Women's health and COVID-19. *Frontiers in Global Women's Health*, *1*. https://doi.org/10.3389/fgwh.2020.570666

Tinker, A. M. (1980). Towards a political economy of accounting: An empirical illustration of the Cambridge controversies. *Accounting, Organizations and Society*, *5*(1), 147–160. https://doi.org/10.1016/0361-3682(80)90031-8

Tiron-Tudor, A., & Faragalla, W. A. (2022). Intersections of women's identities in professional accountancy careers. *Qualitative Research in Accounting and Management*. https://doi.org/10.1108/QRAM-02-2021-0038

Twyford, E. J., Tanima, F. A., & George, S. (2022). Critical race theory, counter-accounting, and the emancipatory potential of counter-stories. *Accounting, Auditing & Accountability Journal*, *35*(9), 330–358. https://doi.org/10.1108/AAAJ-12-2020-5035

Weeks, J. (2018 [1980]). Capitalism and the Organisation of Sex. In G. L. Collective (Ed.), *Homosexuality* (pp. 11–20). London: Verso.

Westbrook, L. (2023). The matrix of violence: Intersectionality and necropolitics in the murder of transgender people in the United States, 1990–2019. *Gender & Society*, *37*(3), 413–446. https://doi.org/10.1177/08912432231171172

Willis, E. (1984). Radical feminism and feminist radicalism. *Social Text* (9/10), 91–118. https://doi.org/10.2307/466537

World Health Organisation. (WHO) (2021). *Violence against Women Prevalence Estimates, 2018.* Geneva. https://www.who.int/news-room/fact-sheets/detail/violence-against-women

Zanghellini, A. (2020). Philosophical problems with the Gender-Critical feminist argument against trans inclusion. *SAGE Open*, *10*(2). https://doi.org/10.1177/2158244020927029

5

POSTCOLONIAL, DECOLONIAL, TRANSNATIONAL, ISLAMIC AND MUSLIM FEMINISMS IN ACCOUNTING

Introduction

This chapter addresses the relevance of non-Western feminisms – postcolonial, decolonial, transnational, Islamic and Muslim – to accounting. Accounting technologies have been implicated in the pursuit of colonialism and repressive regimes, resulting in the exploitation and dehumanisation of workers, indentured labourers or Indigenous Peoples. The chapter opens with some theoretical explanations of postcolonialism and decolonisation, before exploring their relevance to accounting technology and the accounting profession. As well as being constitutive of inequalities, accounting techniques can also be used to redress inequalities and offer ways of resisting colonial legacies in postcolonial contexts. However, despite the interaction of gender, race and class in the positioning of women as subaltern, oppressed and 'othered' under postcoloniality, and the repressive role of capitalism in exploiting women, feminist approaches to understanding these issues in the accounting context are underutilised. This chapter argues that transnational feminism, with its anti-racist and anti-capitalist stance, is highly relevant to accounting and provides six applications of transnational feminism to accounting. It also addresses the potential for the application of Islamic and Muslim feminisms to accounting. The chapter culminates with a discussion of the role of feminisms 'from the margins' in promoting social justice in accounting and outlines a set of principles for decolonising accounting research practice.

Postcolonialism and decolonisation

The concepts of postcolonialism and decoloniality both emerged from political developments which contest the colonial world order arising from

DOI: 10.4324/9781032636603-5

European imperialism and empire building (Bhambra, 2014). Postcolonial can refer to different aspects of colonialism: the position of a former colony that has now become an independent state; the perspective of people who were once colonised; or critics of colonialism, whether they were actually colonised or not (Young, 2020). Decolonisation refers to the need to revoke residual social, cultural and political attitudes or institutional practices that persist in a postcolonial context, especially those with racist underpinnings (Young, 2020). According to Bhambra (2014), postcolonialism was first developed by diasporic Middle Eastern and South Asian scholars addressing the impact of being made to feel like interlopers in their own countries, originating from colonial oppression of the nineteenth and twentieth centuries, whereas decoloniality emerged from scholars from South America, where European invasions began in the fifteenth century. Both postcolonial and decolonial movements contest the cultural, socio-economic, institutionalised and material elements of colonial dominance, history, knowledge and power.

Colonisation can take two very different forms, which influence approaches to postcolonialism and decoloniality. The first occurs when imperialist colonial powers occupied another country, exploiting its natural assets, people and environment for their own gain or trade, but subsequently (mostly) leave, ceding their powers and granting independence to the nation state albeit with the legacy of colonialism in place (Young, 2020). Young (2020) argues that India (under Portuguese, Dutch and British rule), Indo-China (under French rule) or Indonesia (under Dutch rule) are examples of such colonies. The colonial legacy takes the form of continuing cultural, political, social and economic influences, which persist even when national sovereignty has been re-established, yet are potentially eroded over time.

The second form of colonisation occurs when (White, European) settlers invade or settle in a country with the intention of adopting it as their permanent home. Within settler colonialism, land is the key asset of value, meaning that Indigenous Peoples who have relationships with or hold the land are destroyed, moved off or exploited (Arvin, Tuck, & Morrill, 2021), often resulting in genocide, slaughter or enslavement. Examples of such settler colonialism occurred in the Americas, the Caribbean, Australasia, the Middle East and parts of Africa, although in some settler colonies, such as Algeria, Kenya and Zimbabwe, Indigenous Peoples were able to regain control (Young, 2020). A challenge for postcoloniality arising from this kind of colonisation is the continual loss of land rights, downplaying of Indigenous culture and knowledge, and underlying subjugation or marginalisation on racial or ethnic lines that persists into the present. This leads some Indigenous studies scholars to question the nature of how colonialism is actually past or post. For example, Rowe (2021, p. 248) cites Kathryn Trees, an Aboriginal writer, who asks: 'Does postcolonial suggest colonialism has passed? For whom is it "post"? Surely not for Australian Aboriginal people at least, when land rights, social justice, respect and equal opportunity for most does not exist'. Trees' conclusion is that postcolonialism is a White concept formulated by the West to represent itself in non-imperialist terms (Rowe, 2021; Trees & Nyoongah, 1993). Much of the legacy of settler colonialism is not only physical dominance over land or organisation of institutions, but a more insidious, ideological form of control or 'civilising', which persists in people's thinking, in the undervaluing of Indigenous knowledge systems and in forms of inequitable stereotyping and racialisation that persist from colonisation to the present-day consciousness (Mignolo, 2012).

Decolonisation

Decolonisation is the process by which colonised peoples retake or reaffirm their own cultures and knowledge. While decolonisation is important in a postcolonial context where colonisers have ceded a nation state back to an independent condition, it is particularly relevant to forms of settler colonialism where settler dominance has subjugated, suppressed or altered Indigenous knowledge, culture and experience. As a result, much of the theory of decolonisation emerged from reflections on the violence suffered by South Americans under colonisation, during which the 'otherness' of Indigenous Peoples was constructed as they were rendered different or invisible in relation to the perspectives of European colonisers (Cuenca Botey & Célérier, 2023).

The powerful linkages between coloniality and 'modernity', meaning the capitalist, hierarchical logic of Eurocentric rationality, are explored by sociologist Aníbal Quijano, who argues that the 'coloniality of power is based upon "racial" social classification of the world population under Eurocentred world power' (Quijano, 2007, p. 171). He argues that knowledge based on Eurocentric rationality became established as a universal paradigm of knowledge under coloniality, in such a way that coloniality and modernity can barely be distinguished and are one and the same. Colonial power, Quijano (2007, p. 177) argues, 'produced distorted paradigms of knowledge and spoiled the liberating promises of modernity', which requires 'the destruction of the coloniality of world power' through a process of epistemological decolonisation. Building on this, Mignolo (2012, p. xvii) conceptualises decoloniality as what he calls 'border thinking', that is, 'thinking and doing decolonially', which, he suggests, means 'unveiling the logic of coloniality and delinking from the rhetoric of modernity' (Mignolo, 2012, p. xviii). In other words, moving away from the idea that capitalist development and growth are inevitable and restoring colonised subaltern knowledge and different visions of life. Such understanding of the colonial matrix of power is essential in appreciating contemporary global inequalities and their historical origination (Bhambra, 2014). To address this dominant conceptualisation of culture, knowledge, development and progress under/coloniality/modernity requires complete decolonisation in society. As such, 'Latin American decolonial thinking involves challenging the five ideologies of modernity – Christianity, Liberalism, Marxism, Conservatism, and Colonialism – when recognizing pluriversality of knowledges otherwise' (Sauerbronn et al., 2024, p. 5).

In order to embark on a process of decolonisation, the inclusion of Indigenous knowledge is vital in order to develop a history that represents Indigenous experience (Bryer, 2023) and authentically represents those who were colonised (Macleod, Bhatia, & Liu, 2020). Such knowledge may surface when produced through a feminist lens that places people identifying as women and their experiences at the centre of knowledge production, with new imaginaries that challenge colonial legacies. However, decolonisation may also require the colonised to free themselves psychologically from the culturally ingrained perspectives of the colonisers (Young, 2020), to challenge 'the psychic effects of internalized colonisation' (Rowe, 2021, p. 247) that become ingrained through centuries of Indigenous suppression. Perhaps more important, and more current in the contemporary European context, decolonisation requires the colonisers to reflect on their own role in the process and outcomes of colonisation, in terms of the lasting effects of cultural, economic and political dominance, with their resultant racial and geopolitical consequences in the world order.

Postcolonialism, decoloniality and gender

Given the forms of colonisation above, a significant aim of postcolonialism is to reclaim Western-biased precolonial history and to rewrite colonial discourses and analysis by exposing and questioning the implied assumptions of such dominant histories and discourses (Al-wazedi, 2020). However, the challenge is to rewrite new postcolonial histories that validate people marginalised by colonisation without simultaneously essentialising them, which can have the effect of perpetuating the power of colonisation and its categorisations (Dozono, 2022). In such a vein, Edward Said's widely known and influential work, *Orientalism*, illustrates and critiques Western stereotypical and racist assumptions of the Orient, and their 'dehumanising ideology' (Said, 1979, p. 27), which renders the 'Oriental' or Arab simultaneously exotic yet threatening. Said sees colonialism being perpetuated in Western epistemological and cultural domination of the Orient that negates its own language and ways of knowing, resulting in knowledge being aligned with a ruling elite (Said, 1979). Moreover, although gender is not the focus of Said's text, he notes that women within the context of Orientalism are perceived as sensual, backward and fecund, constructed as 'other' not only to men but to the hegemonic discourse of Western femininity.

Building on decolonial theory, Lugones (2010, 2016) addresses what she terms 'the coloniality of gender', putting gender at the heart of any colonial power relations, as race was central to Quijano's 'coloniality of power' (Mendoza, 2016). Lugones (2016) argues that the biological, dimorphic categorisation of sex into two binary categories – male and female – originates in part from colonisation and Eurocentred global capitalism, as many Indigenous Peoples did not resort to the sexual binary in the way they understood gender. Moreover, she argues that gender systems imposed by colonialism were the starting point for the subordination of females, even resulting in the overturning of more egalitarian or matriarchal societies (Lugones, 2016). To understand and decolonise from the coloniality of gender requires a form of feminism that Lugones calls 'decolonial feminism', meaning addressing:

> the oppression of women who have been subalternized through the combined processes of racialization, colonization, capitalist exploitation, and heterosexualism...understand[ing] the oppressive imposition as a complex interaction of economic, racializing, and gendering systems.
>
> *(Lugones, 2010, p. 747)*

Thus, Mendoza (2016) argues that Lugones' (2010, 2016) theory of the coloniality of gender shows how the colonised were dehumanised and helps us to understand how in contemporary society feminicide, trafficking and violence persist heavily against non-Westernised women. In other words, there is an argument that colonialism imposed the binary, rationalised, essentialised, sexual categorisations that culminated in the European Enlightenment and subsequent modernity (see Chapter 2) on to the colonised in ways that persist in postcolonial periods.

In the remainder of this chapter, I address the relationships between postcolonialism, decolonisation and accounting, including the role and application of feminisms – postcolonial feminism, transnational feminism and Islamic and Muslim feminisms – in the accounting context.

Postcolonialism and accounting

Postcolonialism and accounting technologies

This section addresses the influence of colonisation on global accounting technologies, a growing theme in the contemporary accounting literature on the history of accounting development and the perpetuation of postcolonial power relations. Although global politics and economic power has shifted over the last century, reflected in the growth of economies such as India, Brazil and China, international capital markets and institutions continue to be dominated by pro-Western policies (Michie, 2011). As Young (2020, p. 7) puts it:

> The West is no more homogeneous than the South. However it not only retains much of its economic power, it also still controls the normative framework of global institutions and structures, from accounting to commerce to the Internet to legal systems to universities.

Therefore, Hopper, Lassou, and Soobaroyen (2017) argue that globalised accounting technologies, mobilised, for example, through neoliberal normative Financial Reporting Standards, wield a strong influence on what and how developing countries have to report in terms of a financial account. Similarly, management accounting systems, applied to the internal management of companies in developing countries, tend to be produced through the legacies of colonial regimes that fail to take account of postcolonial cultural, economic and political contexts requiring more localised management accounting (Hopper et al., 2009).

These problems of the colonisation of accounting technologies occur in many colonial and postcolonial contexts. For example, Davie (2000, p. 330) argues that 'the practice of accounting became involved in the production of a calculative knowledge of imperialism' in Fiji, referring to the means by which accounting systems were imposed on the Indigenous Chiefs during colonisation by the British, meaning that accounting became a key tool in expanding the Empire. In sub-Saharan Africa, Tawiah et al. (2022) argue that in colonial periods the development of accounting systems and practices was heavily influenced by economic policy, governance systems, education and language imposed by the colonisers, whereas in post-independent postcolonial periods the effects of foreign aid, foreign trade liberalisation, membership of international associations and the prevalence of foreign ownership influence the persistent domination of Western modes of thinking under globalisation. Similarly, in Jamaica, financial accounting practices and reporting benefitted the interests of colonisers, which independence did not diminish; instead, global reporting requirements and practices have tended to embed further the Westernised influence of global accounting technologies and the international requirements of capital markets in the country's development (Bakre, 2008).

However, these colonial influences on accounting technology reflect an underpinning more sinister role for accounting in the perpetuation of colonisation. Accounting became a technology that subjugated and dehumanised people through its derogatory racialisation by colonial oppressors in ways that continue to sustain injustices in today's society. Accounting is not an impartial and objective practice, and its calculative practices can support the commodification and obfuscation of humanity under conditions of slavery, for example. Studies support these assertions. For example, forms of government accounting and taxation in Brazil illustrate the active institutionalisation of slavery by counting slaves as an economic commodity (Rodrigues & Craig, 2018). Accounting records surviving from a Portuguese chartered company depict its slave trading operations, including allocations of clothing, food and water to slaves enduring inhumane conditions on board slave ships (Pinto & West, 2017). Power and Brennan's (2022) study of the annual reports of the British South Africa Company (BSAC) during colonisation of Southern Rhodesia (now Zimbabwe) illustrates how quantification of the deaths of Indigenous People resulted in silencing their representation and masking the company's profit motives and means of operation, rendering the reports a tool of colonial propaganda. Similarly, Jensen, Agyemang, and Lehman's (2021) study of a Danish slave trading company illustrates how accounting systems did not simply ignore the exploitation and violence meted out to slaves, but were actively used to obfuscate mistreatment, including falsifying records that noted slaves as dead rather than killed by beating from their traders, in ways that exemplify the use of accounting as a partisan tool of power. The authors argue that research needs to continue to address how accounting is implicated in contemporary, persistent issues of racialisation, violence and injustice (Jensen et al., 2021). Neu (2000, p. 268) goes further to argue that accounting technologies, embedded in the financial incentives and subsidies provided to Indigenous Peoples in Canada post colonisation, promote the outcomes of 'reproductive genocide, cultural genocide and ecocide', given their linkage with harmful practices and the loss of land and livelihoods.

Colonialism, postcolonialism and accounting technologies therefore have a powerful and constitutive role in the creation and perpetuation of inequalities, mostly on racial terms, which it is important to acknowledge before going on to address the role of feminism in this context. It is also pertinent to address how colonialism and postcolonialism influenced the development of the accounting profession itself.

Postcolonialism and the accounting profession

Chapter 2 addressed the early development in Western contexts during the nineteenth century of what is now the modern global accounting profession. Given the earlier emergence of colonialism from within Europe, supported by accounting technologies, and the power and precedence of institutions such as the British Empire culminating in the nineteenth century, it is also evident that the accounting profession was also implicated in maintaining a postcolonial world order that upholds the colonisers.

Studies indicate that this postcolonial perpetuation of Western style professional accounting can take a number of forms. First, it dominates the approach to the training and development of accounting professionals, as seen in Annisette's (2000) study of how the Association of Chartered Certified Accountants (ACCA) came to dominate the certification of accountants in Trinidad and Tobago, a former British colony, preventing the country's own intention to provide localised accountancy education and qualifications. Second, the implementation of globalised accounting standards, competitive threats to local firms by international firms and the need to adhere to changes in training is perceived as a form of Western imperialism, representing continued postcolonial Anglo-American dominance, by accountants in Middle Eastern, Islamic contexts (Gallhofer, Haslam, & Kamla, 2011). Third, even in contemporary professions in countries such as Canada, long-held 'social identity markers of the colonial archetypical accountant', representing an ideal White male of British heritage, are perpetuated by professional and business discourses, meaning that in order to succeed, migrant non-White accountants have to adapt their self-presentation to mimic this archetype (Thomson & Jones, 2016, p. 63). Postcolonial theory underpins an evaluation of these phenomena, drawing attention to the persistence of colonial legacies within a globalised accounting profession.

Accounting and Indigenous Peoples

Several studies have specifically addressed accounting research and Indigenous Peoples (Vidwans & De Silva, 2023). More than 25 years ago, Gallhofer and Chew (2000) noted the possibly contentious and political dimensions associated with scholars who are not Indigenous researching Indigenous Peoples and their culture, in effect speaking for them. Yet they argued that in the light of injustices and threats to Indigenous Peoples from Western capitalism and imperialism, researchers have a responsibility to contribute to awareness raising and enhanced understanding of these issues (Gallhofer & Chew, 2000). It is important to recognise that some, if not most, Indigenous Peoples continue to suffer from economic and social deprivation arising from settler colonialism of various forms (Rowe, 2021).

Contemporary accounting research tends to be more focused on research 'by' rather than 'for' Indigenous Peoples (Buhr, 2011; Vidwans & De Silva, 2023). Some Indigenous accounting methods, such as oral Aboriginal accounting, have been diluted by the dominance of written Westernised accounting (Lombardi, 2016), However, Maori researchers have sought to develop their own methodologies that encompass their own practice and policies, known as Kaupapa Maori research (McNicholas & Barrett, 2005). Collaborations between Indigenous and non-Indigenous Peoples can support new thinking in respect of accounting, as seen in Finau et al.'s (2023) account of an Australian project aiming to incorporate cultural connections to land with national accounting systems, despite it problematising significant differences between Indigenous and Western worldviews. Yet, Dhillon (2020) argues, giving an example of a North American environmental science partnership consisting of Indigenous and non-Indigenous climate scientists, it is important not to allow ideas about traditional values to obfuscate continuing settler dominance in such partnerships.

In this section, I have spent some time contextualising the role of accounting technologies in colonialism and the perpetuation of colonisation in postcolonial periods, together with accounting's postcolonial influence on the profession itself and in relation to Indigenous Peoples. Understanding the globalised power of accounting as a tool and technology of dominance on societies, cultures and economies, both historically and contemporaneously, is essential in addressing the role of accounting in causing and perpetuating inequalities. And yet, although the above research addresses the interaction of accounting and colonialism illustrating how colonisation relies on racist and ethnocentric repression and devaluation, it does not address the issue of gender. Nor does it utilise feminist theory to support a critique of colonisation. There is some postcolonial accounting research that addresses gender issues, which I consider below, but the majority is focused on accounting as a tool of globalised capitalism.

However, as I have argued throughout this text, feminist theory can bring new insights and activism to bear on complex problems facing women in various societies. I now go on to explore the relevance of various feminisms – postcolonial feminism, transnational feminism and Muslim/Islamic feminism – to accounting in postcolonial and globalised contexts.

Postcolonial feminism

Ghandi (2019) argues that both postcolonialism and feminism have been concerned with defending marginalised 'others' within repressive structures of domination but their interaction has been contentious, as postcolonial nationalism, which aims to reclaim national culture and politics, can potentially clash with perspectives on the gendered position of women. The concept of the 'other' in postcolonial feminism is therefore not straightforward. Coloniality tended to represent non-Western peoples as 'other' in relation to Eurocentric or Western colonisers, as the dominated, conquered or enslaved. However, as Ghandi (2019) points out, citing Prakash (1995), colonisation:

> ...enacted another kind of violence by instituting 'enduring hierarchies of subjects and knowledges – the coloniser and the colonised, the Occidental and the Oriental, the civilised and the primitive, the scientific and the superstitious, the developed and the developing'.
>
> *(Ghandi, 2019, p. 15; Prakash, 1995, p. 3)*

In postcoloniality, this discourse continued with colonial legacies ensuring that the other continued to be considered as culturally exotic, 'reiterating European superiority over Oriental backwardness' (Said, 1979, p. 7) in terms that reify European culture and ensure colonised peoples and cultures remain secondary.

Feminist theory is also concerned with liberating marginalised others from oppression, most notably women (although it could include marginalised others such as trans people) dominated by structures, cultures and practices developed and controlled by men. Postcolonial feminism starts with the assumption that its politics and critique are imbued with the legacies of colonialism and by the institutional national infrastructures that were conferred by previous colonial powers to elite, typically male groups (Young, 2020). It therefore criticises coloniality and the hegemonic power established by Indigenous men under postcoloniality, who were occupied with rebuilding their nation after imperialist oppressions (Al-wazedi, 2020). It tends to analyse the material, cultural and social conditions affecting women in the postcolonial environment. These are important considerations to address, with awareness that in creating new national politics, systems and infrastructures under postcoloniality, women may be marginalised or, worse, dominated.

However, early postcolonial feminist theory and scholarship originated from the perspectives of Western feminists (Al-wazedi, 2020; Brannelly & Boulton, 2017) rather than postcolonial women emerging from coloniality. Although feminism is not homogeneous, as I have discussed throughout this book, postcolonial feminist scholarship tended to represent the position of liberal feminism, with its egalitarian Western values. The interaction of postcolonialism and feminism within postcolonial feminism gave rise to a Western conceptualisation of what Mohanty termed, in her influential critique, 'the production of the "Third World Woman" as a singular monolithic subject in some recent (Western) feminist texts' (Mohanty, 1984, p. 333). In her well-known essay, *Under Western Eyes*, Mohanty (1984) argued, the discursive construction of women of the 'Third World'[1] becomes its own form of colonisation, by assuming the homogeneity of their oppression without taking account of the historically constituted material reality of different groups of women. The effects of this can be summed up as follows:

> This fascination with the colourful exoticism of native women only serves to satisfy the voyeuristic desire of western women. The consciousness of difference sets up an implicit cultural hierarchy: western feminists have the privilege of preparing the path to liberation for their 'unfortunate sisters'.
>
> *(Riyal, 2019, p. 83)*

Postcolonial feminism focused on what was termed the 'double colonisation' of women through colonial power dynamics and also by patriarchy, although it was often Western conceptualisations of oppression under patriarchy (Ghandi, 2019). The 'third world woman' is subjected to both raced and gendered connotations which render her 'othered' by colonialism and feminism alike. Gayatri Spivak's critique of alterity, or the state of otherness, addresses this tension where the voices of postcolonial women themselves are underrepresented and lost in the debate (Spivak, 1988). In her most well-known essay, *Can the Subaltern Speak?*, Spivak provides a sweeping analysis of what she terms epistemic violence arising from the 'remotely orchestrated, far-flung, and heterogeneous project to constitute the colonial subject as Other' (Spivak, 1988, p. 76), which results in the experience of the 'gendered subaltern', or the marginalised, postcolonial woman, being silenced within the academic field. Moreover, given the racial and ethnic underpinning of much colonialism, where Whiteness is associated with the consolidation and maintenance of colonial power (López, 2005), as non-White races were essentially oppressed by White races, postcolonial feminism's tendency is to 'assign[ing] race to "others"' (Tlostanova, Thapar-Björkert, & Koobak, 2019, p. 83), as if Whiteness does not have any racial connotations or origins. Feminism too often associated with White Western women's perceptions, thus 'othering' any women who are different (Manning, 2018). In this way, colonialism is potentially perpetuated by the very postcolonial feminist approaches that seek to deconstruct it.

Some feminists, therefore, prefer to take an explicitly decolonial rather than postcolonial approach. Decolonial feminism has two broad aims: first, to deconstruct dominant forms of feminism primarily from the USA and Europe which tend to 'advertently or inadvertently replicate colonialist and racist ideologies' and, second, to challenge decolonial theory that often ignores the implications of gender (Macleod et al., 2020, p. 289). Decolonial feminism challenges the notion of the 'other', instead positioning non-Western women as having their own agentic experiences and identities (Manning, 2018). Moreover, using decolonisation as a lens to approach intersectionality supports an ontological and epistemological analysis that goes beyond Western perspectives of gender, race and class (Dibavar, 2022). A decolonial feminist approach explicitly embraces Indigenous knowledge and overturns the dominance of US or Eurocentric epistemologies that risk being dominant in a postcolonial feminist approach.

However, despite these critiques of postcolonial feminism, it has the potential to draw attention to the powerful role of colonialism in gendered oppression and its lingering effects in postcolonial societies, as they rebuild their national identities. Contemporary postcolonial politics are often deeply contextualised dependent on the specific conditions in postcolonial states, where localised gender politics can form part of the transformation (Young, 2020). Young argues that postcolonial feminism in the contemporary context of the postcolonial, rather than the West, addresses the situation of the ordinary woman in context, while relating her position to broader issues giving rise to a more powerful collectivity to work 'against a colonial legacy that was itself powerfully patriarchal, institutional, economic, political and ideological' (Young, 2020, p. 115). It then becomes much closer to a transnational approach, relating to alliances of people working together in forms of activism to work against colonial legacies, which I discuss below, after having first illustrated the influence of postcolonial feminism on accounting.

Postcolonial accounting research on gender

Although I have illustrated that a body of research exists addressing postcolonialism and accounting technologies, postcolonialism and the accounting profession, and accounting and Indigenous Peoples in postcolonial contexts, this tends not to address gender, although there are some exceptions, including a minority of feminist studies, which I will illustrate. My argument, as I will go on to articulate further in this chapter, is that feminist theory can bring more politically oriented insights to analysis of gender in accounting.

Globalisation threatens to silence local voices (Gallhofer et al., 2011), at least in the way that colonialism often ignores or misunderstands colonised peoples, or makes it structurally difficult for oppressed groups to make themselves heard, especially when they are in a minority in the professional space. With this in mind, McNicholas, Humphries, and Gallhofer's (2004) study of Maori women in the accountancy profession of Aotearoa/New Zealand aims to give them a 'voice' and 'listen to their stories' in a postcolonial context that continues a strong colonial legacy towards Indigenous groups. Rather than imposing a Western-centred form of postcolonial feminist theory, McNicholas et al. (2004) draw from Maori feminism, which recognises that Maori women's experiences are different from non-Maori women (who may be culturally complicit in the continued dispossession of Maori women), that Maori oppression is rooted in gender, race and class, and heavily associated with Maori collective self-determination and spirituality. Rooting the study in Indigenous postcolonial perspectives and feminism allows for a more nuanced and politically sensitive examination of Indigenous experience in the accounting profession.

Postcolonial research, even without an explicit feminist orientation or theorisation, can elucidate how accounting calculations and technologies are implicated in the construction of gender. Davie's (2017) study of Indian indentured workers illustrates how accounting instruments for management and control constituted and perpetuated gendered and sexualised ideologies in an imperial context using normative concepts of colonial masculinity as a form of imperial power that subjugated not only indentured women but also men. However, when theorised through a postcolonial feminist lens, as in Ranasinghe and Wickramasinghe's (2020) study of tea-plucking women in Sri Lanka, forms of resistance can be identified. The study shows that accounting management controls and technologies, which exert control on the pickers through fear and discrimination as well as weights and measurements, can be resisted by the women through confrontation and compromises, supported by their own use of a contextual variant of neoliberalism that subverts their own budgets and targets to allow some emancipatory actions (Ranasinghe & Wickramasinghe, 2020).

Decolonising accounting

Decolonisation originates from a different perspective to postcolonialism as I outlined earlier. It focuses on an active process of decolonisation of knowledge, mind and body, delinking from colonial world systems, and an embracing of 'pluriversality' and 'transculturality' (Sauerbronn et al., 2024). In other words, decolonial movements address both theory and praxis, in ways that recognise the interconnectedness of people with each other, with their context and within their struggles.

Decolonising accounting can take a number of forms. Although the term decolonisation is often used to address the education curriculum, which in the case of accounting requires highlighting its role in the neoliberal agenda (Alawattage et al., 2021), I am not addressing accounting education in this text. Rather, I explore the decolonisation of knowledge to provide diverse and contextualised epistemology and praxis, engagement with decolonising accounting as a profession and academia and the decolonisation of language.

Decolonising accounting research

Calls for a decolonising accounting research agenda emerged in Brazil in 2017, arguing for alternative decolonial epistemologies (Sauerbronn, Ayres, & Laurenço, 2017). The Latin American decolonial epistemology movement (DEM) promotes epistemic disobedience that allows scholars to emphasise the local context and interact with diverse perspectives including as participants in social movements in liberationist, situated praxis (Sauerbronn et al., 2024). Yet, decolonising accounting research need not ignore all Western perspectives. In an argument for the value of 'Mestizo thought', the hybridised cultures and intellectual ideas that emerged in Latin America over centuries after colonisation, in the production of critical accounting research, Cuenca Botey and Célérier (2023) caution against capitalist modes of research production, colonialism and masculinity being reproduced in what purports to be decolonial research, illustrating that reflexive approaches to research are needed to avoid the reproduction of domination in research itself. What is important in decolonial research is to take a programmatic approach that facilitates delinking/disengagement from colonialism, problematises how the accounting is produced and for whom and engages with oppressed or exploited peoples in forms of praxis (Ramírez-Henao & Sánchez-Guevara, 2023). Such approaches would lend themselves well to analysis of how accounting technologies support gender exploitation and domination, although to date accounting research has not embraced this agenda from a decolonial perspective.

Decolonising accounting as a profession and in academia

As I identified above there is little postcolonial research that is explicitly feminist in accounting. There is also a dearth of decolonial feminist research on the accounting profession, perhaps reflecting the dominance of quantitative and functionalist paradigms in accounting research. However, some research is emerging from Latin America, particularly Colombia and Brazil, on gender challenges in the accounting profession and accounting academia that are more oriented to decolonial feminist perspectives. Colombian studies indicate that accounting academia poses many gendered challenges for women who are in the minority (Chamorro González, Jacinto, & Peñaloza, 2020) and that women in public accounting are subjected to significant gender pay gaps (Restrepo Quintero & Isaza Castro, 2019).

Studies emerging from Brazil are more explicitly feminist. For example, Casa Nova's (2022) study of women's career trajectories in Brazilian accounting academia illustrates that, although they still face challenges, their representation is supported by earlier feminist struggles. Women resist sexist socialisation practices and sexist underlying values in Brazilian accounting that influence perceptions of their abject bodies, through the use of feminist support networks and feminist values (Lima, Casa Nova, & Vendramin, 2024). Although she does not explicitly use a postcolonial or decolonial feminist lens, preferring instead a poststructuralist approach, ground-breaking feminist research by da Silva (2016) on the interaction of race and gender in Brazilian accounting conceptualises a 'tetos de vitrais' – a stained glass ceiling – that encapsulates the challenges facing them that deny their professionalisation through a process of psychological violence. Women in accounting have to resist racialisation as well as sexualisation in accounting (da Silva, 2019), in a context where political representation and racial democracy for Afro-descended women is weak and continues to favour White males (da Silva, Casa Nova, & Carter, 2016).

While acknowledging the challenges of producing research on gender and accounting in some postcolonial contexts, there is an opportunity for further work to support uncovering how understandings of gender, race and class are derived from colonisation, with deeply entrenched cultural perspectives deriving from slavery. Moreover, these perspectives interact with postcolonial neoliberal demands for productivity and 'success' that perpetuate these sexist and symbolically violent cultural norms existing in accounting academia and the profession. Hence, a decolonial approach delinking from colonialism and working communally towards engaged praxis for accounting holds great possibilities.

Decolonising language in accounting

A further area of decolonisation to consider is around the hegemonic use of the English language in globalised societies, as well as in accounting practice and academia. In relation to postcolonial contexts, Alawattage and Fernando (2017, p. 8) argue that the continued use of the English language in corporate social and environmental reporting is 'an apparatus of power-knowledge signifying a "postcolonial encounter"' that they suggest negates local values, language and ontological positioning in favour of global neoliberal hegemony and the reproduction of postcolonial difference, which stifles meaningful debate and actions. English linguistic capital is legitimised as essential to professional accountants' status even in countries where it is not the formal or foremost language, meaning that the less proficient in English are marginalised or forced to employ hybrid linguistic practices (Aburous & Kamla, 2022).

Choice of language and how it is translated can have significant effects on its understandability and acceptance, which can have political and gendered outcomes. In this regard, de Onís (2019) illustrates the case of the role of language in abortion rights in the USA, where 'pro-choice' is the term preferred by mostly White, privileged mainstream feminists, framed in legal access and personal choice. However, she argues, 'choice' alienates many Latina women, whose culture holds reverence for family, but who are also subjected to numerous systemic inequalities, linked to poverty, lack of access to healthcare, legal status, racism and sexism, amongst others. For these women, *justica reproductiva*/reproductive justice is a much more meaningful term that encapsulates a broader social justice perspective and resists forming a linguistic boundary around abortion choices that further excludes marginalised groups (de Onís, 2019).

The hegemony of the English language is foremost in academic research, conditioning writing and influencing the production of knowledge (Komori, 2015; Lehman & Tienari, 2024). In order to decolonise language, some journals have begun to publish versions of journal articles in other languages[2] (Husillos, Larrinaga, & Martínez, 2024). Translation of language is inevitable in accounting research, in fieldwork and in the production of published research, and is imbued with socio-cultural, subjective and ideological processes, which can be particularly problematic where translation is embedded in the interpretive process and may inadvertently reproduce cultural hegemonies (Evans, 2018). Lack of equivalence in translated terms can be a problem, although this can be mitigated by the retention of original terms (Evans & Kamla, 2018). However, the greater challenge pertains to how researchers act as 'cultural brokers' between different languages and contexts (Kamla & Komori, 2018) and requires relational or intersubjective reflexivity (Haynes, 2023; Lehman & Tienari, 2024) when working within and across cultures. Evans (2018) argues that there is an opportunity for accounting research to:

> ...more widely draw upon insights from the interfaces with gender studies, cultural studies and post colonialism. There is, more specifically, scope for research on how language choice and grammatical structures impact on gender roles and power relations between men and women, and how and to what extent we can capture this in translation.
>
> *(Evans, 2018, p. 1863)*

Decolonising language requires attention to how translation can reproduce hegemonic representations of the colonised and acknowledgement that language is an important part of identity and that meaning may be perceived differently in different languages (Evans, 2018).

Again, although there is some striking work on decolonisation and its relevance to accounting, decolonial feminism is not explicitly addressed in the accounting context. It would be a powerful lens with which to further understand and problematise the decolonisation of language and cultural practices in the accounting context, which particularly pertain to women, women's histories and women's rights. I now turn to transnational approaches to feminism to apply them to accounting.

Transnational feminism

Transnational feminism emerged from feminist postcolonialism and feminist approaches to decolonisation (Briggs, 2016), with some scholars grouping them together as transnationality and postcoloniality both address gendered aspects of globalisation (Grosser & Moon, 2019). While transnational feminism addresses the oppressive nature of globalisation, racism and inequality, its focus on the inequities of modern global capitalism and their interaction with gender foregrounds matters of justice and agency. Transnational feminism aims to highlight the diversity of gendered experiences occurring in both Northern and Southern regions, refuting the notion that women share the same oppressions and exploitations within different geopolitical contexts, and focuses on intersectionality, social justice and activism (Zerbe Enns, Díaz, & Bryant-Davis, 2021).

Transnational feminism emphasises issues that transcend nation state boundaries, the *trans*national element, and therefore is of particular interest in addressing the political economy of migration, the state of refugees or oppressions of those who live and work on the margins of state and organisation. This includes, for example, the case of migrant women workers, who may face oppressions in both the places they left and the new economies in which they work (Briggs, 2016). Under global capitalism, labour markets and labour conditions are embedded in several sources of inequality arising from the interactions of race, gender, class, privilege or lack of privilege. Although it incorporates an element of intersectionality (see Chapter 4), transnational approaches to feminism go beyond identity issues to emphasise the systemic and embedded nature of various axes of oppression under capitalism, while encompassing forms of collective activist praxis committed to social justice. Transnational feminist decoloniality therefore focuses on 'antiracist, anti-capitalist, and anti-imperial interventions in theory, practice and activism' (Pal & Nieto-Fernandez, 2024, p. 60).

One of the key theorists in transnational feminism is Chandra Talpade Mohanty, whose influential text *Feminism without borders: Decolonizing theory, practicing solidarity* is widely recognised as shaping the field, and in which she asks the key question:

> What would an economically just and socially just feminist politics look like? It would require a clear understanding that being a woman has political consequences in the world we live in; that there can be unjust and unfair effects on women depending on our economic and social marginality and/or privilege.
>
> *(Mohanty, 2003a, p. 3)*

She outlines the underlying ideologies of sexism, racism, misogyny and heteropatriarchy that fuel these challenges and inflame violence against women, embedded in 'regressive politics of ethnic nationalism and capitalist consumerism' (Mohanty, 2003a, p. 3) and outlines her vision for moving away from these problems. Mohanty's proposals lie in feminist scholarship and practice which enhances solidarities and mutual accountabilities between and within different communities, decolonisation that includes enhancing collective democratic processes as well as self-reflexive transformations and anti-capitalist critique that 'demystifies' the values of capitalism in global societies (Mohanty, 2003a). In a subsequent reflection on *Under Western Eyes*, she reinforces her argument for the interaction of particularity of experience with analysis of global, economic and political frameworks *within*, rather than against, a framework of global solidarity and shared values between feminists across borders (Mohanty, 2003a, 2003b). Transnational feminism, therefore, goes beyond borders of nation state, geopolitics and forms of established knowledge. 'Borderland thinking is useful in many ways: as a way of considering complex hybrid identities, understanding oppression, framing resistance and empowerment, and conceptualizing activism' (Zerbe

Enns et al., 2021, p. 17). In this sense, transnational feminism is perhaps less of a theory and more of an approach to research, practice and activism that is anti-racist, decolonising, democratic, relational against repressive systems underpinned by capitalism.

Yet, transnational feminism is not without its critics (Briggs, 2016). A focus on solidarities can be construed as imposing a degree of universality on the experience of women rather than exposing contextual, geopolitical difference. A key tenet of transnational solidarity is anti-racism, but this can be experienced entirely differently by women of different races, where, even with reflexivity (Haynes, 2023), White women cannot understand the experience of institutionalised racism or fully comprehend their complicity in its perpetuation. Any suggestion of universal sisterhood belies the reality of women's experiences (hooks, 2000). Transnational feminism, it is argued, can obscure more localised resistance (Briggs, 2016) and tends to stem from a 'Western-centric frame that continues to represent itself as universal and delocalised' (Tlostanova et al., 2019, p. 82). Some of the institutions that support transnational activities, such as nongovernmental organisations (NGOs), or international organisations such as the World Bank or the United Nations, are themselves perceived as being overly neoliberal, reinforcing global capitalism or neo-imperialism (Briggs, 2016).

Yet, there are many elements of transnational feminism that have particular relevance to the accounting context.

Transnational feminism and accounting

There is no apparent research in the accounting context which is underpinned explicitly by transnational feminism. Yet, I argue, transnational feminism has a strong resonance with many challenges in which accounting is involved, particularly in relation to global capitalism, which take a number of forms.

First, transnational feminism highlights the threats pertaining to women on a global scale, which transcend national borders. The rise and prominence of misogyny, propagated by social media, is pervasive and influential on the socialisation of young men and boys. Much of this is commodified and marketised, for example, through pornography, in the 'common interests of capital (e.g. profit, accumulation, exploitation)' (Mohanty, 2003a, p. 140), underpinned by accounting technologies and sexual ideologies that intertwine.

Second, transnational feminism highlights the global means of production that pertain to women workers, consumers and citizens across borders. This could relate, for example, to the role of global supply chains and the opportunities, or lack of, for feminist solidarities and ethical practices that can occur under global capitalism. There is a role for accounting and accountability research in exposing, addressing and resisting exploitative practices, as well as providing counter accounts of alternative practice or resistance.

Third, transnational feminism is explicitly anti-racist, an agenda which, as was discussed in Chapter 4, is sorely needed given the poor record of the accounting profession on race, and the accounting's complicity in the underpinning of colonialism with racialisation, as discussed earlier in this chapter. Moreover, Mohanty (2013) cautions against the depoliticisation of anti-racist agendas, in times of increasing national security-driven agendas. In other words, the rise of the nationalist neo-right makes anti-racist feminism all the more necessary.

Fourth, transnational feminism is anti-capitalist, thereby offering opportunities for critical accounting to interrogate its neoliberal values and operations, particularly applying it to 'discourses of consumerism, ownership, profit, and privatization...the collapse of notions of public and private good, and the refashioning of social into consumer identities' (Mohanty, 2003a, p. 9).

Fifth, transnational feminism draws attention to the marginalisation of people under globalisation through the interaction of their gender, race and class. It can then be applied to an accounting analysis of migration, migrant labour, professional or lower paid labour, and the ideological construction of identities and values in the way that workers are constituted.

Finally, transnational feminism can be utilised to critique neoliberal ideologies, institutional practices and problematic democratisation, which draws from cross-border perspectives. Examples of accounting work in this space include Tanima, Brown, and Dillard's (2020) analysis of how a microfinance NGO in Bangladesh was dominated by neoliberal perspectives that prevented more enabling alternative actions and da Silva et al.'s (2016) study of the problematic political representation of women of Afro-descent in Brazil due to wider postcolonial challenges that require racial democratisation. This last suggestion for the application of transnational feminism to accounting is perhaps where accounting research has produced the greatest volume of work, on NGOs, on the sustainable development goals (SDGs) and on neoliberalism more generally.

In all these six areas, there is great potential to apply the tenets of transnational feminism to analysis of accounting technologies and the accounting profession.

Islamic and Muslim feminisms

A common theme in feminist research is addressing female subordination, but as I have argued throughout this book and we have seen earlier in this chapter regarding colonisation, it is important to take account of the particular context in which women are living, to understand the constraints and norms that they live within and to evaluate their agency in defying their subordination. This is also the case in Islamic contexts, where the meaning of feminism has constituted several forms (Hesová, 2019; Kamla, 2019; Karam, 1998), as it also does, in different ways, in non-Muslim countries or in Western contexts. In addition, not all Islamic countries operate in the same way with the same cultural norms and interpretations of Islam. The geographic area of feminism related to Islam is wide, including Asian, African, Arab countries but also Western contexts (Grami, 2013).

Following Karam (1998), Kamla (2019) notes that feminism in the Arab world tends to fall into three movements: secular, Islamist and Muslim feminisms. Secular feminism relates to support for women's rights, but from outside of organised religion, which is viewed instead as a personal matter of belief (Glas & Alexander, 2020; Kamla, 2019). Secular feminism is socially reformist but concentrates on the struggle for rights in the public sphere rather than within the domestic and private sphere (Hesová, 2019).

To address the difference between Islamist and Muslim feminisms requires an understanding of the position of women within Islam and within the Quranic scriptures (Al-wazedi, 2020). Many verses of the Quran stress gender equality, asserting that women and men are endowed with the same and equal potential as human beings, and establish the notion of egalitarian ethics within Islam (Shahin, 2020). However, misinterpretations of fundamental Islamic texts, such as the Quran and Hadith (prophetic sayings and actions that become traditions) (Mutaqin, 2018), which can be interpreted as free from patriarchalism, have given rise over centuries of Islamic jurisprudence to patriarchal readings (Denny, 2022). This is said to arise from traditional readings of the text which do not examine content and context together to prevent undermining the universality of the text, although what was deemed universal was directed by men whose interpretation favoured their own superiority, especially as particular words in the Quran may have multiple meanings or interpretations (Shahin, 2020). Moreover, these interpretations have become embedded in social, cultural and political norms, resulting in a predominant conservative tradition that collectively naturalises and essentialises women differently to men in Islamic societies (Sirri, 2020), albeit subtly differently in various geographical contexts.

Hence, both Islamic and Muslim feminisms challenge and resist the traditional and patriarchal characteristics of Islamic religion and politics (Sirri, 2020), arguing for a revised independent jurisprudential interpretation and critical reasoning on religious texts, or the practice of ijtihad, with a feminist lens (Althalathini, Al-Dajani, & Apostolopoulos, 2022; Keddie, 2018; Khader, 2016). However, Islamic and Muslim feminisms differ, with Islamic feminists not 'distinguishing between women's oppression and socio-political oppression as a whole' and Muslim feminists arguing that resistance is both possible and desirable within an Islamic framework (Kamla, 2019, p. 56). As Khader (2016, p. 747) puts it, 'not all Muslim feminists are Islamic feminists', as some are more aligned with the secular and oppose patriarchy on multiple grounds without accepting that 'the Qur'an is the only or primary source of moral truth'.

Islamic feminism can be a contentious term, with a perceived incompatibility between the two terms; that is, *Islam* as a religious belief and *feminism* as an international, legal and civil movement that rejects the introduction of religion into the struggle of women, and some conservative and fundamentalist Islamists reject feminism entirely as a product of Western imperialism (Grami, 2013) It is perceived as a postcolonial importation of Western feminist ideas into Muslim contexts, potentially threatening Islamic culture and society, or as a means of challenging Islam and reinforcing its stereotype as a discriminatory religion (Hesová, 2019). However, while some Muslim researchers in the Arab world identify with Islamic feminism, others reject it and avoid using it (El-Saadi, 2014). Nonetheless, Tlaiss and McAdam (2020) make clear that many contemporary Islamic feminists claim the term, arguing strongly that the Quran emphasises gender equality between men and women, but has been interpreted to promote ideological manifestations of patriarchy, requiring the deconstruction of the legitimacy of patriarchy from Islam. Traditionalism and feminism need not be opposed, Khader (2016) argues, if grounded in moral Islamic epistemology. Islamic feminists aim to reinterpret their culture in order to incorporate it within a civilised, culturally authentic and Islam-based reformulation of the perspective of gender and, in the process, achieve their alienated rights (El-Saadi, 2014).

It is perhaps because of this element of contention that some feminists prefer the term Muslim feminism to describe resistance strategies within an Islamic framework that promotes a more ethical and egalitarian re-interpretation of religious texts, challenging traditional interpretations (Kamla, 2019, 2024). It potentially avoids reducing women's identity to a single identifier pertaining to religion, risking essentialising women as objects of religion with little agency, when they may represent many different tenets of culture (Tadros, 2015). Muslim feminism can be used broadly and inclusively to pertain to highly religious Muslims who support feminism (Glas & Spierings, 2019), enabling the wider interaction between religion, politics, society and gender to be addressed, but also enabling women to be perceived as having agency to challenge gendered patriarchal norms. Muslim feminism resists and challenges fundamentalist identity politics, allowing for more intersectional thinking (Al-wazedi, 2020). Moreover, Glas and Spierings' (2019) analysis of public opinion data within the Middle East and North Africa (MENA) region shows that one in five Arab Muslims combine high attachment to Islam with support for feminism, gender equality and women's empowerment. Muslim women leaders are seen to promote religious ethical principles of equity, inclusivity, hard work, integrity and fairness, which can be used to resist subordinate identities (Khalil & DeCuir, 2018).

Accounting in Muslim contexts

There is currently little research in the accounting literature which addresses either accounting as a technology or accounting as a profession in predominantly Muslim countries. Women's financial literacy is weak in some Islamic contexts requiring intervention to support its development (Abdo Alaghbari, Abdullah Othman, & Mohd. Noor, 2021). Forms of Islamic banking and financing have been found to support women's empowerment in the public sphere but less so in domestic settings (Mboutchouang Kountchou et al., 2023), although it is beyond the scope of this book to address banking methods. There is also a body of literature on women's entrepreneurship in Islamic contexts, where entrepreneurial activity in the form of running small businesses is often more culturally acceptable than employment in mixed gendered businesses (see, for example, Alkhaled, 2021; Essers & Benschop, 2009; Tlaiss, 2019). Islam has been found to influence entrepreneurial activity in Arab countries in the way in which Muslim women entrepreneurs maintain Islamic values in their business activities (Tlaiss, 2015). However, despite Islamic guidelines towards fairness and justice, tribal customs in a country such as Jordan continue to restrict women's employment opportunities through patriarchal interpretations of Islam (Koburtay, Syed, & Haloub, 2020). It is unsurprising perhaps, given the structural and cultural issues identified above, that more critical articles on Islamic accounting – defined as research on accounting in Islamic financial institutions or within Muslim countries – are in the minority, with only four articles focusing on gender issues in 30 years, according to Alam (2022). However, the extant research on gender issues and accounting in Muslim countries is focused on the employment of female accountants and takes a feminist lens, which offers a contextually specific yet politically informed stance on their experiences.

Much of Rania Kamla's earlier work focuses on Syria, prior to the Syrian civil war which began in 2011. She explores the experiences and attitudes of Syrian women accountants to wearing the hijab, finding that some veiled women were able to use this practice to make it more acceptable within their own patriarchal context to access a working environment, but were then denied career progress due to the increased influence of Western accounting firms who appeared to prefer non-veiling (Kamla, 2012). Women's bodies and the way they are presented continue to be sites of contention within feminism, as some Northern liberal feminists consider the wearing of the hijab as oppression of women, while Southern or Muslim feminists may consider it as a representation of Islam that reflects their personal empowerment, as well as, for some, a symbol of resistance to Islamophobia and colonisation (Heshmati, Ali, & Pitre, 2021). Kamla's (2012) study is grounded in postcolonial feminism and argues that rather than focusing overly on arguments over the hijab, research should address the socio-political, cultural and global conditions that pertain to the marginalisation of women accountants in Muslim contexts. She argues that capitalism and patriarchy intertwine to produce the subordination of Muslim women, as professional accounting has become increasingly commercialised in Arab contexts resulting in discrimination based on gender and socio-economic position (Kamla, 2014). Even in an entirely different context from the West, and although they operate differently in this Muslim context, gender and class structures intersect to reproduce privilege in the accounting profession, as was also seen in Chapter 3. However, grounding her analysis in Muslim feminism, Kamla (2019) illustrates how Syrian women accountants mobilise resistance against patriarchal interpretations of women's roles by countering and challenging traditional interpretations, using their Islamic ethical framework as part of their identity construction as professional Muslim women.

Sian et al. (2020) also explore the interaction of gender, politics and religion in experiences of women auditors in another Muslim context, Saudi Arabia. Drawing from an Islamic feminist perspective that allows for cultural and social difference between men and women, their study illustrates the creation of a 'feminine version' of audit that enables the female auditors to negotiate gendered constraints around guardianship, family honour, dress code and client relationships, but which limits their experience to the forms of professional work allowed by specific interpretations of Islam, interconnecting with cultural and political conventions in the Saudi content. In Saudi Arabia, the gendered segregation of working space within the professional environment of Big Four audit firms, dictated by the State, produces a female-only section that marginalises women to the periphery of core professional activities (Agrizzi, Soobaroyen, & Alsalloom, 2021).

Feminisms 'from the margins' for social justice in accounting

Having explained the theoretical orientation and application of postcolonial, decolonial, transnational and Islamic or Muslim feminisms to accounting, this section considers their implications and relevance, and culminates in some principles for the decolonisation of accounting research as scholarly practice. Addressing the section as *feminisms 'from the margins'* does not in any way reflect that the feminisms in this chapter – postcolonial, decolonial, transnational and Islamic or Muslim – are marginal. They reflect the concerns and heritage of millions of women around the globe. However, these feminisms and the women's interests that they represent tend to be marginalised in the mainstream accounting literature, if they are addressed at all. This reflects the continued dominance of liberal feminism in accounting research (as discussed Chapter 3), which tends not to take account of non-Western contexts or address the concerns of non-White Western women, despite the social, economic, political and cultural issues that other feminist theories can elucidate. Moreover, liberal approaches to feminism tend to 'other' those who are perceived as different, rendering them marginalised outsiders. This chapter draws in these feminisms 'from the margins' to address their potential for accounting research.

As I identified earlier, accounting technologies are heavily implicated in the implementation and perpetuation of colonialism, both during colonisation and in postcolonial contexts. The interaction of gender, race and class in repressive regimes, such as slavery and colonisation, or in exploitation under global capitalism, is of interest to feminists globally, and also highly relevant to accounting scholars. There is, however, little accounting research which makes explicit use of postcolonial, decolonial, transnational and Islamic or Muslim feminisms. Anglocentrism is heavily persistent in international accounting research (Komori, 2015). Some accounting research identifies as postcolonial and addresses gender but is not explicitly feminist. Further research emerging from postcolonial contexts addresses gender but is not grounded in postcolonial, decolonial or feminist theory. Transnational feminism has not been explicitly utilised in respect of accounting, despite my earlier evaluation of its potential to critique the oppressive elements of globalisation, capitalism and neoliberalism, underpinned by accounting technologies and the accounting profession. Islamic or Muslim perspectives within accounting research are rare, despite Kamla's (2015) argument that intellectual Muslim debates, with their emphasis on spirituality, ethics and liberation theology, can challenge the domination of Western accounting's modes of thinking.

This lack of feminist accounting research drawing from postcolonial, decolonial, transnational and Islamic or Muslim could derive from a number of causes. First, it may reflect that accounting researchers do not perceive any benefit from a feminist orientation and theoretical analysis, or feminist researchers do not perceive the relevance of feminism to accounting. My aim in the book has been to redress this issue and demystify feminism and accounting, while illustrating their potential for social justice. Second, it may reflect the challenge of undertaking and publishing feminist research on accounting in contexts where quantitative approaches to accounting research heavily predominate, and where international journals tend to reproduce dominant English-language, Westernised approaches to research. Third, it could reflect the challenge of applying feminism within particular contexts. For example, some researchers do not wish to (Sirri, 2020), or are advised not to (Dambrin & Lambert, 2012), label their research as feminist, for ideological or professional reasons. Some postcolonial researchers, for example, even when they acknowledge gender issues under postcolonialism, may be loath to replicate the critique of importing Western concepts on to non-Western women.

However, I argue that each of the feminisms in this chapter has its own potential to illuminate and address inequalities arising from the use of accounting technologies and within accounting as a profession. These feminisms support contextually specific, collective and individualised means of challenging repressive forces and exercising agency and resistance, in support of forms of social justice. Islamic and Muslim feminisms allow for resistance *within* an Islam religious framework that supports Muslim authenticity yet challenges repressive cultural norms. Moreover, I identified six ways in which transnational feminism can support an analysis and critique of the application of accounting to the interaction of gender, race and class subsumed within global capitalism. These were highlighting global threats to women, highlighting the global means of production that pertain to women workers consumers and citizens, promoting anti-racism, critiquing capitalism and accounting's role in it, understanding accounting's role in the marginalisation of peoples and the role of accounting in upholding neoliberal ideologies. Transnational feminism particularly focuses on social justice achieved through feminist practice within everyday actions, in collective movements and in scholarly practice (Mohanty, 2003a), all of which are relevant to the application of feminist practice in the discipline of accounting.

Within postcolonial and decolonial feminisms, the role of research and practice on accounting as a technology and accounting as a profession would entail an approach to social justice that puts the perspective of postcolonial raced and classed women at the forefront. That is, in relation to people living in a nation state that was once colonised or in a state where European settlers have long resided; or people striving to decolonise their institutions, politics and culture, as well as their own minds and identities to recognise the legacies therein; or people working collaboratively across borders of geography, knowledge and institution to transform their societies and economies. This type of postcolonial politics:

> ...stands for empowering the poor, the dispossessed and the disadvantaged, for tolerance of difference and diversity, for the establishment of minorities' rights, women's rights, LGBTQ+ rights, and cultural rights within a broad framework of democratic egalitarianism that refuses to impose alienating Western ways of thinking on tricontinental societies.
>
> *(Young, 2020, p. 112)*

Furthermore, I argue that accounting as a research field can benefit from some feminist principles which support its scholarly decolonisation. These are to:

- Embrace alternative, feminist ways of thinking and knowing that move accounting away from its traditional functionalist paradigm towards a social justice agenda;

- Identify research projects that address the role of accounting in creating or perpetuating forms of power relations (whether colonial, gendered, raced or classed);
- Reject raced, classed and gendered power relations within accounting academia itself to promote a more egalitarian and supportive approach to researching, writing and reviewing;
- Respect research in other languages in order to undermine the perpetuation of coloniality by using the English language as the primary mode of publication and production;
- Reject the reducibility of gender to a binary variable, preferring more nuanced, fluid approaches;
- Embrace Indigenous and decolonised perspectives; and
- Embrace intersubjective research which is reflexive on its own positionality (on this point, see, Haynes, 2023).

Together, these principles support solidarities among accounting scholars, which have the potential to promote more compassionate, engaged, reflexive and less imperialist modes of research production.

Conclusion

This chapter has addressed the contribution of non-Western feminist perspectives to accounting research, specifically postcolonial, decolonial, transnational, Islamic and Muslim feminisms. It illustrated that accounting technologies played a pivotal role in the processes and politics of colonisation, postcoloniality and decolonisation. Colonisation played a constitutive role in the construction of gendered, raced and classed identities that still persist and are reflected in the dominant positioning of accounting under postcolonialism. Yet these feminist perspectives are not widely utilised in accounting research. The chapter made the argument for the relevance of such feminisms, including six applications of transnational feminism to accounting. It culminated with a synthesis that makes the case for feminisms 'from the margins' in relation to accounting for social justice, and identified some principles for decolonising accounting research practice more generally.

Notes

1 I have used Mohanty's own term 'Third World', which she points out is used critically, with awareness that it implicitly reinforces economic, cultural and ideological hierarchies between countries labelled 'third' or 'first' world [Mohanty, C. T. (1984). Under Western eyes: Feminist scholarship and colonial discourses. *Boundary* 2 (12/13), 333–358. https://doi.org/10.2307/302821]. Subsequently, Mohanty argued that she preferred the terms North/South or particularly One-Third/Two-Thirds Worlds to denote communities of people

situated as social majorities/minorities in different ways [Mohanty, C. T. (2003b). "Under Western Eyes" revisited: Feminist solidarity through anticapitalist struggles. *Signs: Journal of Women in Culture and Society*, *28* (2), 499–535. https://doi.org/10.1086/342914]. Other contemporary usage would be developing/developed countries or emerging economies.

2 Critical Perspectives on Accounting and Gender, Work & Organization.

References

Abdo Alaghbari, L. M., Abdullah Othman, A. H., & Mohd. Noor, A. B. (2021). Challenges and difficulties facing Islamic financial inclusion in women's economic empowerment in Yemen: Qualitative approach. *International Journal of Business Ethics and Governance*, *4*(3), 91–114. https://doi.org/10.51325/ijbeg.v4i3.80

Aburous, D., & Kamla, R. (2022). Linguistic tensions in a professional accounting field: English linguistic capital, hierarchy, prestige, and distinction among accountants. *Contemporary Accounting Research*, *39*(2), 1120–1149. https://doi.org/10.1111/1911-3846.12751

Agrizzi, D., Soobaroyen, T., & Alsalloom, A. (2021). Spatiality and accounting: The case of female segregation in audit firms. *Accounting, Organizations and Society*, 101238. https://doi.org/10.1016/j.aos.2021.101238

Al-wazedi, U. (2020). Postcolonial Feminism. In N. A. Naples (Ed.), *Companion to Feminist Studies* (pp. 155–173). Chichester: John Wiley & Sons.

Alam, M. S. (2022). 30 Years of research in Islamic accounting: A literature review. *PSU Research Review*, ahead-of-print. https://doi.org/10.1108/PRR-05-2021-0024

Alawattage, C., Arjaliès, D.-L., Barrett, M., Bernard, J., Casa Nova, S. P. d. C., Cho, C. H., Cooper, C., Denedo, M., D'Astros, C. D., Evans, R., Ejiogu, A., Frieden, L., Ghio, A., McGuigan, N., Luo, Y., Pimentel, E., Powell, L., Pérez, P. A. N., Quattrone, P., Romi, A. M., Smyth, S., Sopt, J., & Sorola, M. (2021). Opening accounting: A manifesto. *Accounting Forum*, *45*(3), 227–246. https://doi.org/10.1080/01559982.2021.1952685

Alawattage, C., & Fernando, S. (2017). Postcoloniality in corporate social and environmental accountability. *Accounting, Organizations and Society*, *60*, 1–20. https://doi.org/10.1016/j.aos.2017.07.002

Alkhaled, S. (2021). Women's entrepreneurship in Saudi Arabia: Feminist solidarity and political activism in disguise? *Gender, Work & Organization*, *28*(3), 950–972. https://doi.org/10.1111/gwao.12626

Althalathini, D., Al-Dajani, H., & Apostolopoulos, N. (2022). The impact of Islamic feminism in empowering women's entrepreneurship in conflict zones: Evidence from Afghanistan, Iraq and Palestine. *Journal of Business Ethics*, *178*, 39–55. https://doi.org/10.1007/s10551-021-04818-z

Annisette, M. (2000). Imperialism and the professions: The education and certification of accountants in Trinidad and Tobago. *Accounting, Organizations and Society*, *25*(7), 631–659. https://doi.org/10.1016/S0361-3682(99)00061-6

Arvin, M., Tuck, E., & Morrill, A. (2021). Decolonizing Feminism. Challenging Connections between Settler Colonialism and Heteropatriarchy. In C. R. McCann, S.-k. Kim, & E. Ergun (Eds.), *Feminist Theory Reader. Local and Global Perspectives* (5th ed., pp. 169–180). Abingdon: Routledge.

Bakre, O. M. (2008). Financial reporting as technology that supports and sustains imperial expansion, maintenance and control in the colonial and post-colonial globalisation: The case of the Jamaican economy. *Critical Perspectives on Accounting*, *19*(4), 487–522. https://doi.org/10.1016/j.cpa.2006.09.002

Bhambra, G. K. (2014). Postcolonial and decolonial dialogues. *Postcolonial Studies*, *17*(2), 115–121. https://doi.org/10.1080/13688790.2014.966414

Brannelly, T., & Boulton, A. (2017). The ethics of care and transformational research practices in Aotearoa New Zealand. *Qualitative Research*, *17*(3), 340–350. https://doi.org/10.1177/1468794117698916

Briggs, L. (2016). Transnational. In L. Disch & M. Hawkesworth (Eds.), *The Oxford Handbook of Feminist Theory* (pp. 991–1010). Oxford University Press. https://doi.org/10.1093/oxfordhb/9780199328581.013.49

Bryer, A. (2023). Critical accounting as an Indigenous project. *Critical Perspectives on Accounting*, *93*, 102579. https://doi.org/10.1016/j.cpa.2023.102579

Buhr, N. (2011). Indigenous peoples in the accounting literature: Time for a plot change and some Canadian suggestions. *Accounting History*, *16*(2), 139–160. https://doi.org/10.1177/1032373210396334

Casa Nova, S. P. d. C. (2022). "Ridin' down the highway" – Reflections on the trajectories of women professors in academia. *Advances in Scientific and Applied Accounting*, *15*(2), 030–046/047–062. https://doi.org/10.14392/asaa.2022150202

Chamorro González, C., Jacinto, R. A. P., & Peñaloza, L. V. (2020). Women Accountants in Academic and Research Spaces in Colombia. In C. R. Lehman (Ed.), *Resistance and Accountability* (Vol. 22, pp. 23–34). Leeds: Emerald Publishing Limited. https://doi.org/10.1108/S1041-706020200000022002

Cuenca Botey, L. E., & Célérier, L. (2023). On the relentless labour of deconstructing domination logics: The case of decolonial critical accounting research in South America. *Critical Perspectives on Accounting*, *93*, 102599. https://doi.org/10.1016/j.cpa.2023.102599

da Silva, S. M. C. (2016). *Tetos de vitrais: Gênero e raça na contabilidade no Brasil* [Tese de Doutorado em Controladoria e Contabilidade: Contabilidade, Universidade de São Paulo]. Faculdade de Economia, Administração e Contabilidade.

da Silva, S. M. C. (2019). Nenhum Saber a Menos! *Sociedade, Contabilidade e Gestão*, *14*(4). https://doi.org/10.21446/scg_ufrj.v14i4.31348

da Silva, S. M. C., Casa Nova, S. P. d. C., & Carter, D. B. (2016). Brazil, Racial Democracy? The Plight of Afro-descendent Women in Political Spaces. In *Accounting in Conflict: Globalization, Gender, Race and Class* (Vol. 19, pp. 29–55). Emerald Group Publishing Limited. https://doi.org/10.1108/S1041-706020160000019003

Dambrin, C., & Lambert, C. (2012). Who is she and who are we? A reflexive journey in research into the rarity of women in the highest ranks of accounting. *Critical Perspectives on Accounting*, *23*(1), 1–16. https://doi.org/10.1016/j.cpa.2011.06.006

Davie, S. S. K. (2000). Accounting for imperialism: A case of British-imposed Indigenous collaboration. *Accounting, Auditing & Accountability Journal*, *13*(3), 330–359. https://doi.org/10.1108/09513570010334900

Davie, S. S. K. (2017). Accounting, female and male gendering, and cultural imperialism. *Accounting, Auditing & Accountability Journal*, *30*(2), 247–269. https://doi.org/10.1108/AAAJ-08-2012-01080

de Onís, K. M. (2019). Lost in Translation. Challenging (White, Monolingual Feminism's) <choice>; with *Justica Reproductiva*. In T. Oren & A. L. Press (Eds.), *The Routledge Handbook of Contemporary Feminism* (pp. 77–93). Abingdon: Routledge.

Denny, F. M. (2022). Muslim ethical trajectories in the contemporary period. *Encyclopedia of Religious Ethics*, 586–594. https://doi.org/10.1002/9781118499528.ch69

Dhillon, C. M. (2020). Indigenous feminisms: Disturbing colonialism in environmental science partnerships. *Sociology of Race and Ethnicity*, 6(4), 483–500. https://doi.org/10.1177/2332649220908608

Dibavar, A. (2022). (Re)Claiming gender: A case for feminist decolonial social reproduction theory. *Global Constitutionalism*, *11*(3), 450–464. https://doi.org/10.1017/S2045381721000216

Dozono, T. (2022). Race and the evidence of experience: Accounting for race in historical thinking pedagogy. *Critical Studies in Education*, *63*(4), 468–484. https://doi.org/10.1080/17508487.2021.1899951

El-Saadi, H. (2014). Islamic Feminism in Egypt: Between Acceptance and Rejection. In J. S. Makdisi, N. Bayoumi, & R. R. Sidawi (Eds.), *Arab Feminisms: Gender and Equality in the Middle East* (1 ed., pp. 305–316). London: I.B.Tauris.

Essers, C., & Benschop, Y. (2009). Muslim businesswomen doing boundary work: The negotiation of Islam, gender and ethnicity within entrepreneurial contexts. *Human Relations*, *62*(3), 403–424. https://doi.org/10.1177/0018726708101042

Evans, L. (2018). Language, translation and accounting: Towards a critical research agenda. *Accounting, Auditing & Accountability Journal*, *31*(7), 1844–1873. https://doi.org/10.1108/AAAJ-08-2017-3055

Evans, L., & Kamla, R. (2018). Language and translation in accounting: A scandal of silence and displacement? *Accounting, Auditing & Accountability Journal*, *31*(7), 1834–1843. https://doi.org/10.1108/AAAJ-09-2018-020

Finau, G., Jarvis, D., Stoeckl, N., Larson, S., Grainger, D., Douglas, M., Ewamian Aboriginal, C., Barrowei, R., Coleman, B., Groves, D., Hunter, J., Lee, M., & Markham, M. (2023). Accounting for Indigenous cultural connections to land: Insights from two Indigenous groups of Australia. *Accounting, Auditing & Accountability Journal*, *36*(9), 370–389. https://doi.org/10.1108/AAAJ-08-2022-5971

Gallhofer, S., & Chew, A. (2000). Introduction: Accounting and Indigenous peoples. *Accounting, Auditing & Accountability Journal*, *13*(3), 256–267. https://doi.org/10.1108/09513570010334081

Gallhofer, S., Haslam, J., & Kamla, R. (2011). The accountancy profession and the ambiguities of globalisation in a post-colonial, Middle Eastern and Islamic context: Perceptions of accountants in Syria. *Critical Perspectives on Accounting*, *22*(4), 376–395. https://doi.org/10.1016/j.cpa.2010.09.003

Ghandi, L. (2019). *Postcolonial Theory. A Critical Introduction* (2nd ed.). New York: Columbia University Press.

Glas, S., & Alexander, A. (2020). Explaining support for Muslim feminism in the Arab Middle East and North Africa. *Gender & Society*, *34*(3), 437–466. https://doi.org/10.1177/0891243220915494

Glas, S., & Spierings, N. (2019). Support for feminism among highly religious Muslim citizens in the Arab region. *European Journal of Politics and Gender*, 2(2), 283–310. https://doi.org/10.1332/251510819X15538590890492

Grami, A. (2013). Islamic feminism – A new feminist movement or a strategy by women for acquiring rights? *Contemporary Arab Affairs*, 6(1), 102–113. https://doi.org/10.1080/17550912.2012.757851

Grosser, K., & Moon, J. (2019). CSR and feminist organization studies: Towards an integrated theorization for the analysis of gender issues. *Journal of Business Ethics*, *155*(2), 321–342. https://doi.org/10.1007/s10551-017-3510-x

Haynes, K. (2023). Reflexivity and academic identity in accounting: Intersubjective reflexive identity work as a feminist academic. *Accounting, Auditing & Accountability Journal*, *36*(5), 1379–1395. https://doi.org/10.1108/AAAJ-10-2022-6099

Heshmati, S., Ali, S. R., & Pitre, S. (2021). Transnational feminism and the policing of Muslim women's bodies: Implications for therapy. *Women & Therapy*, *44*(1–2), 47–62. https://doi.org/10.1080/02703149.2020.1775012

Hesová, Z. (2019). Secular, Islamic or Muslim feminism? The place of religion in women's perspectives on equality in Islam. *Gender a výzkum/Gender and Research*, *20*(2), 26–46. https://doi.org/10.13060/25706578.2019.20.2.482

hooks, b. (2000). *Feminist Theory from Margin to Center*. London: Pluto Press.

Hopper, T., Lassou, P., & Soobaroyen, T. (2017). Globalisation, accounting and developing countries. *Critical Perspectives on Accounting*, *43*, 125–148. https://doi.org/10.1016/j.cpa.2016.06.003

Hopper, T., Tsamenyi, M., Uddin, S., & Wickramasinghe, D. (2009). Management accounting in less developed countries: What is known and needs knowing. *Accounting, Auditing & Accountability Journal*, *22*(3), 469–514. https://doi.org/10.1108/09513570910945697

Husillos, J., Larrinaga, C., & Martínez, D. (2024). Language was always a companion of the Empire. *Critical Perspectives on Accounting*, *100*, 102753. https://doi.org/10.1016/j.cpa.2024.102753

Jensen, M. L., Agyemang, G., & Lehman, C. R. (2021). Accountabilities, invisibilities and silences in a Danish slave trading company on the Gold Coast in the early 18th century. *Critical Perspectives on Accounting*, *77*, 102181. https://doi.org/10.1016/j.cpa.2020.102181

Kamla, R. (2012). Syrian women accountants' attitudes and experiences at work in the context of globalization. *Accounting, Organizations and Society*, *37*(3), 188–205. https://doi.org/10.1016/j.aos.2012.02.002

Kamla, R. (2014). Modernity, space-based patriarchy and global capitalism: Implications for Syrian women accountants. *Accounting and Business Research*, *44*(6), 603–629. https://doi.org/10.1080/00014788.2014.933401

Kamla, R. (2015). Critical Muslim intellectuals' thought: Possible contributions to the development of emancipatory accounting thought. *Critical Perspectives on Accounting*, *31*, 64–74. https://dx. doi.org/10.1016/j.cpa.2015.01.014

Kamla, R. (2019). Religion-based resistance strategies, politics of authenticity and professional women accountants. *Critical Perspectives on Accounting*, *59*, 52–69. https://doi.org/10.1016/j.cpa.2018.05.003

Kamla, R. (2024). Muslim Women Accountants: The Unknown Feminists. In H. Vollmer (Ed.), *Handbook of Accounting in Society* (pp. 226–238). Cheltenham: Edward Elgar Publishing.

Kamla, R., & Komori, N. (2018). Diagnosing the translation gap: The politics of translation and the hidden contradiction in interdisciplinary accounting research. *Accounting, Auditing & Accountability Journal*, *31*(7), 1874–1903. https://doi.org/10.1108/AAAJ-08-2017-3067

Karam, A. M. (1998). *Women, Islamisms and the State: Contemporary Feminisms in Egypt*. London: Palgrave Macmillan.

Keddie, A. (2018). Disrupting (gendered) Islamophobia: The practice of feminist ijtihad to support the agency of young Muslim women. *Journal of Gender Studies*, *27*(5), 522–533. https://doi.org/10.1080/09589236.2016.1243047

Khader, S. J. (2016). Do Muslim women need freedom? Traditionalist feminisms and transnational politics. *Politics & Gender*, *12*(4), 727–753. https://doi.org/10.1017/S1743923X16000441

Khalil, D., & DeCuir, A. (2018). This is us: Islamic feminist school leadership. *Journal of Educational Administration and History*, *50*(2), 94–112. https://doi.org/10.1080/00220620.2018.1439904

Koburtay, T., Syed, J., & Haloub, R. (2020). Implications of religion, culture, and legislation for gender equality at work: Qualitative insights from Jordan. *Journal of Business Ethics*, *164*(3), 421–436. https://doi.org/10.1007/s10551-018-4036-6

Komori, N. (2015). Beneath the globalization paradox: Towards the sustainability of cultural diversity in accounting research. *Critical Perspectives on Accounting*, *26*(0), 141–156. https://doi.org/10.1016/j.cpa.2014.09.005

Lehman, I. M., & Tienari, J. (2024). What do you mean? Linguistic sensitivity and relational reflexivity in scholarly writing. *Organization*, *0*(0), 13505084241233956. https://doi.org/10.1177/13505084241233956

Lima, J. P. R. d., Casa Nova, S. P. d. C., & Vendramin, E. d. O. (2024). Sexist academic socialization and feminist resistance: (De)constructing women's (dis)placement in Brazilian accounting academia. *Critical Perspectives on Accounting*, *99*, 102600. https://doi.org/10.1016/j.cpa.2023.102600

Lombardi, L. (2016). Disempowerment and empowerment of accounting: An Indigenous accounting context. *Accounting, Auditing & Accountability Journal*, *29*(8), 1320–1341. https://doi.org/10.1108/AAAJ-08-2015-2167

López, A., J. (2005). Introduction: Whiteness after Empire. In A. López, J. (Ed.), *Postcolonial Whiteness. A Critical Reader on Race* (pp. 1–30). Albany and New York: State University of New York Press.

Lugones, M. (2010). Toward a decolonial feminism. *Hypatia*, *25*(4), 742–759. https://doi.org/10.1111/j.1527-2001.2010.01137.x

Lugones, M. (2016). The Coloniality of Gender. In W. Harcourt (Ed.), *The Palgrave Handbook of Gender and Development* (pp. 13–33). London: Springer. https://doi.org/10.1007/978-1-137-38273-3_2

Macleod, C. I., Bhatia, S., & Liu, W. (2020). Feminisms and decolonising psychology: Possibilities and challenges. *Feminism & Psychology*, *30*(3), 287–305. https://doi.org/10.1177/0959353520932810

Manning, J. (2018). Becoming a decolonial feminist ethnographer: Addressing the complexities of positionality and representation. *Management Learning*, *49*(3), 311–326. https://doi.org/10.1177/1350507617745275

Mboutchouang Kountchou, A., Haruna, A., Tekam Oumbé, H., & Wirajing, M. A. K. (2023). Women empowerment in Africa: Can we rely on Islamic finance? *Journal of Islamic Accounting and Business Research*, ahead-of-print. https://doi.org/10.1108/JIABR-06-2023-0175

McNicholas, P., & Barrett, M. (2005). Answering the emancipatory call: An emerging research approach 'on the margins' of accounting. *Critical Perspectives on Accounting*, *16*(4), 391–414. https://doi.org/10.1016/S1045-2354(03)00098-4

McNicholas, P., Humphries, M., & Gallhofer, S. (2004). Maintaining the Empire: Maori women's experiences in the accounting profession. *Critical Perspectives on Accounting*, *15*(1), 57–93. https://doi.org/10.1016/S1045-2354(03)00007-8

Mendoza, B. (2016). Coloniality of Gender and Power: From Postcoloniality to Decoloniality. In L. Disch & M. Hawkesworth (Eds.), *The Oxford Handbook of Feminist Theory* (pp. 100–121). Oxford: Oxford University Press. https://doi.org/10.1093/oxfordhb/9780199328581.013.6

Michie, J. (2011). Globalisation: Introduction and Overview. In J. Michie (Ed.), *The Handbook of Globalisation* (2nd ed., pp. 1–16). Cheltenham: Elgar. https://doi.org/10.4337/9780857931443

Mignolo, W. (2012). *Local Histories/Global Designs*. Princeton: Princeton University Press.

Mohanty, C. T. (1984). Under Western eyes: Feminist scholarship and colonial discourses. *Boundary*, 2(12/13), 333–358. https://doi.org/10.2307/302821

Mohanty, C. T. (2003a). *Feminism without Borders: Decolonizing Theory, Practicing Solidarity*. Durham and London: Duke University Press.

Mohanty, C. T. (2003b). "Under Western Eyes" revisited: Feminist solidarity through anticapitalist struggles. *Signs: Journal of Women in Culture and Society*, *28*(2), 499–535. https://doi.org/10.1086/342914

Mohanty, C. T. (2013). Transnational feminist crossings: On neoliberalism and radical critique. *Signs: Journal of Women in Culture and Society*, *38*(4), 967–991. https://doi.org/10.1086/669576

Mutaqin, Z. Z. (2018). Culture, Islamic feminism, and the quest for legal reform in Indonesia. *Asian Journal of Women's Studies*, *24*(4), 423–445. https://doi.org/10.1080/12259276.2018.1524549

Neu, D. (2000). Accounting and accountability relations: Colonization, genocide and Canada's first nations. *Accounting, Auditing & Accountability Journal*, *13*(3), 268–288. https://doi.org/10.1108/09513570010334126

Pal, M., & Nieto-Fernandez, B. (2024). Politics of transnational feminism to decolonize feminist organizational communication: A call to action. *Management Communication Quarterly*, *38*(1), 60–85. https://doi.org/10.1177/08933189231161620

Pinto, O., & West, B. (2017). Accounting, slavery and social history: The legacy of an eighteenth-century Portuguese chartered company. *Accounting History*, *22*(2), 141–166. https://doi.org/10.1177/1032373217696512

Power, S. B., & Brennan, N. M. (2022). Accounting as a dehumanizing force in colonial rhetoric: Quantifying native peoples in annual reports. *Critical Perspectives on Accounting*, *87*, 102278. https://doi.org/10.1016/j.cpa.2020.102278

Prakash, G. (1995). After Colonialism. In G. Prakash (Ed.), *After Colonialism. Imperial Histories and Postcolonial Displacements* (pp. 3–18). Princeton: Princeton University Press.

Quijano, A. (2007). Coloniality and modernity/rationality. *Cultural Studies*, *21*(2–3), 168–178. https://doi.org/10.1080/09502380601164353

Ramírez-Henao, D. F., & Sánchez-Guevara, A. (2023). The roles of accounting in the racial organization of work. *Critical Perspectives on Accounting*, *98*, 102661. https://doi.org/10.1016/j.cpa.2023.102661

Ranasinghe, S. B., & Wickramasinghe, D. (2020). Unveiling a postcolonial neoliberalism: Hybridised controls and emancipatory potentials for tea-plucking women in Sri Lanka. *Accounting, Auditing & Accountability Journal*, *34*(3), 651–679. https://doi.org/10.1108/AAAJ-12-2018-3785

Restrepo Quintero, K., & Isaza Castro, J. G. (2019). ¿De lo masculino a lo femenino? Reflexiones sobre el mercado laboral de la contaduría pública. *Revista Científica General José María Córdova*, *17*(27), 527–553. https://doi.org/10.21830/19006586.385

Riyal, A. (2019). Post-colonialism and feminism. *Asian Social Science*, *15*(11), 83–88. https://doi.org/10.5539/ass.v15n11p83

Rodrigues, L. L., & Craig, R. (2018). The role of government accounting and taxation in the institutionalization of slavery in Brazil. *Critical Perspectives on Accounting*, *57*, 21–38. https://doi.org/10.1016/j.cpa.2018.02.001

Rowe, A. C. (2021). Settler Xicana. Postcolonial and Decolonial reflections on Incommensurability. In C. R. McCann, S.-k. Kim, & E. Ergun (Eds.), *Feminist Theory Reader. Local and Global Perspectives* (5th ed., pp. 247–252). Abingdon: Routledge.

Said, E. (1979). *Orientalism*. New York: Vintage Books.

Sauerbronn, F. F., Ayres, R. M., da Silva, C. M., & Lourenço, R. L. (2024). Decolonial studies in accounting? Emerging contributions from Latin America. *Critical Perspectives on Accounting*, *99*, 102281. https://doi.org/10.1016/j.cpa.2020.102281

Sauerbronn, F. F., Ayres, R. M., & Laurenço, R. L. (2017). Postcolonial and decolonial perspectives: A proposal for a research agenda in accounting in Brazil. *Custos & Agronegocio*, *13*(3), 120–148.

Shahin, F. (2020). Islamic feminism and hegemonic discourses on faith and gender in Islam. *International Journal of Islam in Asia*, *1*(1), 27–48. https://doi.org/10.1163/25899996-01010003

Sian, S., Agrizzi, D., Wright, T., & Alsalloom, A. (2020). Negotiating constraints in international audit firms in Saudi Arabia: Exploring the interaction of gender, politics and religion. *Accounting, Organizations and Society*, *84*, 101103. https://doi.org/10.1016/j.aos.2020.101103

Sirri, L. (2020). *Islamic Feminism: Discourses on Gender and Sexuality in Contemporary Islam*. Abingdon: Routledge.

Spivak, G. C. (1988). Can the subaltern speak? In C. Nelson & L. Grossberg (Eds.), *Marxism and the Interpretation of Culture* (pp. 271–313). Basingstoke: Macmillan Education.

Tadros, M. (2015). From Secular Reductionism to Religious Essentialism. In R. Baksh & W. Harcourt (Eds.), *The Oxford Handbook of Transnational Feminist Movements* (pp. 651–667). Oxford: Oxford University Press.

Tanima, F. A., Brown, J., & Dillard, J. (2020). Surfacing the political: Women's empowerment, microfinance, critical dialogic accounting and accountability. *Accounting, Organizations and Society*, *85*, 101141. https://doi.org/10.1016/j.aos.2020.101141

Tawiah, V., Oyewo, B. M., Doorgakunt, L. D. B., & Zakari, A. (2022). Colonisation and accounting development in Sub-Saharan Africa. *Cogent Business & Management*, *9*(1), 2087465. https://doi.org/10.1080/23311975.2022.2087465

Thomson, K., & Jones, J. (2016). Colonials in camouflage: Metonymy, mimicry and the reproduction of the colonial order in the age of diversity. *Critical Perspectives on Accounting*, *35*, 58–75. https://doi.org/10.1016/j.cpa.2015.05.001

Tlaiss, H. A. (2015). How Islamic business ethics impact women entrepreneurs: Insights from four Arab Middle Eastern Countries. *Journal of Business Ethics*, *129*(4), 859–877. https://doi.org/10.1007/s10551-014-2138-3

Tlaiss, H. A. (2019). Contextualizing the career success of Arab women entrepreneurs. *Entrepreneurship & Regional Development*, *31*(3–4), 226–241. https://doi.org/10.1080/08985626.2018.1551790

Tlaiss, H. A., & McAdam, M. (2020). Unexpected lives: The intersection of Islam and Arab women's entrepreneurship. *Journal of Business Ethics*, *171*, 253–272. https://doi.org/10.1007/s10551-020-04437-0

Tlostanova, M., Thapar-Björkert, S., & Koobak, R. (2019). The postsocialist 'missing other' of transnational feminism? *Feminist Review*, *121*(1), 81–87. https://doi.org/10.1177/0141778918816946

Trees, K., & Nyoongah, M. (1993). Postcolonialism: Yet another colonial strategy? Span: Journal of the South Pacific Association for Commonwealth Literature and Language Studies, (36), 1–7.

Vidwans, M., & De Silva, T.-A. (2023). Indigenous peoples and accounting: A systematic literature review. *Accounting History*, *28*(2), 232–261. https://doi.org/10.1177/10323732231158406

Young, R. J. C. (2020). *Postcolonialism* (2nd ed.). Oxford: Oxford University Press.

Zerbe Enns, C., Díaz, L. C., & Bryant-Davis, T. (2021). Transnational feminist theory and practice: An introduction. *Women & Therapy*, *44*(1–2), 11–26. https://doi.org/10.1080/02703149.2020.1774997

6

INFLUENCES OF POSTSTRUCTURALIST FEMINISMS ON IDENTITIES, SEXUALITIES AND EMBODIMENT IN ACCOUNTING

Introduction

This chapter addresses the influence of poststructuralist feminisms on how identities are constructed and experienced, and how people with different sexualities are positioned, within the accounting context. Poststructuralism has widely influenced critical accounting research focusing on discursive effects of language and its interaction with power relations. However, poststructuralist feminist approaches, while theoretically powerful, have been less prevalent, potentially because feminists are concerned with lived experience and the potential for overcoming oppressions, which may not be apparent under discursive analysis. Nonetheless, the chapter illustrates the rich influence of and potential for feminist poststructuralist approaches to understanding identities and sexualities in accounting. Drawing particularly from the work of Judith Butler, it shows how binary constructs and cis-heteronormativities can be disrupted and subverted, applying queering to understandings of gender and identity in accounting. The chapter also addresses the physical body and embodiment in the accounting context, arguing that one can read the culture of accounting through the physical body and that more attention needs to be paid to sexist oppressions involving the body. Although not all the research discussed in this chapter is explicitly poststructuralist feminist, its influence is nonetheless important and hence I begin with a discussion of poststructuralist feminism.

Poststructuralist feminism

Poststructuralism is an intellectual movement that has been influential within social science since the late 1980s (Alvesson & Due Billing, 2009).

DOI: 10.4324/9781032636603-6

Poststructuralist feminism draws its origins from poststructuralist theory, which is influenced by several prominent theorists, particularly Saussure (1966), Derrida (1978) and Foucault (1980) (Benschop & Verloo, 2016). Although such theorists pay little, if any, attention to gender *per se*,[1] their underlying concepts of language, discourse and meaning are central tenets of poststructuralism and poststructuralist feminism. Ferdinand de Saussure's theory of structural linguistics suggests that language structured meaning rather than reflected an intrinsic meaning, which then influenced the poststructuralist perspective on language systems and discourses (Weedon, 1997). From a poststructuralist perspective, language is not a neutral and simple reflection of a reality (Alvesson & Due Billing, 2009). Language has no fixed meaning but is constructed and acquired through social relations; therefore, it is necessary to address 'in what specific contexts, among which specific communities of people, and by what textual and social processes has meaning been acquired?' (Scott, 1988, p. 35). Jacques Derrida addressed this by focusing on understanding language as text, which constitutes the social world, and can therefore be deconstructed to reveal the discursive relations inherent within it that challenge and reveal ambivalence in meaning (Benschop & Verloo, 2016). Discourse in poststructuralism is a 'historically, socially, and institutionally specific structure of statements, terms, categories and beliefs' that underpin meaning (Scott, 1988, p. 35). Discourse does not reflect a neutral reality but is contextually specific; therefore, it can have the effect of forming and reflecting a 'truth' in the consequences arising from it (Alvesson & Due Billing, 2009). Michel Foucault illustrates how discourses are imbued with power relations that constitute and govern individual subjects (Weedon, 1997). For Foucault, meanings are contested within discursive fields of force that rely on claims to knowledge embedded in institutions (Scott, 1988), and it is relations between these institutions that defines how knowledge is produced (Calás & Smircich, 1999).

Based on these principles of poststructuralism, for poststructuralist feminists, conceptualisations of men and women are not based on pre-existing truths that define an essential character, but are the products of language, discourse and culture. Hence, they argue for new ways of understanding sex, gender and difference by combining postmodernism and feminism, which takes account of the cultural specificity of difference societies, temporal periods and groups (Fraser & Nicholson, 1990). Gendering processes occur through cultural and discursive practices, so that individuals come to understand themselves and are perceived by others as gendered. Meanings are constructed through binary oppositions and contrasts in language, where a dominant meaning is established in opposition to the other, such as in the terms masculine/feminine, mind/body, culture/nature, reason/emotion, reflecting a cultural representation, which in turn establishes how relations between men and women are understood (Scott, 1988). Poststructuralist feminism challenges these binary constructions of meaning, and, through the deconstruction of language, identifies the hierarchies that constitute and privilege one position at the expense of another being silenced or negated. Hence, 'the binary logic of gender' is deconstructed allowing for a more sophisticated and subversive conceptualisation of gender (Benschop & Verloo, 2016, p. 106). This is why early poststructuralist feminists such as Flax (1987, p. 627) assert: 'Gender can no longer be viewed as a simple and natural matter of fact'. Poststructuralism allows for the analysis of gender in ways that are 'independent from particular sexed bodies... as the linguistic turn moved the concerns of feminist theory from the body of women to the body of the text' (Calás & Smircich, 1999, p. 660). For poststructuralist feminists, therefore, gender is not a fixed, homogenous characteristic, but is fluid, multiple, discursive and subjective.

The postmodern turn has heavily influenced modern culture, social science and science in its questioning of the nature and representation of reality (Ward, 1997). Poststructuralist theory challenges the privileged status of the 'reasoning subject', which in Western philosophy tends to be implicitly male, while poststructuralist feminism contests the authority, truth and power of knowledge about gender (Weedon, 1997). However, poststructuralist feminism, while potentially theoretically and philosophically powerful, has been contentious in its application to the experiences of women. Feminists from all positions have long fought to improve the lives, status and suffering of women against discrimination, sexism and violence and it is not always clear how destabilising discourses focus on social and political solutions to these issues. This causes Alvesson and Due Billing (2009, p. 41) to distinguish between a 'strong' and a 'weak' version of poststructuralist feminism, where the strong form focuses entirely on a discursive level, deconstructing claims within language, whereas the weak or soft form recognises both discursive constructs and forms of material reality. This means that it can simultaneously work towards understanding rhetorical constructs *and* political change in various forms.

In the remainder of the chapter, I will illustrate and evaluate the application of, and the potential for, poststructuralist feminism in accounting. I will highlight where, despite a lack of explicit poststructuralist feminist research and practice, the concepts of poststructuralist feminism have influenced, or could influence further, knowledge on the accounting profession and practice.

Poststructuralist feminism in accounting

Poststructuralist theorists, such as Foucault, have been widely used in critical accounting research, sparking debate between postmodern, Marxist and humanist scholars (Hoskin, 1994; Vollmer, 2019). Foucault's concept of governmentality, or how people are guided to conduct and manage themselves, is central to debates on how accounting practices contribute to the disciplining of organisations and individuals (McKinlay & Pezet, 2010). Some of Foucault's specific concepts support detailed analyses of critical incidents in which accounting is implicated. For example, his notion of 'apparatuses of security', applied to the way government managed movement and circulation of people during the Covid pandemic, helps to illuminate practices of accountability within government (Ahrens & Ferry, 2021). Similarly, a Foucauldian critique of market liberalism supports an analysis of the causes and effects of the Grenfell Tower disaster in 2017 (Funnell & Jupe, 2022).

However, explicitly poststructuralist feminist approaches to accounting and gender have been little used. Exceptionally, more than 30 years ago, Hammond and Oakes' (1992) article presented 'some feminisms and their implications for accounting practice'. They identified the promise of feminist poststructuralism in challenging essentialism and recognising that women are culturally constructed. They highlighted that 'the purpose of feminist poststructuralism is to make apparent the fact that more than one discourse is possible, thereby showing that the dominant discourse is not the only one available', illustrating that language is a site of political struggle (Hammond & Oakes, 1992, p. 57). In respect of accounting, they argue that 'practitioners should recognise that accounting is a language; it is used to legitimate corporate action. What is measured and disclosed is as important as what is not measured or disclosed' (p. 60) and they conclude that, aligned with poststructuralist feminism, 'accounting must be recognised as a language used for the benefit of the dominant group' which can thus be challenged (Hammond & Oakes, 1992, p. 66).

Despite this argument that poststructuralist feminism illuminates the discourses of accounting, few studies have made explicit reference to this approach to feminism, even when considering the breadth of research on gender and accounting as identified in this book. Although there is an important contemporary debate in accounting about the hegemony of the English language in research practices and publications, as was discussed in Chapter 5 (see, for example, Evans & Kamla, 2018; Husillos, Larrinaga, & Martínez, 2024; Kamla & Komori, 2018), this does not take a poststructuralist perspective on language as discourse, and is not specific to gender. Walker (2008) laments the lack of historical accounting research adhering to feminist approaches to history or even deploying theories of gender, suggesting that poststructuralist approaches are potentially significant for understanding gendered histories of accounting by drawing attention to the way in which the language and practice of accounting could be gendered.

A poststructuralist perspective, which considers language as discourse, primarily influences understanding of how the world is produced, but it is often combined with analysis of how people experience it, in the softer form of poststructuralist feminism highlighted by Alvesson and Due Billing (2009).

In this way both cultural and social analysis combine to allow for the constitutive nature of language in contributing to how different worlds emerge, while also seeking explanations for lived experience. An example of this blended approach is Nganga et al.'s (2023) study of women's doctoral education in accounting academia in Brazil, focusing on work-life conflict. They blend the use of constructionism and feminist poststructuralism to understand the process of construction of meanings (attributed to the doctoral students by themselves and by others) in their formation and socialisation as accounting academics, to interpret the conflict experienced between academic and personal lives (Nganga et al., 2023).

My own autoethnographical research on sexual symbolism in an accounting firm (Haynes, 2013b) illustrates how various discursive elements such as language, images and use of space become symbolic, ingrained, normalised and constitutive of behaviours and culture. For example, I draw attention to the 'inherently sexual use of language with frequent reference to colloquial terms for sex and for female genitalia – "No swearing in front of the ladies!"' (Haynes, 2013b, p. 385). I also illustrate how the use of sexualised images and artefacts, incongruously placed within the back-office spaces of the accounting firm, serve to construct and perpetuate dominant hierarchies and binary oppositions between masculine and feminine, legitimating the organisational superiority of men and the subordination of women. Cultural norms, such as these, are difficult to address, being construed as neutral, taken for granted, natural or usual, or even, in the case of sexualised calendars, acceptable 'gifts from clients'. This was despite a female counterculture and male ambivalence, both of which tended to reinforce the norms rather than resulting in challenging the meanings underpinning them. My research in this study was not defined as explicitly poststructuralist, although it was defined as feminist, but in its critique of the discursive elements, it is clearly influenced by the poststructuralist turn in finding language and symbols constitutive of meanings. I argue that discourse can form a deliberate or unconscious means of exerting gendered dominance, hence I show in this study the effects of such discourse in three interrelated ways:

i as a means of marginalising and oppressing those within the organisation who fall outside its dictates;
ii as part of a process of gendering identities;
and
iii as a mechanism for, and representation of, the operation of gendered power relations (Haynes, 2013b, p. 391).

Yet, in common with many other feminists, I find it is not sufficient to address the cultural representations and discursive construction of women; I also wish to address the *effects* of these discourses on lived experience, the use of agency and resistance. In this study, these were illustrated using autoethnographical vignettes, and a discussion of them, which illustrate affect, frustration, resistance and transformation, such as in this example:

> I could fight against the dominant cultures of the organisation, but by doing so my sense of isolation and exclusion became all the more profound. I was fairly miserable there for much of the time. I could adjust my actions and reactions to be acceptable to the group culture, but this meant rejecting aspects of my own sense of identity. I could pretend to attitudes I did not have or hide those I do. These options led to feelings of inauthenticity, of acceptance being conditional, and of poor self-esteem, all of which affected my sense of self-identity. I did not want to have to dissemble or to become a kind of person I did not want to be, in order to avoid being marginalised. Acceptance, rejection and exclusion shape identities...It was part of a process which saw me finally leaving professional accountancy for academia.
>
> *(Haynes, 2013b, p. 391)*

A reflection on this quote some 12 years after it was published illustrates some of the tensions in poststructuralist feminism that continue to persist and perhaps explains why so few accounting feminists make use of 'strong' philosophical feminist poststructuralism which focuses on discourse entirely. As I grappled with in this quote, the lived experience of accountants reflects agency – 'actions and reactions'; 'identity'; 'authenticity' and marginalisation within 'dominant cultures'. For many feminists, myself included, these issues reflect a social order which is inherently social and political and thus requires a political solution, even when the constitutive nature of language is recognised. Hence, in the remainder of this chapter, I will go on to discuss some of the influences of poststructuralist feminism and its interrelationship with identity within the accounting context. This will begin with a discussion of the influence of Judith Butler's work on performativity and accountability, before addressing identity politics, non-heteronormative identities in accounting and embodiment.

Butler: performativity and accountability

Judith Butler's reconceptualisation of gender and her theory of performativity have been highly influential on poststructuralist and feminist thought. Originating in her 1990 text, *Gender Trouble*, and developed subsequently, gender performativity is how 'gender is manufactured through a sustained set of acts, posited through the gendered stylization of the body' (Butler, 1990, p. xv). Performativity is not a singular act but a reiteration of a norm or set of norms (Butler, 1993). Performativity is not the same as performance, but it is the constant repetition of acts and routines of gender that then actually produce and reproduce gendered norms and identities. Or, as Lorber (2012, p. 285) describes, performativity is 'the unconscious process of reenactment that makes gendered selves that reiterate social norms of femininity and masculinity and inscribes femaleness and maleness on the body and heterosexuality on the psyche'. Butler argues: 'there is no gender identity behind the expressions of gender; that identity is performatively constituted by the very "expressions" that are said to be its results' (Butler, 1990, p. 34). This performance of gender has the effect of producing a gendered identity rather than the other way round, which is what causes the issue of 'gender trouble' (Butler, 1990; Ehlers, 2016; Lorber, 2012).

In *Bodies that Matter*, Butler goes on to elaborate that the subject is produced within 'a gendered matrix of relations', hence it is important to query how bodies are legitimated or abjected within those 'regulatory norms', and how they are governed by 'heterosexual hegemony in what qualifies as a viable body' (Butler, 1993, p. 16). 'The body becomes its gender through a series of acts which are renewed, revised, and consolidated through time' (Butler, 2020, p. 523). In other words, she claims that bodies are not naturally sexed but are constituted as sexed through gendered performativity, which claims binary sex as the norm, and those who do not conform, or 'fail to do their gender right are regularly punished' (Butler, 2020, p. 522). Heteronormative performativity is created through the ritualised and repetitive enactment of binary gender and heterosexual sexuality, which are not innate, but a product of such performativity.

Butler's concept of performativity, however, allows for more innovative and subversive performance of acts other than the heteronormative binary. Performing gender or sexuality differently, or what is termed 'queering' in queer theory, can be subversive (Lorber, 2012) and reflects a form of resistance to traditional gender norms. While heteronormativity is performatively constituted as normative through the use of language, it can be disrupted by overturning its use and presenting it back in an affirmative form, such as the use of the word 'queer' which had pejorative connotations being used to celebrate diverse sexualities (Rumens & Lewis, 2023). Butler's work contests the norms of gender, sexuality and culture (Butler, 1990), and the way in which 'performativity starts to describe a set of processes that produce ontological effects, that is, that work to bring into being certain kinds of realities or... that lead to certain kinds of socially binding consequences' (Butler, 2010, p. 147).

Butler's prolific work ranges across numerous areas of philosophy, feminism and poststructuralism, which can be applied to accounting and its related concept of accountability. In *Giving an Account of Oneself* (Butler, 2005), she discusses the nature of the self and the difficulties in being morally accountable to oneself and others. She argues that 'narrative capacity constitutes a precondition for giving an account of oneself and assuming responsibility for one's actions through that means' (Butler, 2005, p. 15). Despite individuals thinking that they ought to be able to give an account of themselves, this is a 'difficult, if not impossible, norm to satisfy' (Butler, 2005, p. 42), because the self is never fully coherent and cannot maintain a solid self-identity at all times. What Butler terms 'ethical violence' occurs as a result because people condemn themselves for failing to live up to their own expectations and condemn others for what they perceive as their unethical conduct. However, Butler (2005, p. 42) suggests that individuals can counter ethical violence through a position of 'humility and generosity alike', humility towards oneself and generosity to others, and 'it is on the basis of this susceptibility over which we have no choice that we become responsible for others' (Butler, 2005, p. 88).

Butler's (2005) philosophical understanding of *Giving an Account of Oneself* can essentially be interpreted as being about accountability, a concept closely related to accounting, since rendering an account is central to reporting practices, as discussed in Chapter 1. I further discuss how accountability is central to social and environmental reporting in Chapter 7, reflecting on going beyond economic responsibilities. Accountability may be enacted through reporting by a company to stakeholders (Brennan & Solomon, 2008) or it can reflect a need for greater transparency between one party and another, as Killian (2015) argues in her damning account of the nature of the Magdalen laundries in Ireland. In Butlerian terms, Messner (2009) points to the ethical importance of recognising the limited nature of accountability in providing a reason to another for one's behaviour.

Victoria Pagan, Stefanie Reissner and I applied Butler's theory to our study of the experiences of sustainability and humanitarian advocates participating in the World Economic Forum, a heavily corporatised context which often challenged their own values (Pagan, Haynes, & Reissner, 2023). We demonstrate their difficulties in being accountable to themselves and to the sustainability and humanitarian causes they represent, resisting temptation to condemn themselves for compromising their own values, or condemning the other corporate representatives for not having the same priorities. This is illustrated by the participants' reflections on their struggles and actions, for example:

> there are these contradictions which we all have to struggle with and it's always a balancing act, so you think first are you crossing any moral red line for oneself? (Sam)
>
> they might not agree with me because they may not see change happening in the way I see change ... it is more of a story of cooperation and the more you cooperate the more you can push people, you just do it... (Katherine)

> overall, it is better to have something that is deficient and can be criticised rather than not have anything, because then you will be operating in silos... at least there is a platform where we can go and to challenge. So overall it is important. (Tristan)
>
> *(Pagan et al., 2023, p. 267)*

In other words, in an empirical application of Butler's theory, we illustrate the struggle to resist ethical violence but show how trying to be 'accountable selves' is a process that Butler (2005, p. 103) terms 'becoming human' and leads to a greater sense of human responsibility. Although Butler's *Giving an Account of Oneself* is grounded in philosophy and is not a feminist work, nor is our own article, I raise it here to illustrate the possibilities arising from the application of her powerful oeuvre to the discipline of accounting that can expand our understanding of self, other, the subject, discourse and personhood. Yet, as Carter and Toms (2010) point out, Judith Butler's work has only begun to influence accounting explicitly from around that date, excepting Haynes' (2008a) research on bodies, which is discussed below, and Messner's (2009) work on accountability. Gendered performativity can have the effect of imbuing accounting workspaces with power relations that produce and reaffirm gender divisions (Carmona & Ezzamel, 2016).

Performativity v. doing gender

I think it is important to distinguish between performativity, as defined by Butler, and 'doing gender', as coined by West and Zimmerman in the 1970s, in which they 'distinguished between sex, sex categorisation, and gender' (West & Zimmerman, 2009, p. 113), and suggested that rather than masculinity and femininity being 'natural, essential properties of individuals', they are instead, interactional, 'social, properties of a system of relationships' (p. 114). They emphasise the importance of understanding that the 'oppressive character of gender rests not just on difference but the inferences from and the consequences of those differences...supported by historical and structural circumstances' (West & Zimmerman, 2009, p. 117). The concept of 'doing gender' emerged from the social sciences and is social constructionist, whereas performativity emerged from the humanities (Lorber, 2012), honed by Butler's poststructuralist feminist philosophy. Doing gender requires attention to gendering processes and practices embedded in routine everyday interactions (Benschop & Verloo, 2016). It can be performative, in the sense of 'doing' gendered roles in ways that are, or are not, 'fitted to situations and modified or transformed as the occasion demands' (West & Zimmerman, 1987, p. 135).

Doing gender lends itself to understanding how gender is performed in organisational contexts, including the accounting context. For example,

Adapa, Rindfleish and Sheridan (2016) draw on the concept to explain the absence of women from senior roles in Australian regional accounting firms, illustrating how gender is enacted through structures, hierarchies and identities in ways that shape expectations of women's roles. Similarly, also understanding gender as socially and historically constituted and from a 'doing gender' perspective, the hegemonic masculinity of management accountants tends to prevail despite some caring attributes such as empathy being construed as important (Ala-Heikkilä, Lämsä, & Järvenpää, 2024).

Butler's performativity, however, is not the same as doing gender and is not simply a performance of gender; it is the routinisation of acts that actively creates gender, since for Butler there is no pre-existing sex/gender distinction (Butler, 1990). In Butler's conceptualisation of performativity, 'to be socially understood as a feminine subject, then, an individual must reproduce the norms associated with femininity, and it is this activity that *makes* her gendered a woman' (Ehlers, 2016, p. 358, italics in original). Performativity can therefore be subversive, overturning a gender order, questioning heteronormativity and its psychic effects. Butler's conceptualisation of performativity and its relation to identities being produced through acts, language and gestures (McKinlay, 2010) has perhaps had the most influence on accounting research, particularly her poststructuralist contestation that gender identities are unstable, not fixed or binary, and cannot be reduced to an essential essence. The next section addresses the influence of poststructuralism on identity generally before discussing how this might relate to accounting and accountants.

Poststructuralist feminism's influence on understanding identity in accounting

Poststructuralist conceptions of meaning and poststructuralist feminism clearly have implications for conceptualisation of identity. As Ehlers (2016) explains, although different types of feminists have resisted essentialisation and universalism as women by addressing their own particular differences (based on, for example, race, class or sexuality), they tend to accept some kind of identification on which to base solidarities or political identities. Levels of identity range over the individual, group/occupational/professional, organisational and societal/cultural, with theories covering numerous traditions (Corlett et al., 2017). The main areas of dispute can be characterised between the broad categories of humanism and poststructuralism concerning

> the extent to which human beings actively create the social worlds they inhabit through their everyday social encounters; and secondly, the way in which the social context of structures, culture and institutions (such as the accounting profession) moulds and forms social activity.
>
> *(Haynes, 2008b, p. 623)*

In humanist forms of identity theory, the self is an agentic, rational subject, whose inner essentialist nature can express itself and is free to follow its own desires and fulfil its potential as a human being (Elliott, 2001; Sarup, 1996). Hence, the self is an ongoing project, which demands the active participation of the subject and allows for levels of individual agency (Giddens, 1991). The question from a sociological perceptive is how that inner, agentic self can operate within the confines or structures in which it finds itself. Weedon (1997) explains the assumptions from this perspective as being that rational individuals have the potential for self-development given the right context, with language being a tool for self-expression. The implications for feminism are seen in liberal feminism with its demands for equal opportunities to give a right to self-actualisation and autonomy (see Chapter 3); in Marxist feminism, which focuses on critiquing capitalist means of production rather than sexual difference between men and women (see Chapter 4); in some radical feminism, which focuses on women's assumed essence (see Chapter 4); and in affinity eco-feminism (see Chapter 7), which assumes women's unique relationship and affinity with nature.

However, poststructuralism has challenged the assumption that people have coherent unified identities (Weedon, 1997). The subject under poststructuralist theory has no fundamental essence but is the product of discourse (Davies & Gannon, 2011). Poststructuralists, therefore, reject the concept of identity as a form of categorisation, as it negates differences and is bound up in relations of power and knowledge that have produced such an identity. As a result, poststructuralist theorists prefer the term 'subjectivity' rather than 'identity' to denote 'the ways individuals are subjected to and participate in forming themselves in relation to dominant cultural knowledges, discourses, and practices' (Ehlers, 2016, p. 357). Subjectivity, according to Weedon (1997, p. 32), 'is used to refer to the conscious and unconscious thoughts and emotions of the individual, her sense of herself and her ways of understanding her relation to the world'. In poststructuralist analysis, agency is limited and only occurs when 'speaking subjects are aware of the different ways in which they are made subject' and thus disrupt current discourses and invent 'new subject positions', so that they have 'a sense of oneself as one who can go beyond the given meanings in any one discourse' (Davies, 1991, pp. 50–51).

Scholars of gender and identity influenced by poststructuralist feminism, therefore, consider gender as produced by culture and discourse, and fluid and emergent, rather than fixed and innate. Even the sexed body is construed as gendered through discourse because it is constrained by heterosexual discourse that requires conformity to either binary gender (Ehlers, 2016). Hence, poststructuralist theorists, such as Butler, are more concerned with how power relations shape discourses than they are with the essence of identity or the self-identification of gender. From this arises the questioning of gendered identity that exercises some gender-critical feminists (Zanghellini, 2020) and, certainly in the UK at least, has driven a 'moral panic whereby conservative thinkers and some feminist activists are joining forces with the aim of resurrecting gender binaries' (Hines, 2020, p. 699) amid a populist backlash against identity politics. Ehlers (2016, p. 359, italics in original) gives a useful summary of the impact of poststructuralist feminist theory on gendered identity and identity politics:

> [first] to question the identity 'woman' *occasions the possibility* of reimagining what gender might *mean* and how it might be *lived*. Second, it is both possible to recognize the contingency of gender while at the same time struggling against the terms that regulate and constrain gendered life. And third, poststructuralist theorists seek to imagine other forms of solidarity that might be cultivated, such that, rather than rallying around a supposed common identity individuals might instead rally around common goals (that are not linked necessarily to identity – such as childcare needs, the mitigation of violence, etc).

In the remainer of this section, I will address the influence of poststructuralism and poststructuralist feminism in our understanding of identity and the implications for accounting. I have already discussed, largely from a social constructionist perspective, how accountants are socialised into being professional accountants in Chapter 3. However, my focus in this section is to explore the effects of poststructuralist fluidity and emergence on accountants' identities, as a product of discourse.

According to Brouard et al. (2017), the professional identity of accountants is formulated from two main influences: first, wider society, which includes governments, clients, the general public and media, and, second, the accounting profession itself, in terms of accounting firms, professional accounting bodies or associations, other employers of accountants and the individual accountants themselves. They suggest that both society and the profession influence accountants' professional identity directly, but society also influences the accounting profession indirectly partly because the relationship between the profession and society can viewed as a social contract (Brouard et al., 2017), meaning that the profession receives the benefit of legitimation and status in return for its expertise and responsibility. Various factors relating to the profession, such as the failure of a professional firm (such as Arthur Anderson following the Enron scandal) (Gendron & Spira, 2010), the merger of various professional accounting associations (Guo, 2018) or the shifting nature of the profession with the advent of new technologies (Tomo, 2023), mean that professional identity can come under threat of destabilisation. Identity threats occur when there is a perceived harm to values, meanings or enactments of identities (Petriglieri, 2011).

However, shifts to identity can also occur to professional accountants from influences outside the profession. While society and the profession may influence professional identity, it is hard to disentangle personal identity from professional, since how we are gendered, raced, classed or perceived as abled/disabled, and the political ramifications of these characteristics, affects the way we are perceived in society and our experiences in the accounting profession, as I have discussed in this text in Chapters 3 and 4. Feminists have long argued that society, and indeed the accounting profession, are not gender-neutral. Professional identities may be gendered due to archetypes and stereotypes associated with masculine and feminine social and cultural norms within professions and professional services firms (Haynes, 2013a). Yet, the interaction of the professional and the personal in terms of identity has rarely been addressed, with the focus in much of the accounting literature tending to be on experience rather than identity.

Thus, in a study of the impact of motherhood on professional accountants' identities, I address the juxtaposition, fluidity and transformation of identity occurring during a time of change (Haynes, 2008b). The study addresses the prevalent cultural discourses of professionalism and mothering which influence the accountants' identities. For example, from a professional perspective, the women in the study are subjected to cultural norms of long working hours, availability to clients and working away from home. Senior women are culturally presented as career 'role models' – a 'high-flyer' – which reinforces high expectations. Professional discourses around maternity leave are that the women were 'skiving', 'gadding about', 'having a great time' at the expense of their work. Moreover, the participants' perceptions of motherhood are influenced by moral discourses of the ideal mother, or what one participant defines as being the 'perfect' mother, despite the oppressive, exhausting workload:

> 'I want the best for my child. I'm making most of his food... so in some ways I could argue that I'm making it harder for myself. I have great intentions of using terry towelling nappies...that's more washing and stuff, but it's something I've chosen to do, so I've got to do it' (Judith).
>
> *(Haynes, 2008b, p. 632)*

Their own memories of being mothered provide coercive prescriptions of gendered behaviours. For example, a participant references an ideal childhood that she is unable to replicate as a working professional accountant for her own child, leading to a sense of consternation and guilt:

> My mum never worked, you know, she was always there when I came home from school, you know, the house was always warm, the lights were

> always on, all those sort of things. ...I worry that he's going to miss out on that (Maureen).
>
> *(Haynes, 2008b, p. 632)*

After coming back to work after having their babies, the women felt transformed, 'often using a discourse that encompassed reference to changes experienced between a pre and post-child self' (p. 636): '...my old self'; 'I was a different person'.

> The relationship between these two selves, professional accountant and mother, is complex, with women all too commonly experiencing self-doubt and guilt in the transformation and negotiation process between the two identities, rooted in the social and cultural practices and expectations of professional work and motherhood.
>
> *(Haynes, 2008b, p. 637)*

Although this study was not positioned as a poststructuralist feminist research project, it is evident that it is influenced by elements of poststructuralist theory on the self. It assumes the self as fluid and shaped by prevailing cultural discourses, allowing for not one fixed identity but multiple selves that are juxtaposed and intertwined. It examines identity and the self as a process of becoming, a 'process of connecting personal and social change' (Haynes, 2008b, p. 638). If I were to carry out this project again, I would potentially be more explicit on this discursive construction and performative quality of gendered identity that it raises. However, the study shows the ways in which the women accountants *become* mothers and the gendered expectations placed on them from discourses of 'good' professional accountant inherent in the profession and 'good' mother prevailing in society.

Next in this chapter I will also go on to discuss the relations between identity, sexuality and accounting.

Queering identity and gender in accounting

Poststructuralist feminism and the emergence of queer theory have influenced the way we think of identity and sexuality. These theories 'attack the gender order directly by multiplying gender categories and undermining the boundaries between women and men, female and male, heterosexual and homosexual...making room for new kinds of relationships and multiple sexualities' (Lorber, 2012, p. 13). A logic of sexual attraction that presupposes binary oppositional categories of gender is overturned by poststructuralist feminism, and queer theory is a poststructuralist mode of critique that challenges assumptions about sex, gender and sexuality (Benschop & Verloo, 2016). According to Rumens (2016, p. 115), queer theory's central analytic aim is 'the deconstruction of categories of knowledge and identities that are taken for granted, considered natural and beyond contestation'. Hence, heteronormativity and performativity are core concepts in queer theory, critiquing fixed identities and broadening perspectives on diversity (Bendl, Fleischmann, & Hofmann, 2009). Butler's strong influence on queer theory is evident in these concepts, from her identification and critique of the 'heterosexual matrix' (Butler, 1990) and the normalising of gender and desire into heteronormative binaries through the 'materialisation of regulatory norms that are in part those of heterosexual hegemony' (Butler, 1993, p. 15).

I have already discussed, particularly in Chapters 2 and 3, the masculinity of the accounting profession, but I want to extend this debate in this chapter to the cis-heteronormativity of the accounting profession. In a text on feminist theories and their relation to accounting, I consider it essential to include non-binary, non-cis and non-heterosexual perspectives, given that they too are oppressed through normative gendered assumptions. In this I concur with Butler who argues that feminism is a means of countering repressive norms that limit the experience of gender along with other identities:

> That feminism has always countered violence against women, sexual and nonsexual, ought to serve as a basis for alliance with these other movements, since violence against bodies is part of what joins anti homophobic, antiracist, feminist, trans, and intersex activism.
>
> *(Butler, 2004b, p. 9)*

Moreover, in a chapter on poststructuralism and identity, it is appropriate to consider that professional firms wield considerable resources in their discursive representation, meaning that the inclusion of a wider variety of perspectives offers an alternative reality.

Non-cis-heteronormative identities in accounting

Research on non-heteronormative and non-cis identities within the accounting context has gained traction only in the last decade and then it is in a considerable minority compared with the much higher amount of research on gender, mostly focusing on women. Rumens' (2016) article was a critical provocation to accounting scholarship of the value of queer theory within studies of accounting, countering the view, through their silence on sexuality, that accounting firms and places of work are asexual. He argues that queer theory disrupts heteronormativity and challenges the ontology of heterosexuality, thus 'disturbing deeply entrenched epistemological and ontological premises upon which accounting studies... rest' (Rumens, 2016, p. 115). He maintains that by *not* accounting for LGBTQI+ people in research, characteristics and stereotypes go unchallenged, sexualities are perceived as a private issue with no public relevance, yet 'in accounting work contexts, sexual and gender stereotyping can potentially hinder identity development, well-being, career mobility and work performance' (Rumens, 2016, p. 116). His erudition of the value of queer theory and his provocation to accounting scholars of gender to be more reflexive on the potential for perpetuating heteronormative assumptions was a timely call for broader research on how the accounting profession and technologies of accounting perpetuate heteronormativity.

Since then, a body of work is beginning to emerge on non-heteronormative identities in the accounting profession, which, although not defined as feminist, often uses queer theory or is influenced by a poststructuralist perspective, which focuses 'on the fragmented, shifting complexity of meanings (rather than on universal notions of centralized order)' (Bendl et al., 2009, p. 626). 'Queering' can include the need to disrupt, subvert, open up or overturn established norms and taken-for-granted ways of thinking, rather than pertaining only to the position of queer-identifying people (Ghio, McGuigan, & Powell, 2023). In any case, McGuigan and Ghio (2018) caution against treating the LGBTQI+ community as a homogeneous group in any process of 'queering accounting', but to allow for sexual diversity, fluidity, intersectionality and multiple heterogenous perspectives. Their point is well made since, as I have discussed in this text, many feminists have also opposed the identification of women as a homogenous group, which negates their possible multiple differences. They also argue for embracing multiple worldviews both in the profession and in accounting research, together with breaking the overlap between heterosexuality and heteronormativity, since they argue: 'Given the presence of implicit and explicit coercive heteronormative aspects within the accounting profession and the associated pressure to conform, heterosexuality may include sites for disruption to the constituted organizational regimes' (McGuigan & Ghio, 2018, p. 629).

Research is emerging on the experiences of LGBTQI+ accountants in the profession and the role of firms in supporting this community. In French audit firms, gay and lesbian employees were found to conceal their sexualities and personal identities, and thus experience significant discomfort, due to the stereotyping and heteronormative homo-sociality they faced, which reflects a heterosexual perception of what represents professional identity and success (Stenger & Roulet, 2018). In the context of Australia, which legislated for marriage equality in 2017, Egan's (2018) research examines publicly available discourse from the Big Four and other large accounting firms' statement on the nature and drivers of diversity initiatives for LGBTQI+ staff. He finds that suggestions, from the employers' perspective, for a more inclusive professional workplace culture are under way but detail on actual policies is scarce and there is a risk of shifting responsibilities for improvement to the LGBTQI+ staff themselves. Throughout the 2010s, the

Big Four firms in Australia sought to redress perceptions of their 'male, pale and stale' image, offering hope of change to LGBTQI+ employees, which was negated by a persistence of business case logics and silence by the end of the decade (Egan & Voss, 2023b). Nonetheless LGBTQI+ staff navigated 'the shifting technologies of client power', meaning how people manage themselves and their behaviours, resulting in some limitations to client privileges for those who disagreed with the changing social attitudes around sexuality and gender at the time of the marriage equality legislation in 2017 (Egan & Voss, 2024). The 'promise of happiness' (p. 2040) offered to LGBTQI+ staff in accounting is evidenced by progressive and supportive statements regarding legislative change by the firms, 'emerging allies and visible LGBTIQ+ staff' (p. 2041); however, any evolution of workplace norms tended to focus on 'narrow opportunities for gay men, with less on offer for individuals of intersectionality, including ethnically diverse and female individuals' (Egan & Voss, 2023a, p. 2045), meaning that gendered norms persist.

What is notable in the research of Egan and Voss, apart from their access to powerful data from LGBTQI+ individuals, is the situating of their work in poststructuralist theorisations (albeit not explicitly feminist), which clearly evidences the shifting focus within sexuality and identity studies to fluidity and non-heteronormativity. Hence, the articles above are underpinned by theorisations from queer theory and Butler (1990) (Egan, 2018); Butler (2004a), in turn, is influenced by Levinas (1991) (Egan & Voss, 2023b); Foucault's (1990) technologies of power and governmentality (Egan & Voss, 2024) and Ahmed's (2010) *Promise of Happiness*, located in feminist and queer theory. This indicates the richness of the potential for poststructuralist theorising in understanding subjectivities and discourse around gender, sexuality and power in the context of accounting.

It is worth noting, however, that much of the research on non-heteronormative identities in accounting thus far has been able to take place in countries where, despite the findings of continued discomfort and problematisation of professional accounting workplaces, LGBTQI+ employees live in a context where their sexuality is legal and broadly tolerated, when in some countries it remains illegal and subject to persecution. It is also notable that in those studies above which drew from the perspective and experiences of LGBTIQ+ participants, the experiences of gay men are in the majority. This could be for a number of reasons, including relative larger numbers, or a lack of feeling of safety in self-disclosing sexualities and volunteering to take part in research. Egan (2018) found that the diversity discourses coming from large professional firms tended to omit the terms 'transgender', 'intersex' and 'queer' on their websites as if this were a step too far in challenging dominant cultural norms. This suggests some kind of hierarchy of acceptability of diverse sexualities in accounting. Moreover, Egan and Voss (2023b) note the ethical challenges of asking participants to self-disclose sexualities and gender identities, and recognise the potential for 'survivorship bias', where only those participants who are able to survive in the accounting firms and are willing to be interviewed tend to take part.

The more underresearched area of identity is around cisnormativity and the experiences of trans people, bearing in mind that trans people can also reflect a range of sexualities. Transgender people are subjected to a 'matrix of violence' intersecting with a form of necro-politics or the use of socio-political power to determine whose lives are deemed less worthy than other individuals in society (Westbrook, 2023). Violence occurs both literally and symbolically. Cisnormativity in workplace cultures generally tends to sustain discrimination towards trans people and gender non-conforming employees (Anderson, 2023). Moreover, research on trans women of colour in the USA finds they face multiple forms of discrimination through economic exclusion, a racially gendered glass ceiling and employment constraints (Greene & Ervin, 2024). Currently, research on trans people in accounting is fairly minimal (Egan & Voss, 2023b). As Chamorro González, Patiño-Jacinto & Reiss (2024) point out in their research on Colombia, it is not always possible to find lesbian, transsexual, queer, transgender or intersex accountants, who are undoubtedly present in the accounting profession, willing to take part in research, especially in less accepting contexts. Despite this, research on the experiences of trans people in accounting and in education is emerging in Brazil, a country with exceptionally high murder and suicide rates amongst trans people (Círico, 2024). Furthermore, innovative work using music lyrics is widening awareness of the oppression to and resistance by trans or gender non-conforming people in Brazil that opens new avenues of social awareness and understanding of minority groups within accounting (Círico, Galvão, & Casa Nova, 2024). Such work on non-cis-heteronormative identities in accounting provides a further opportunity to address how the accounting profession and use of accounting technologies promote or exacerbate power relations and inequalities (Haynes, 2025).

Bodies/embodiment in accounting

The body is of interest across a number of theoretical approaches: for example, in social theory illustrating how bodies are positioned sociologically (Dale, 2001; Shilling, 2012); in postcolonial studies and critical race theories, which show how bodies are raced and/or exploited (Lugones, 2016; Said, 1979) and in French psychoanalytical feminism, such as Irigaray's interpretation of desire, sexual difference and sexuality (Irigaray, 1985; Ives, 2016). Feminist approaches to the body and embodiment are rich and diverse, challenging cognitive-based knowledge through an 'emphasis on the primacy of embodied experience' (Fotaki & Pullen, 2024, p. 601). The notion of embodiment emphasises the lived body and how we know the world through bodily perceptions (Haynes, 2008a). Moreover:

> Embodiment is a central concern of feminist theory insofar as the body is a site for the symbolic construction of sexual difference, a ground for political exclusion or inclusion, a locus of subjectivity, a prospect for self-realization, and the material focus of many labors that typically fall to women and/or define femininity.
>
> *(Threadcraft, 2016, p. 207)*

Poststructuralist feminist conceptualisations of the body and embodiment have influenced an emphasis on disrupting the binary, focusing on the discursive construction of power, and addressing multiple subjectivities. Particularly, poststructuralist feminist approaches to the body challenge assumptions of a masculine default disembodied human subject (Fotaki & Pullen, 2024). Susan Bordo's (1993) work *Unbearable Weight*, for example, offers an influential analysis of the discursive cultural construction of women's bodies under a male gaze, with the often detrimental consequences arising from a Western cultural need to maintain a slim, 'feminine' body. Bordo (1993), like many other feminists influenced by poststructuralism, draws from Foucault's conceptualisation of power to explore this discursive construction of femininity expressed within and through the body. Her work is insightful in understanding the influence of modern culture in commodifying the body, requiring the need to work on the body, which may have detrimental effects if regimes of body maintenance, such as diet and exercise, are taken too far. However, Davis (2007) argues that in focusing on the power of cultural discourses to influence women's bodily experiences and practices, it is important not to lose sight of women's agency in making choices about their personal empowerment.

In the context of accounting, Ingrid Jeacle might agree with Davis since her analysis of the historical operating results of US store cosmetic departments from 1930 to 1980 supports her argument that the accounting numbers reflect the demands of a powerful female consumer (Jeacle, 2006). She counters the practice of 'making up' the face as being symptomatic of capitalist exploitation or masculine domination of women, represented in Marxist critique of the beauty industry and in Foucauldian feminist critiques of cultural norms, and instead argues for an 'alternative reality', evidenced by the accounting numbers, where women are 'intelligent players in a consumer world' (Jeacle, 2006, p. 104). While I do not disagree with the latter point, in a postfeminist culture, where feminism seems, to many, to have lost its relevance, it is also pertinent to emphasise the influence of cultural media in constituting:

> femininity as a bodily property; the shift from objectification to subjectification; the emphasis upon self surveillance, monitoring and discipline; a

> focus upon individualism, choice and empowerment; the dominance of a makeover paradigm; a resurgence in ideas of natural sexual difference; a marked sexualisation of culture; and an emphasis upon consumerism and the commodification of difference.
>
> *(Gill, 2007, p. 149)*

These elements of contemporary neoliberal society show how prevailing cultural norms and discourses continue to sexualise and commodify bodies, and particularly women's bodies, in ways that underlie inequality, even when women are exercising choice. It is interesting, however, to ascertain the role of accounting's calculative practices in mobilising decisions which pertain to the body. In addition to her (2006) study on the placing of cosmetics counters, Jeacle (2003) examines how accounting technologies in the form of workroom costs and alteration costs in the manufacture of ready-to-wear garments formed the construction of a standardised body and the implementation of standard body sizes, which still lie at the core of contemporary perceptions of the human body.

Despite the potential for calculative practices to be interrogated in our understandings of the body, few studies seek to make this leap. Nor has research on the accounting profession tended to address the body or embodiment of the accounting professional in much detail. While, as this text has shown, characteristics of professionals might include being gendered, raced or classed (see Chapter 4), or being of various sexualities, as discussed earlier in this chapter, understanding these characteristics, identities or subjectivities in relation to the physical body is rarely addressed.

What I find particularly interesting about bodies is not their biology, but a combination of how it feels to live in a body and how that body is perceived and interpreted by others. Instead of being abstract and disembodied, our bodies are visceral, fleshy, leaky and a source of embodied knowledge. By embodied knowledge, I mean the way that we can experience and know things through our bodies. This can apply to the common life experiences of illness, wellness and ageing, but for women also has the added possible dimensions of menstruation, pregnancy, childbirth, breast-feeding and menopause. We also attain embodied knowledge in our physical sensations of work, such as tiredness, aches or lightness on achieving a task. To explore these types of embodied knowledge often requires a theoretical and methodological positioning that is phenomenological, to understand the body as subjectively lived and experienced, although interpretations need not be limited to one individual (see, for example, Abdellatif & Haynes, 2025). When we address how others perceive bodies, then the norms, values and structural conditions under which those bodies operate are pertinent, and can be interpreted through different theoretical positions, such as, for example, social constructionism, emphasising the role of culture and context in constructing meanings, or poststructuralism, emphasising the discursive constitution of power and hierarchies. The two positions – how we experience the body and how others perceive us – are, of course, mutually constitutive rather than independent.

In accounting research, however, focus on the body and embodiment is minimal. There is a set of work focusing on the experiences of disabled accountants in the UK, which gives attention to how bodies are perceived in the accounting profession when differently abled. This work focuses on a social model of disability which focuses on the physical or attitudinal barriers in society which affect people with impairments; under this model it is this failure to accept people with impairments that creates 'disability' rather than the impairments themselves (Duff, Ferguson, & Gilmore, 2007). Understandably, by using this model, the focus is on the barriers created for disabled people in accounting rather than their experiences of their own bodies. Despite equality rights legislation in the UK, firms have minimal understanding of disability with little focus on disability in their personnel policies, and perceptions that the employability of disabled people in accounting is problematic, due to the need to visit clients and work as a team (Duff & Ferguson, 2007; Duff et al., 2007). When addressing the perceptions of disabled accounting professionals rather than the firms, research finds that accountants feel that their bodies do not conform to the expected norm, but the focus is mostly on institutional practices that exclude or marginalise them in accounting, arising from discrimination, stereotyping or a lack of support (Duff & Ferguson, 2011a, 2011b). This focus is not surprising, given the social model of disability.

However, in thinking about how bodies are experienced and perceived in accounting, it would be interesting to extend Butler's concept of performativity to able-bodiedness. One could argue that it is the performative repetitive acts enacted by 'abled' bodies that produce the norms of able-bodiedness and thus the concept of 'disability', as Butler argues they do for gender, as masculinities and femininities (Butler, 1990). Ability/disability becomes another binary constructed through discourse which reflects hierarchical positioning and the operation of power relations. Disrupting discourses around this binary could allow for subjective experiences of differently abled bodies while subverting cultural norms, as has occurred with disruption to non-binary, non-heteronormative approaches within queer theory.

Other work on the accounting profession focuses on the body from a social constructionist gendered perspective. My own research on the gendered embodiment of accounting professionals during pregnancy and early motherhood suggests that the juxtaposition of these forms of embodiment – as professional and as mother – is simultaneously a mechanism of social control and self-expression for women (Haynes, 2008a). Control is exercised, for example, by the need to wear appropriate professional clothing, as 'our bodies are a medium of culture representing the symbolic forms of the context we are embedded in' or to have bodies that behave in particular ways, such as having the right kind of presence or voice – 'Speak up, speak up' (Haynes, 2008a, p. 336). During pregnancy and early motherhood, women were very aware of their corporeality, with additional incidences of bodily issues – 'tiredness, weight gain, varicose veins, backache, heartburn, sickness, constipation, increased need to urinate' (p. 337) – that intruded into professional life, although women could also draw on their embodied gendered identities to negotiate their own social positioning either within or outside the profession. Ultimately, 'the symbolic values attached to bodily forms, appearance and attributes were identified as particularly relevant to the identity of accounting professionals, with the body playing a complex role in the exercise of power and the reproduction of social inequalities' (Haynes, 2008a, p. 337).

In a further study addressing the physical body and its interaction with professionalism for women lawyers and accountants, I found that women have to balance and control negatively construed aspects of femininity, such as being overweight or having too 'shrill' or 'strident' a voice, with displaying positively construed forms of masculine embodiment, such as having a degree of 'authority' or being 'presentable to a client' in order to be taken seriously (Haynes, 2012). Using Bourdieu's theorisation of social and physical capital in the field of accounting, one can argue that embodied identity remains resolutely gendered (as well as raced and classed) (Haynes, 2008a, 2012), which reflects a shift in forms of social and professional closure from the entry point of the professions (see Chapter 2) to more implicit and subtle forms of social closure in the pursuit of promotion and prestigious areas of work (Haynes, 2013a). However, one can also see that there is a discursive construction of what makes an acceptable body in professions. Discourses around women being 'not traditionally professional, or too casual, or too sort of trendy', not wearing 'gigantic shoes', showing 'professional demeanour', needing to appear 'fit and healthy', and not being so authoritative that they are perceived as 'a bitch' illustrate that the conceptualisation of professional in the presentation of the body is essentially masculine, which women are judged against in terms of their femininity (Haynes, 2012).

Bitbol-Saba and Dambrin's (2019) study argues that much accounting research focusing on the client addresses firms' rhetorical discourses in positioning the client as an abstract controlling device, whereas they address how the bodies of female auditors are brought into play in interactions with the client. Drawing from theorisations from Goffman (1977) on interaction and gender, they find that female auditors make use of their bodies during audit interactions with clients by playing on their stereotypical features (being blonde or appearing young) and body language (using big smiles) to build trust and elucidate information from the clients. However, the auditors were aware of having to do this, in playing the game, and their bodies being instrumentalised by their firms in getting difficult audits done and generating new clients. Moreover, they found that such instrumentalisation leads to objectification and often sexual harassment from clients, ultimately normalising a male hegemonic order. Bitbol-Saba and Dambrin therefore position their contribution as a feminist critique of patriarchy that reveals:

> the invisible order of male domination that shapes social interaction in accountancy, uncovering what is being done in the name of efficiency and operational performance and emphasising the tacit expectations of the professional service culture that set up women as sexual objects.
>
> *(Bitbol-Saba & Dambrin, 2019, p. 16)*

In the context of Brazil, Lima, Casa Nova, and Vendramin (2024) find that accounting doctoral programmes reproduce social norms and discourses on the sexual division of labour that suggest academics can embody either a productive (read masculine) body or a reproductive (read feminine) body. Moreover, women academics' bodies are sexualised and objectified, rendered 'other' and subjected to multiple elements of sexist violence, through masculinised environments, 'old boys' clubs' and harassment, to the extent that they may have to silence themselves and hide their bodies in masculine dress codes to survive (Lima et al., 2024).

However, the women in these studies counter or resist abjection arising from objectification of their bodies in ways that they can: through building feminist networks and dissembling with their bodies (Lima et al., 2024) or through using body techniques of stereotypical femininity in agentic ways that nonetheless could be regarded as freely made choices or tactics within a postfeminist climate, or continually shaped by structural constraints (Bitbol-Saba & Dambrin, 2019; Haynes, 2017). In an autoethnographical study, I discuss how I resisted sexist aggression during a position of academic leadership, drawing from an incident at a meeting where I faced aggressive tactics of 'barracking, yelling, hectoring…':

> The aggression expressed, the shouting, pacing, waving arms, and looming near by a man who shouts louder and stands larger, is a power struggle against my female representation. Suppressing my voice by talking over it and not giving me space to respond is a silencing action.
>
> *(Haynes, 2024, p. 2293)*

I discuss how one form of resistance is through embodied affective authenticity, refusing to take on masculine symbolism in presentation of the self, even if this does not conform to the norms of the organisation. Resistance can be *through* the body:

> My body is mine – tall height, blond hair, feminine dress, breasts that have fed babies, eyes that cry tears, voice that is quiet – and I will not moderate it for the organization.
>
> *(Haynes, 2024, p. 2296)*

It is notable, however, that such forms of resistance in these three studies are largely individualised, where the onus remains on women themselves to navigate sexist cultures and manage their own embodiment rather than through any wider organisational change. That sexism continues to occur in organisations, which include accounting organisations, is no real surprise. The #MeToo movement illustrated the prevalence of sexual harassment in organisations and societies around the world (Alcade & Villa, 2022), which extends to women, trans people, LGBTQI+ people and other minorities. I address further the integrated role of accounting and feminism to provide a collective and systemic response to inequalities and oppressions through forms of resistance and emancipatory activism in the final chapter of this book. However, I conclude this current chapter by evaluating the emancipatory potential of poststructuralist feminism for accounting.

The emancipatory potential of poststructuralist feminism for accounting

Poststructuralist feminism may not have the collective focus of other feminisms: for example, the more radical approaches to feminism against neoliberalism, the sense of shared political struggle against capitalism under Marxist feminism or the shared solidarities against oppressions deriving from race (see Chapter 4 for all these) or postcoloniality (see Chapter 5). This is perhaps why it has not been adopted so widely in accounting research that focuses on the social and political effects of accounting technologies and the role of the profession. However, poststructuralist feminism has emancipatory potential for accounting. Poststructuralism illustrates that language and its expression in discourse is not neutral but is embedded with underlying meaning that reveals relations of power. Therefore, under poststructuralism, language is ontologically significant. Binaries that are taken for granted, such as masculine/feminine or mind/body, are actually value-laden with cultural significance. The value of poststructuralist feminism is that it points out how discourses are gendered, such that they produce, as well as reflect, meanings and hierarchies of power. By exposing how discourse, gender and power are interrelated to produce a 'reality', solutions to overcome these normative assumptions can be imagined.

Butler's (1990) work is particularly influential in this regard, since her concept of performativity argues that it is the very performance of repetitive acts that constructs understandings of binary gender, where no essential gendered reality pre-exists. Moreover, she extends this to the regulatory norms proscribing a heterosexual identity as the ideal. These arguments subvert our understanding of gender as a binary and as a heterosexual orientation. Moreover, queer theory addresses sexualities as identities and a queer perspective can refer to highlighting and invoking issues of power, which challenges cis-heteronormativities. A key contribution of poststructuralist feminism is to challenge the fixed or essentialised nature of identity, instead moving to conceptualise subjectivities as fluid and unfixed. Where poststructuralist discursive analysis is less prevalent is in relation to race, perhaps because racial and intersectional oppressions are perceived as structurally and politically constituted, thus requiring political outcomes and more overtly political and racialised feminisms. It is important to note the potential, however, for deconstruction to disrupt and dismantle not only masculine, heterosexual hegemonies but also the discursive construction relating to other norms, for example, around race or dis/ability.

In relation to the body and embodiment, while phenomenological approaches to research support an understanding of what it is like to live in that body, *be* that body, which is an important facet of human experience, poststructuralist approaches help to understand how discourses around the body imbue it with cultural norms about acceptable bodies. Where the discourse is gendered, it can have the effect of reinforcing the underlying preference for the male body, promoting a form of hegemonic masculinity. Women's bodies are expected to be presented and used differently – through exaggerated femininity, vulnerability or reproductive capacities, or as sexual objects – which renders them oppositional to the male norm and potentially subject to harassment, literal or symbolic violence. Although much of the research on bodies and embodiment in accounting is not explicitly poststructuralist in its theoretical orientation, some emphasis on the discursive construction of normative bodies supports increased awareness and understanding of difference and hierarchical power relations, which can promote an emancipatory perspective.

In extending the emancipatory potential of poststructuralist feminism further in relation to accounting, I offer the following reflections and five suggestions:

First, understanding norms and culture as discursively constructed illustrates the power of language and discourse in creating hierarchies of power. That is, as identified by Hammond and Oakes (1992), language can reflect a dominant position but is also open to challenge in political struggle. In constructing accounting technologies or calculative practices, or in reporting practices, language can reflect those hierarchies. Poststructuralist feminist approaches to deconstruction can reveal the inherent logics and thereby challenge them. Similarly, revealing how discourses maintain a masculine hegemony or a colonialist legacy within the accounting profession can also be used to subvert them.

Second, it is possible to conduct research that not only reveals discursive constructions of power, for example, in the ways in which accounting professionals are positioned or behave, but also has political intent to change the underlying structures which allow this. The so-called 'weak' version of poststructuralist feminism (see Alvesson & Due Billing, 2009) can be combined with feminist intent to change the material realities of women's lives through solidarities and collective struggle.

Third, although poststructuralist feminism has tended to apply to the discursive construction or deconstruction of cultural norms relating to women in accounting, in hierarchical opposition to masculine norms and cultures, it is important to recognise that the masculine ideal is predominantly Western, White, middle-class and able-bodied. Undertaking deconstructive analysis that addresses the cultural representation of other subjects, who may be differently raced, classed or dis/abled, can extend the emancipatory potential of poststructuralist feminism to incorporate other forms of oppression and to disrupt wider sets of binary norms.

Fourth, the widening of research on accounting identities in the profession to include non-heterosexual identities is a welcome extension of existing knowledge. The queering of accounting in terms of representing the multiplicity of our professional community, with sexually diverse, intersectional and multiple heterogenous perspectives *and* also by representing the subverting of dominant power relations can only enhance our knowledge of and praxis within accounting. However, while recognising the difficulties of recruiting participants, understanding the experiences of non-cis, fluid or trans accountants is a next necessary step in widening inclusion and diversity in the profession.

Fifth, poststructuralist feminism illustrates the significance of discourse and language in creating power relations and norms. Without in any way suggesting that physical violence, including gender-based violence, is not endemic and reprehensible in our societies, it is also pertinent to reflect on the use of language as violence. What is said and how language is used to take a position, as well as what is silenced and not said, is central to discursive representation. Moreover, violent discourses can mutate into physical violence. Applying these concepts of the potential violence of language to accounting discourses suggests that the way in which financial reporting is carried out, what is represented in the webpages of firms and how professionals themselves both use and are subjected to discourse is an important means of constituting and symbolising cultural values.

Conclusion

This chapter has addressed the influence of poststructuralist feminism on accounting. Although this theoretical approach is not widely used, I argue it has great potential for understanding the discursive construction of cultural representation and power relations in accounting, and it can be combined with feminist intent to improve the material realities of people's lives as well as produce more abstracted discursive analysis. Drawing from Butler's work, the chapter illustrates the impact of poststructuralist feminism on performativity, identity and sexuality. It discusses the relevance of the body and embodiment within accounting technologies and to the experiences of accounting professionals. Finally, the chapter makes five key suggestions for where the emancipatory potential of poststructuralist feminism can be expanded within accounting research.

Note

1 Foucault addresses sexuality in a four-volume work beginning with Foucault, M. (1976 [2020]). *The History of Sexuality 1: The Will to Knowledge*. Penguin Classics. Although not directly about gender, its emphasis on power and sexuality has been of interest to feminists.

References

Abdellatif, A., & Haynes, K. (2025). Be-ing seen: Towards a feminist interpretative phenomenological analysis to researching the marginalised. *Culture and Organization, 31*(1), 64–85. https://doi.org/10.1080/14759551.2024.2378789

Adapa, S., Rindfleish, J., & Sheridan, A. (2016). 'Doing gender' in a regional context: Explaining women's absence from senior roles in regional accounting firms in Australia. *Critical Perspectives on Accounting, 35*, 100–110. https://doi.org/10.1016/j.cpa.2015.05.004

Ahmed, S. (2010). *The Promise of Happiness*. Durham and London: Duke University Press.

Ahrens, T., & Ferry, L. (2021). Accounting and accountability practices in times of crisis: A Foucauldian perspective on the UK government's response to COVID-19 for England. *Accounting, Auditing & Accountability Journal, 34*(6), 1332–1344. https://doi.org/10.1108/AAAJ-07-2020-4659

Ala-Heikkilä, V., Lämsä, A.-M., & Järvenpää, M. (2024). Management accountants—A gendered image. *Critical Perspectives on Accounting, 99*, 102724. https://doi.org/10.1016/j.cpa.2024.102724

Alcade, C. M., & Villa, P.- I. (Eds.) (2022). *#MeToo and Beyond. Perspectives on a Global Movement*. Kentucky: The University Press of Kentucky.

Alvesson, M., & Due Billing, Y. (2009). *Understanding Gender and Organizations* (2nd ed.). London: Sage.

Anderson, K. A. (2023). Cisnormative symbolic colonization and transgender and gender nonconforming individuals in the workplace. *Gender, Work & Organization, 31*(1), 1–15. https://doi.org/10.1111/gwao.13048

Bendl, R., Fleischmann, A., & Hofmann, R. (2009). Queer theory and diversity management: Reading codes of conduct from a queer perspective. *Journal of Management & Organization*, *15*(5), 625–638. https://doi.org/10.5172/jmo.15.5.625
Benschop, Y., & Verloo, M. (2016). Feminist Organization Theories: Islands of Treasure. In R. Mir, H. Willmott & M. Greenwood (Eds.), *The Routledge Companion to Philosophy in Organization Studies* (pp. 100–112). New York and London: Routledge.
Bitbol-Saba, N., & Dambrin, C. (2019). "It's not often we get a visit from a beautiful woman!" The body in client-auditor interactions and the masculinity of accountancy. *Critical Perspectives on Accounting*, *64*, 102068. https://doi.org/10.1016/j.cpa.2018.12.002
Bordo, S. (1993). *Unbearable Weight: Feminism, Western Culture and the Body*. Berkeley: University of California Press.
Brennan, N. M., & Solomon, J. (2008). Corporate governance, accountability and mechanisms of accountability: An overview. *Accounting, Auditing & Accountability Journal*, *21*(7), 885–906. https://doi.org/10.1108/09513570810907401
Brouard, F., Bujaki, M., Durocher, S., & Neilson, L. C. (2017). Professional accountants' identity formation: An integrative framework. *Journal of Business Ethics*, *142*(2), 225–238. https://doi.org/10.1007/s10551-016-3157-z
Butler, J. (1990). *Gender Trouble. Feminism and the Subversion of Identity* (2nd ed.). New York and London: Routledge.
Butler, J. (1993). *Bodies That Matter. On the Discursive Limits of Sex*. New York and London: Routledge.
Butler, J. (2004a). *Precarious Life: The Powers of Mourning and Violence*. New York: Verso.
Butler, J. (2004b). *Undoing Gender*. London: Routledge.
Butler, J. (2005). *Giving an Account of Oneself*. New York: Fordham University Press.
Butler, J. (2010). Performative agency. *Journal of Cultural Economy*, *3*(2), 147–161. https://doi.org/10.1080/17530350.2010.494117
Butler, J. (2020). Performative Acts and Gender Constitution: An Essay in Phenomenology and Feminist Theory. In C. R. McCann, S.-k. Kim, & E. Ergun (Eds.), *Feminist Theory Reader* (pp. 353–361). Abingdon: Routledge.
Calás, M. B., & Smircich, L. (1999). Past Postmodernism? Reflections and tentative directions. *Academy of Management Review*, *24*(4), 649–671. https://doi.org/10.5465/amr.1999.2553246
Carmona, S., & Ezzamel, M. (2016). Accounting and lived experience in the gendered workplace. *Accounting, Organizations and Society*, *49*, 1–8. https://doi.org/10.1016/j.aos.2015.11.004
Carter, C., & Toms, S. (2010). The contours of critical accounting. *Critical Perspectives on Accounting*, *21*(3), 171–182. https://doi.org/10.1016/j.cpa.2010.02.001
Chamorro González, C., Patiño-Jacinto, R. A., & Reiss, L. K. (2024). Personas LGBTIQ+ en las firmas de contabilidad y auditoría en Colombia, percepciones y su rol laboral. *Cuadernos de Contabilidad*, *25*, 1–25. https://doi.org/10.11144/Javeriana.cc25.plfc
Círico, J. (2024). *Vozes da resistência: vivências de pessoas transgêneras e travestis na contabilidade brasileira [Voices of resistance: experiences of transgender and transvestite people in Brazilian accounting]* [PhD, Universidade Federal de Uberlândia]. Uberlândia, Brazil.

Círico, J., Galvão, A. A., & Casa Nova, S. P. d. C. (2024). Carta Aberta: (In)visibilizing transgender bodies in organizations. *Organization*, in press, 13505084241275780. https://doi.org/10.1177/13505084241275780

Corlett, S., McInnes, P., Coupland, C., & Sheep, M. (2017). Exploring the registers of identity research. *International Journal of Management Reviews*, *19*(3), 261–272. https://doi.org/10.1111/ijmr.12149

Dale, K. (2001). *Anatomising Embodiment & Organisation Theory*. New York: Palgrave.

Davies, B. (1991). The concept of agency: A feminist poststructuralist analysis. *Social Analysis: The International Journal of Social and Cultural Practice* 30, 42–53.

Davies, B., & Gannon, S. (2011). Feminism/Poststructuralism. In B. Somekh & C. Lewin (Eds.), *Theory and Methods in Social Science* (2nd ed., pp. 312–319). Los Angeles, London and New Delhi: Sage.

Davis, K. (2007). Reclaiming Women's Bodies: Colonialist Trope or Critical Epistemology? In C. R. McCann, S.-K. Kim, & E. Ergun (Eds.), *Feminist Theory Reader. Local and Global Perspectives* (5th ed., pp. 385–395). New York and London: Routledge.

Derrida, J. (1978). *Writing and Difference*. Chicago: University of Chicago Press.

Duff, A., & Ferguson, J. (2007). Disability and accounting firms: Evidence from the UK. *Critical Perspectives on Accounting*, *18*(2), 139–157. https://doi.org/10.1016/j.cpa.2005.09.002

Duff, A., & Ferguson, J. (2011a). Disability and the professional accountant: Insights from Oral Histories. *Accounting, Auditing & Accountability Journal*, *25*(1), 71–101. https://doi.org/10.1108/09513571211191752

Duff, A., & Ferguson, J. (2011b). Disability and the socialization of accounting professionals. *Critical Perspectives on Accounting*, *22*(4), 351–364. https://doi.org/10.1016/j.cpa.2010.12.009

Duff, A., Ferguson, J., & Gilmore, K. (2007). Issues concerning the employment and employability of disabled people in UK accounting firms: An analysis of the views of human resource managers as employment gatekeepers. *British Accounting Review*, *39*(1), 15–38. https://doi.org/10.1016/j.bar.2006.08.003

Egan, M. (2018). LGBTI staff, and diversity within the Australian accounting profession. *Sustainability Accounting, Management and Policy Journal*, *9*(5), 595–614. https://doi.org/10.1108/SAMPJ-07-2017-0069

Egan, M., & Voss, B. d. L. (2023a). Ephemeral promises of happiness: Coming out in the Australian accounting profession into the late 2010s. *Gender, Work & Organization*, *30*(6), 2033–2048. https://doi.org/10.1111/gwao.13043

Egan, M., & Voss, B. d. L. (2023b). Redressing the Big 4's male, pale and stale image, through LGBTIQ+ ethical praxis. *Critical Perspectives on Accounting*, *96*, 102511. https://doi.org/10.1016/j.cpa.2022.102511

Egan, M., & Voss, B. d. L. (2024). LGBTIQ+ staff and shifting client power within professional services firms. *Accounting, Auditing & Accountability Journal*, *37*(6), 1537–1557. https://doi.org/10.1108/AAAJ-01-2023-6257

Ehlers, N. (2016). Identities. In L. Disch & M. Hawkesworth (Eds.), *The Oxford Handbook of Feminist Theory* (pp. 346–366). Oxford: Oxford University Press. https://doi.org/10.1093/oxfordhb/9780199328581.013.18

Elliott, A. (2001). *Concepts of the Self*. Cambridge: Polity Press.

Evans, L., & Kamla, R. (2018). Language and translation in accounting: A scandal of silence and displacement? *Accounting, Auditing & Accountability Journal*, *31*(7), 1834–1843. https://doi.org/10.1108/AAAJ-09-2018-020

Flax, J. (1987). Postmodernism and gender relations in feminist theory. *Signs: Journal of Women in Culture and Society*, *12*(4), 621–643. https://doi.org/10.1086/494359

Fotaki, M., & Pullen, A. (2024). Feminist theories and activist practices in Organization Studies. *Organization Studies*, *45*(4), 593–616. https://doi.org/10.1177/01708406231209861

Foucault, M. (1976 [2020]). *The History of Sexuality 1: The Will to Knowledge*. London: Penguin Classics.

Foucault, M. (1980). *Power/Knowledge: Selected Interviews and Other Writings, 1972–1977*. London: Random House.

Foucault, M. (1990). *The History of Sexuality 2: The Use of Pleasure*. New York: Vintage Books.

Fraser, N., & Nicholson, L. J. (1990). Social Criticism without Philosophy. In L. J. Nicholson (Ed.), *Feminism/Postmodernism* (pp. 19–38). New York and London: Routledge.

Funnell, W., & Jupe, R. (2022). The architecture of accounting and the neoliberal betrayal of life. *Critical Perspectives on Accounting*, *89*, 102329. https://doi.org/10.1016/j.cpa.2021.102329

Gendron, Y., & Spira, L. (2010). Identity narratives in turmoil: A study of former members of Arthur Andersen. *Accounting, Organizations and Society*, *35*(3), 275–300. https://doi.org/10.1016/j.aos.2009.09.001

Ghio, A., McGuigan, N., & Powell, L. (2023). The queering accounting manifesto. *Critical Perspectives on Accounting*, *90*, 102395. https://doi.org/10.1016/j.cpa.2021.102395

Giddens, A. (1991). *Modernity and Self Identity*. Cambridge: Polity Press.

Gill, R. (2007). Postfeminist media culture: Elements of a sensibility. *European Journal of Cultural Studies*, *10*(2), 147–166. https://doi.org/10.1177/1367549407075898

Goffman, E. (1977). The arrangement between the sexes. *Theory and Society*, *4*(3), 301–331. https://doi.org/10.1007/BF00206983

Greene, J., & Ervin, W. (2024). The cost of crossing gender boundaries: Trans women of color and the racialized workplace gender order. *Gender, Work & Organization*, 31(6), 2585–2600. https://doi.org/10.1111/gwao.13108

Guo, K. H. (2018). The odyssey of becoming: Professional identity and insecurity in the Canadian accounting field. *Critical Perspectives on Accounting*, *56*, 20–45. https://doi.org/10.1016/j.cpa.2017.10.008

Hammond, T., & Oakes, L. S. (1992). Some feminisms and their implications for accounting practice. *Accounting, Auditing & Accountability Journal*, *5*(3), 52–70. https://doi.org/10.1108/09513579210017389

Haynes, K. (2008a). (Re)figuring accounting and maternal bodies: The gendered embodiment of accounting professionals. *Accounting, Organizations and Society*, *33*(4–5), 328–348. https://doi.org/10.1016/j.aos.2007.04.003

Haynes, K. (2008b). Transforming identities: Accounting professionals and the transition to motherhood. *Critical Perspectives on Accounting*, *19*(5), 620–642. https://doi.org/10.1016/j.cpa.2006.10.003

Haynes, K. (2012). Body beautiful?: Gender, identity and the body in professional services firms. *Gender, Work & Organization*, *19*(5), 489–507. https://doi.org/10.1111/j.1468-0432.2011.00583.x

Haynes, K. (2013a). Gender and Diversity Challenges in Professional Services Firms. In K. Haynes & I. Grugulis (Eds.), *Managing Services: Challenges and Innovations* (pp. 66–82). Oxford: Oxford University Press.

Haynes, K. (2013b). Sexuality and sexual symbolism as processes of gendered identity formation: An autoethnography of an accounting firm. *Accounting, Auditing & Accountability Journal*, *26*(3), 374–398. https://doi.org/10.1108/09513571311311865

Haynes, K. (2017). Accounting as gendering and gendered: A review of 25 years of critical accounting research on gender. *Critical Perspectives on Accounting*, *43*, 110–124. https://doi.org/10.1016/j.cpa.2016.06.004

Haynes, K. (2024). Resisting sexisms, aggression, and burnout in academic leadership: Surviving in the gendered managerial academy. *Gender, Work & Organization*, *31*(5), 2286–2302. https://doi.org/10.1111/gwao.13137

Haynes, K. (2025). The role of accounting in creating, perpetuating and overcoming inequalities: Going beyond discipline, borders and stasis towards accounting as activism. *Gender, Work & Organization*, 32(2), 912–928. https://doi.org/10.1111/gwao.13191

Hines, S. (2020). Sex wars and (trans) gender panics: Identity and body politics in contemporary UK feminism. *The Sociological Review*, *68*(4), 699–717. https://doi.org/10.1177/0038026120934684

Hoskin, K. (1994). Boxing clever: For, against and beyond Foucault in the battle for accounting theory. *Critical Perspectives on Accounting*, *5*(1), 57–85. https://doi.org/10.1006/cpac.1994.1004

Husillos, J., Larrinaga, C., & Martínez, D. (2024). Language was always a companion of the Empire. *Critical Perspectives on Accounting*, *100*, 102753. https://doi.org/10.1016/j.cpa.2024.102753

Irigaray, L. (1985). *Speculum of the Other Woman* (G. C. Gill, Trans.). New York: Cornell University Press.

Ives, K. (2016). *Cixous Irigary Kristeva: The Jouissance of French Feminism* (5th ed.). Kent: Crescent Moon Publishing.

Jeacle, I. (2003). Accounting and the construction of the standard body. *Accounting, Organizations and Society*, *28*(4), 357–377. https://doi.org/10.1016/S0361-3682(02)00021-1

Jeacle, I. (2006). Face facts: Accounting, feminism and the business of beauty. *Critical Perspectives on Accounting*, *17*(1), 87–108. https://doi.org/10.1016/j.cpa.2004.04.006

Kamla, R., & Komori, N. (2018). Diagnosing the translation gap: The politics of translation and the hidden contradiction in interdisciplinary accounting research. *Accounting, Auditing & Accountability Journal*, *31*(7), 1874–1903. https://doi.org//10.1108/AAAJ-08-2017-3067

Killian, S. (2015). "For lack of accountability": The logic of the price in Ireland's Magdalen Laundries. *Accounting, Organizations and Society*, *43*, 17–32. https://doi.org/10.1016/j.aos.2015.03.006

Levinas, E. (1991). *Totality and Infinity: An Essay on Exteriority* (4th ed.). Dordrecht: Springer.

Lima, J. P. R. d., Casa Nova, S. P. d. C., & Vendramin, E. d. O. (2024). Sexist academic socialization and feminist resistance: (De)constructing women's (dis)placement in Brazilian accounting academia. *Critical Perspectives on Accounting*, *99*, 102600. https://doi.org/10.1016/j.cpa.2023.102600

Lorber, J. (2012). *Gender Inequality. Feminist Theories and Politics*. Oxford: Oxford University Press.
Lugones, M. (2016). The Coloniality of Gender. In W. Harcourt (Ed.), *The Palgrave Handbook of Gender and Development* (pp. 13–33). London: Springer. https://doi.org/10.1007/978-1-137-38273-3_2
McGuigan, N., & Ghio, A. (2018). Queering accounting: Opening up and connecting professional services firms. *Sustainability Accounting, Management and Policy Journal*, *9*(5), 625–635. https://doi.org/10.1108/SAMPJ-08-2018-0210
McKinlay, A. (2010). Performativity and the politics of identity: Putting Butler to work. *Critical Perspectives on Accounting*, *21*(3), 232–242. https://doi.org/10.1016/j.cpa.2008.01.011
McKinlay, A., & Pezet, E. (2010). Accounting for Foucault. *Critical Perspectives on Accounting*, *21*(6), 486–495. https://doi.org/10.1016/j.cpa.2009.08.006
Messner, M. (2009). The limits of accountability. *Accounting, Organizations and Society*, *34*(8), 918–938. https://doi.org/10.1016/j.aos.2009.07.003
Nganga, C. S. N., Casa Nova, S. P. d. C., da Silva, S. M. C., & Lima, J. P. R. d. (2023). There's so much life out there! Work-life conflict, women, and Accounting graduate programs (Há Tanta Vida Lá Fora! Work-life conflict, mulheres e pós-graduação em Contabilidade). *Revista de Administração Contemporânea*, *27*(2), e210318. https://doi.org/10.1590/1982-7849rac2023210318.en
Pagan, V., Haynes, K., & Reissner, S. (2023). Accountable selves and responsibility within a global forum. *Journal of Business Ethics*, *187*, 255–270. https://doi.org/10.1007/s10551-022-05286-9
Petriglieri, J. L. (2011). Under threat: Responses to and the consequences of threats to individuals' identities. *Academy of Management Review*, *36*(4), 641–662. https://doi.org/10.5465/amr.2009.0087
Rumens, N. (2016). Sexualities and accounting: A queer theory perspective. *Critical Perspectives on Accounting*, *35*, 111–120. https://doi.org/10.1016/j.cpa.2015.05.003
Rumens, N., & Lewis, P. (2023). Conceptualizing and disrupting heteronormativity as performative in management education: Speech acts and LGBTQ* injurious language. *Academy of Management Learning & Education*, 22(4), 718–734. https://doi.org/10.5465/amle.2021.0480
Said, E. (1979). *Orientalism*. New York: Vintage Books.
Sarup, M. (1996). *Identity, Culture and the Postmodern World*. Edinburgh: Edinburgh University Press.
Saussure, F. D. (1966). *Course in General Linguistics*. New York: McGraw-Hill.
Scott, J. W. (1988). Deconstructing equality-versus-difference: Or, the uses of poststructuralist theory for feminism. *Feminist Studies*, 32–50. https://doi.org/10.2307/3177997
Shilling, C. (2012). *The Body and Social Theory* (3rd ed.). London: Sage.
Stenger, S., & Roulet, T. J. (2018). Pride against prejudice? The stakes of concealment and disclosure of a stigmatized identity for gay and lesbian auditors. *Work, Employment and Society*, *32*(2), 257–273. https://doi.org/10.1177/0950017016682459
Threadcraft, S. (2016). Embodiment. In L. Disch & M. Hawkesworth (Eds.), *The Oxford Handbook of Feminist Theory* (pp. 207–226). Oxford: Oxford University Press. https://doi.org/10.1093/oxfordhb/9780199328581.013.11

Tomo, A. (2023). 'Angry accountants': Making sense of professional identity crisis on online communities. *Critical Perspectives on Accounting*, *95*, 102483. https://doi.org/10.1016/j.cpa.2022.102483

Vollmer, H. (2019). Accounting for tacit coordination: The passing of accounts and the broader case for accounting theory. *Accounting, Organizations and Society*, *73*, 15–34. https://doi.org/10.1016/j.aos.2018.06.003

Walker, S. P. (2008). Accounting histories of women: Beyond recovery? *Accounting, Auditing & Accountability Journal*, *21*(4), 580–610. https://doi.org/10.1108/09513570810872932

Ward, G. (1997). *Postmodernism*. London: Hodder & Stoughton.

Weedon, C. (1997). *Feminist Practice and Poststructuralist Theory* (2nd ed.). Oxford: Blackwell.

West, C., & Zimmerman, D. H. (1987). Doing gender. *Gender & Society*, *1*(2), 125–151. https://doi.org/10.1177/0891243287001002002

West, C., & Zimmerman, D. H. (2009). Accounting for doing gender. *Gender & Society*, *23*(1), 112–122. https://doi.org/10.1177/0891243208326529

Westbrook, L. (2023). The matrix of violence: Intersectionality and necropolitics in the murder of transgender people in the United States, 1990–2019. *Gender & Society*, *37*(3), 413–446. https://doi.org/10.1177/08912432231171172

Zanghellini, A. (2020). Philosophical problems with the Gender-Critical feminist argument against trans inclusion. *SAGE Open*, *10*(2). https://doi.org/10.1177/2158244020927029

7

ECOFEMINISMS, ETHICS OF CARE AND ACCOUNTING *AS* CARE

Introduction

This chapter addresses two key areas of feminist theory, ecofeminism and the ethics of care, and evaluates them in relation to accounting. Ecofeminism addresses the link between the oppression of women and the degradation and exploitation of the environment. Although early ecofeminism in the 1960–1970s may have been considered essentialist, by assuming that women are closer to nature than men (Gaard, 2011), evidence points to women being disproportionately affected by climate change in countries where the effect is the greatest (Pearse, 2017). More recent ecofeminist perspectives focus on the relationship between climate change, capitalism and violence (Mellor, 1997; Mies & Shiva, 2014 [1993]; Oksala, 2018). Given the role of accounting in underpinning global commerce, the chapter addresses the need to consider gendered and other inequalities when accounting for climate change and sustainability. It considers the potential for enhancing the social elements of social and environmental accounting (SEA) to include more representation of, and accounting, for gender.

The ethics of care concept focuses on relations of care, empathy and connectedness, rather than ethics of justice and rights, which underpin human and organisational behaviours. Early ethics of care theory was also critiqued by some feminists for essentialism, where a focus on care, and caring for children and the home, may have provoked assumptions that caring was a female characteristic (Robinson, 2019). However, when applied widely to the politics of morality, care, globalisation and neoliberalism, it offers both a critique of human activity and an innovative way forward towards a more caring future (Robinson, 2011; Tronto, 1993).

DOI: 10.4324/9781032636603-7

In this chapter, I evaluate both of these feminist theories in relation to accounting, finding that they hold great potential for understanding the role and power of accounting, especially calculative practices, in our societies. Despite this, I find that the explicit use of these theories within the accounting literature is relatively low. After discussing the key theoretical points of each of the theories – ecofeminism and ethics of care – and considering their position within accounting, I re-evaluate their feminist credentials in addressing climate change, unsustainability and the need for a more relational, caring global society. I discuss their interaction with accounting within SEA and under capitalist neoliberalism, illustrating the potential for the integration of the two concepts. Finally, I conclude the chapter with a proposal for a new conceptualisation of accounting underpinned by these integrated feminist theories; to move from an accounting *for* care to accounting *as* care.

Ecofeminism

Environmentalists have long been deeply concerned about the degradation of ecological systems and the environment, whether caused by natural disasters, such as hurricanes and floods, or the impact of human activity, such as the use of pesticides, extraction of natural resources and pollution. Rachel Carson's classic book, *Silent Spring* (Carson, 2022), first published in 1962, for example, was influential in exposing and eliminating the harmful effects of DDT pesticide exposure on the land, wildlife and humans. By the 1970s, the impact of greenhouse gases on the climate was firmly established (Blowfield & Murray, 2019) and successive reports by the Intergovernmental Panel on Climate Change (IPCC) backed by the United Nations reveal increased levels of certainty that global warming is a direct effect of anthropogenic climate change (Haynes & Murray, 2015). The IPCC's 4th Assessment Report in 2007 for the first time used the word 'unequivocal' in linking human-induced climate change to global warming giving a probability of 90% for this human impact (IPCC, 2007), with the 5th report in 2013 increasing this level to 95% (IPCC, 2013), and a reassertion that human activities have unequivocally caused global warming, which is central to the 6th report (IPCC, 2023). In other words, shifts in the global climate, and extreme weather events that may once have been termed natural disasters, are more commonly understood as being caused, or at least exacerbated, by human actions causing climate change. Moreover, as discussed in Chapter 1, while environmental degradation and climate change affect all human beings, those in the Global South and particularly women may be disproportionately affected. Women's traditional roles as the primary users and managers of natural resources, primary caregivers and labourers engaged in unpaid labour mean they are involved in, and dependent on, livelihoods and resources that are put most at risk by climate change while simultaneously they are less likely to be involved in decision-making about solutions (United Nations Economic Commission for Africa, 2009).

Against this context, this section addresses the feminist movement known as ecofeminism, which first emerged in the 1970s and drew together aspects of feminism and ecology (see Haynes & Murray, 2015). Essentially ecofeminism:

> '...sees a connection between exploitation and degradation of natural world and the subordination and oppression of women'... [drawing] 'from the green movement a concern about the impact of human activities on the non-human world, and from feminism the view of humanity as gendered in ways that subordinate, exploit and oppress women'.
>
> *(Mellor, 1997, p. 1)*

Within the term ecofeminism, ecosystems and feminism are equally primary, meaning ecology and feminism are integrated (Mallory, 2018). Ecofeminism assumes that there are critical connections between the domination of nature and women, although it can be approached from a range of theoretical positions to explore these connections (Braidotti et al., 1994). As a result, ecofeminism may resonate with some other forms of feminism discussed in this book: for example, Marxist or socialist feminism (Chapter 4), which critiques the powerful role of capital in oppressing women; radical feminism (Chapter 4), which addresses institutionalised patriarchy; or postcolonial/decolonial feminisms that address the links between oppression, race and colonisation (Chapter 5). As ecofeminism tends to be an activist feminism, it has much less resonance with liberal feminism (Chapter 3), which tends to focus on internal reform rather than radical change. Poststructuralist feminism (Chapter 6) tends to focus on the discourses and apparent universal positioning of women under ecofeminism, from which charges of essentialism are posed, as I shall discuss.

Gaard (2011) provides an overview of ecofeminism's origins in the 1970s, to the backlash against it in the 1990s, to its potential positioning in the twenty-first century. She argues that ecofeminism was eclectic in the 1980s encompassing a diverse set of theoretical positions, ranging from cultural, materialist, Marxist to socialist positions, that took account of various economic, material, intersectional and global perspectives (Gaard, 2011). It incorporated activism that focused on unsustainable energy production (as seen with the Greenham Common anti-nuclear protests in the UK), various anti-militaristic peace movements and animal ecofeminism that addressed speciesism, or the domination of human over animal species in ecological systems. Yet, by the 1990s, ecofeminism was perceived as lacking focus, critiqued as drawing too widely across issues, and charged with essentialism and ethnocentrism (Gaard, 2011).

As I discussed in Chapter 1, essentialism relates to sex differences and their essential reducibility to particular characteristics and internalisations of identity. The association of Western dualisms, such as mind/body, masculinity/femininity, reason/emotion, culture/nature, with patriarchy and power relations positions women as both closer to nature and inferior in a masculine hierarchy. Many feminisms, as we have already seen in this book, have fought to prevent women from being reduced to their biology, which is associated with inferior conceptualisations, while also acknowledging women's bodies as a site of struggle and recognising the social construction of gendered structures, cultures and behaviours. Ecofeminism has been accused of essentialism because of the close association claimed by some ecofeminists between women and nature, particularly in what has been termed the nature/culture dualism, where women are associated with nature (base, subordinated, exploited) and men with culture (sophisticated, dominant, powerful) (Irving & Helin, 2018; King, 2018; Mellor, 1997). Mellor (1997) critiques what is termed 'affinity ecofeminism' as promoting the problem of essentialism within ecofeminism, whereby women's supposed affinity with nature, the celebration of women-centred values such as nurturing and caring, the association of women's bodies and spirituality as closer to nature fixes their identities with essentialist traits, which feminists have fought against:

> To argue that women as biologically sexed or socially gendered beings are connected with, or in some way represent, the natural world is seen as dangerous by many feminists. It undermines the struggle that they have waged against the way the identification of women with nature has been used to justify women's subordination.
>
> *(Mellor, 1997, p. 2)*

This essentialisation of women is a reductionist stereotype which risks ignoring social and political influences on women's position.

Moreover, the increasingly poststructuralist turn of the late twentieth and early twenty-first century (see Chapter 6) has provided two major critiques of some forms of ecofeminism. The first is around the use of language or discourse in referring to ecological concepts, where feminised terms signify codes of value or symbolic underpinning meanings. For example, the terms 'Mother Earth' or 'Mother Nature' personify the earth or nature and its ability to sustain life. They both reify nature as a goddess, yet through its feminisation make it vulnerable to degradation, violence and violation. From a poststructuralist perspective, this again suggests that women have a particular relationship or affinity with nature that renders ecofeminism charged with essentialism. Second, poststructuralist feminism charged ecofeminism with false universality in assuming that all women experience their relationships and position in nature in a universal way without accounting for difference based on class, race, global positioning or more localised ecological issues. This charge perhaps arises from the dominance of White Western women in the early ecofeminist movement and its academic orientation (Gaard, 2011), although there were notable exceptions such as Vandana Shiva's work on non-Western contexts, particularly her homeland of India (Mies & Shiva, 2014 [1993]; Shiva, 1988). As well as essentialism, these early Western ecofeminists were charged with ethnocentrism in promoting an idealist, uncritical understanding of women's position within nature in the Global South, without awareness of the social construction of their own Western theoretical and social positioning (Oksala, 2018). This poststructuralist critique, however, remains contentious with a recent resurgence in interest in ecofeminism making claims that some ecological feminists did indeed incorporate poststructuralist insights into the social construction of concepts such as 'nature', without losing sight of the structural materiality of people's lives (Gaard, 2011; Thompson, 2006). As I shall discuss later in this chapter, accounting scholars have also made productive use of poststructuralist feminist theorists, such as Hélène Cixous, in a critique of accounting's relationships with nature.

Ecofeminism, capitalism and climate change

In the third decade of the twenty-first century, the issue of climate change has become an imperative challenge for humankind in its interaction with planetary and ecological systems. The year 2023 was the hottest year on record according to the EU's Copernicus climate intelligence service,[1] close to 1.5 C above pre-industrial levels. Multiple global crises, such as floods, droughts, wildfires and storms, as well as warfare, place human beings in a trepidatious position in relation to their environment. Simultaneously, climate change has a documented gendered character in terms of how women are vulnerable to the effects of climate change and less represented in decision-making, government representation, mitigation and adaptation projects on climate change, not due to their essential characteristics as a group, but due to the socio-economic and cultural circumstances (e.g. poverty, lack of education, lack of access and opportunity, lack of various rights) in which they are situated (Pearse, 2017).

The role of ecofeminism in addressing the challenges of climate change, environmental justice and the unsustainable effects of human actions in relation to the environment therefore takes on a new imperative. As Zoloth (2017, p. 141) asserts:

> In the impending environmental crisis, women and children will be the first to be harmed. All the freedoms we have obtained in the West – all the fine capacities for voice and leadership – will mean little if feminists

> stand by and watch the world warm, the seas rise, the climate change, the refugees struggle, and the world we share disappear.

In contrast to its early origins, more recent ecofeminism has extended its focus to include a critique of globalisation, considering the linkages between exploitation of the natural world and the global exploitation of women (Donovan, 2001).

There remain, however, several perspectives on ecofeminism in its approach towards this ecological crisis. An emphasis on a material ecofeminism stresses the analysis of women's embodiment and social experience to explore dimensions of oppression and exploitation within the human/nature interaction that allows for a focus on women's caring work and reproduction without becoming essentialist by highlighting the social construction of society (Mellor, 1997). According to Oksala (2018), material ecofeminism is empirically grounded, emphasising the actual material conditions of women's interactions with the environment in specific geographical and cultural contexts, but it has a tendency to be descriptive and lacking in theorisation.

A more overtly political perspective on ecofeminism addresses the relationship between nature and the institutional structures of global capitalism. This position within ecofeminism identifies patriarchy as a key source of global environmental destruction through the division of power and labour between men and women, which becomes institutionalised through capitalist economic practices (Federici, 2009; Salleh, 2009). Marxist ecofeminism identifies the systemic logic of capitalism that binds gender oppression and environmental destruction (Oksala, 2018). She argues:

> The Marxist-feminist argument contends that, in addition to the appropriation of surplus value produced by wage-labour, capitalism relies on the ongoing and violent expropriation of women, indigenous peoples, nonhuman animals, and the biosphere. The expropriation of women's reproductive labour is therefore structurally analogous to and historically contemporaneous with the extraction of natural resources.
>
> *(Oksala, 2018, p. 222)*

Both a materialist approach and a Marxist or socialist approach to ecofeminism could be a suitable means of exploring gendered inequalities and ecological degradations, depending on their emphasis on the degree of analysis of embodied human experience or political struggle against capitalist institutions. Yet, as Ariel Salleh, a prominent ecofeminist scholar, argues, ecofeminism offers the potential to synthesise four major social and political issues: the need for focus on the environment; the need for anti-capitalist socialist movements; the challenge of addressing postcoloniality under globalisation; and feminist theorisation, allowing for political analysis of capitalism that combines with the materiality of women's embodied lives (Salleh, 2017). Thus, ecofeminism has resonance with and application to many of the complex, multidimensional, multidisciplinary challenges facing humanity and the environment. Moreover, it gives insight into particular behaviours such as violence.

Ecofeminism and violence

In a classic ecofeminist text originally published in 1993, *Ecofeminism*, Mies and Shiva address the relationship between patriarchal oppression and the destruction of nature, which is imbued with forms of violence (see Mies & Shiva, 2014 [1993]). In their updated 2014 text, Vandana Shiva additionally argues in her new preface that the intensification of global violence against women is connected with undemocratic, unjust and unsustainable neoliberal economic policies, as patriarchy becomes more endemically capitalist (Mies & Shiva, 2014 [1993]). She argues this occurs in four ways, all of which she argues inculcate forms of violence against women: first, that an economic system focusing on growth ignores the contributions of many of the world's women whose work is not counted in measures of GDP; second, that patriarchy under capitalism separates women from the natural resources that they need to thrive; third, that economic 'reforms' such as privatisation tend to solidify the interacting power and control of governments and corporations; and, fourth, that economics under patriarchy commodifies everything, including women's lives and bodies (Mies & Shiva, 2014 [1993]). According to Shiva, increasing economic vulnerability of women makes them more susceptible to forms of violence:

> ...the rape of the Earth and the rape of women are intimately linked – both metaphorically, in shaping worldviews, and materially, in shaping women's everyday lives.
>
> *(Mies & Shiva, 2014 [1993], p. xvi)*

In the same update on their earlier work, Mies, in her new preface (Mies & Shiva, 2014 [1993], p. xxvii), addresses the 'violence against nature, people and future generations.. [through] the restructuring of the whole world economy according to the principles of neoliberalism: globalization, liberalization, privatization and universal competition'. Giving examples of the effects of supply chain issues affecting women in developing countries, she also argues that capitalism fuels violence against women through poverty, adverse working conditions and exploitation.

The notion of violence is a theme that runs through much ecofeminist thinking. It includes the destructive violence that humans impose on natural resources through extraction and pollution. It also addresses the violence of anthropocentrism that prioritises human economic development at the expense of other life forms (Fotaki & Pullen, 2024). It encapsulates the violence of technology intervening on animals, plants, seeds as well as humans (Braidotti, 2016) as well as reproductive technologies (Mies & Shiva, 2014 [1993]) and the exploitation of animals or non-human species (Gaard, 2015), under a commodified and hierarchical patriarchal world order. In this sense, ecofeminism provides insights into the connections between violence against women and violence against animals and the earth (Mallory, 2018).

Having outlined the central tenets of ecofeminist theory, I will address its relevance to accounting and potential application to the discipline, but before doing so, it is necessary to situate ecofeminist accounting in the broader field of SEA and reporting.

SEA and reporting

A strong movement in accounting academia over the last four decades, SEA has addressed new forms of accounting and accountability that focus on bringing social and environmental factors within accounting's remit. Heavily influenced by the prolific work of Rob Gray and members of the Centre for Social and Environmental Accounting Research (CSEAR),[2] it proposed new conceptualisations of accounting and accountability through forms of corporate social reporting, defined as:

> The process of communicating the social and environmental effects of organisations' economic actions to particular interest groups within society and to society at large. As such, it involves extending the accountability of organisations (particularly companies) beyond the traditional role of providing a financial account to the owners of capital, in particular, shareholders. Such an extension is predicated upon the assumption that companies do have wider responsibilities than simply to make money for their shareholders.
>
> *(Gray, Owen, & Adams, 1996, p. 3)*

What SEA aimed to do from its inception was to broaden the relationship between a firm and its wider stakeholders, including the planet itself, by addressing how externalities, such as pollution or effects on natural resources, could be accounted for and reported on. SEA has developed and broadened to become a global movement that addresses the important interaction of accounting and social and environmental issues.

Deegan's (2017) review of 25 years of SEA research finds that it tends to cover three approaches: 'critical' and 'managerial', being two ends of a spectrum on the degree of radical change recommended, with the majority being 'middle of the road', which 'accepts (with some misgivings) the structures, organisations, society and accounting currently obtain but seeks to change them in a manner which privileges social and environmental concerns' (Deegan, 2017, p. 71). It is perhaps not surprising that much research is corporate-centred since it coincides with a shift in SEA reporting over the last three decades whereby, either through mandatory or through voluntary regimes, companies report on environmental, social and governance (ESG) topics. For example, the European Union's Corporate Sustainability Reporting Directive (CSRD)[3] commenced in 2023 requiring most companies with operations in the EU to provide standardised and verified reporting on ESG performance. Previously, various voluntary initiatives such as the Global Reporting Initiative (GRI), amongst others, were utilised to provide frameworks for forms of sustainability reporting. Therefore, SEA research focused on the potential gaps between reporting and performance (Adams, 2004); on who the audience is for such reporting (Spence, 2009); on whether capital markets pay attention to SEA reporting (Murray et al., 2006); on the role of social and natural capital in integrated reporting (Coulson et al., 2015) or on how SEA reporting is implemented in different countries. Moreover, a slew of quantitative work addresses casual links or correlations between various variables of disclosure and performance, which is beyond the scope of this book to address, since I am focusing more critically on accounting. Early critical accountants warned that unless there was a more radical approach to social and environmental issues, business interests would capture the social and environmental agenda (Tinker, Neimark, & Lehman, 1991), and it remains questionable some 35 years later whether these reports change the underlying culture, performance or systems of an organisation. Indeed, although SEA began with an emphasis on 'corporate social *reporting*' (Gray et al., 1996), it has perhaps been subsumed into the whole corporate social *responsibility* (CSR) agenda of companies and an emphasis on CSR or sustainability reporting.

More recent SEA research tends to move away from reporting *per se* to focus more on new ways of accounting, including, amongst others, critiquing accounting's role in addressing the SDGs (Bebbington & Unerman, 2020); the effects of stakeholder engagement in SEA (Kaur & Lodhia, 2017); the role of accounting in developing understanding of and approaches to the Anthropocene[4] (Bebbington et al., 2020); the interaction of accounting and sustainability (Bebbington & Larrinaga, 2014) and the role of more pluralist perspectives in widening SEA (Brown & Dillard, 2013; Brown, Dillard, & Hopper, 2015). These new ways of thinking are important given that, despite a supposed emphasis on nature, Russell, Milne, and Dey's (2017) review of environmental accounting alone over 40 years finds that it tends to emphasise the economic entity and its effects on environmental inputs and outputs rather than actual ecology. Only recently has some innovative research emerged on how accounting as a technology can be mobilised more effectively to address ecological issues more directly (see Jones, 2014). For instance, Cuckston argues that innovation on calculative practice is capable of producing information on risks to biodiversity and the possibility of species loss that can improve conservation (Cuckston, 2018a, 2018b), with novel means of using accounting to value biodiversity ecologically rather than economically (Cuckston, 2019). Accounting practices can be framed as a means of serving human and non-human species in the ecological renewal of the planet (Vollmer, 2021). Marketisation of biodiversity through off-setting schemes, on the other hand, is problematised (Ferreira, 2017).

Moreover, one of the challenges of SEA is what it deems to include in the 'social' element. SEA has tended to focus more firmly on the environment and where it has addressed the social, it has been on (albeit highly important) relationships between accounting and marginalised communities (Angotti et al., 2024; Jayasinghe & Thomas, 2009), human rights (Gallhofer, Haslam, & van der Walt, 2011; McPhail & Ferguson, 2016) or ethics (Lennard & Roberts, 2023). Thomson (2014) makes a plea for social accounting to be reframed firmly as symbolic activism through collective communities of academic research and as transformative educators. Gray et al. (2014) argue that social accounting is a form of speaking truth to power. Some forms of shadow account, an alternative form of account as discussed in Chapter 4, might be deemed a form of SEA. Although there have been calls for more feminist approaches to CSR (Grosser & Moon, 2019; Spence & Taylor, 2024), few scholars have been explicit about the inclusion of any gender or feminist dimensions to the social element of SEA, which represents a different focus. Where gender is addressed in corporate reporting or forms of sustainability reporting, it tends to follow a liberal feminist reformist agenda of compliance to reporting standards and requirements on issues such as numbers of female directors or gender pay gap, or more CSR-related issues, such as women stakeholders as beneficiaries of CSR programmes.

Frustration with the dominance of the environment and the tendency to ignore the social, or at least the social elements that address equality and equity, led to our argument that social justice and equity are at the heart of concepts of sustainability (Haynes & Murray, 2015) and therefore should be addressed in any SEA reporting. We drew from the most widely accepted definition of sustainable development from the Brundtland Report, which suggests sustainability meets 'the needs of the present without compromising the ability of future generations to meet their own needs', and also raises issues of *inter-generational equity*, between present and future generations, and *intra-generational equity*, between different peoples within the current generation (WCED, 1987). We argued that intra-generational equity includes the developed and developing worlds, and peoples within those worlds, who may be different from each other, based on race, religion, ethnicity and gender, but who should be treated with equity and social justice, which would include gender equality and gender justice (Haynes & Murray, 2015).

Moreover, in developing an interdisciplinary exploration of the concept and application of the Circular Economy, I, together with colleagues, proposed a definition that has been widely adopted in Circular Economy research that explicitly includes the social:

> The Circular Economy is an economic model wherein planning, resourcing, procurement, production and reprocessing are designed and managed, as both process and output, to maximize ecosystem functioning and *human well-being.*
>
> *(Murray, Skene, & Haynes, 2017, p. 377, emphasis added)*

We argued that without this social dimension, important moral and ethical issues, such as inter- and intra-generational equity, gender, racial or other forms of diversity, are missing from the concept (Murray et al., 2017) and therefore our definition of the Circular Economy aimed to redress this balance and include social factors.

The above reflects a snapshot of the vast body of research on SEA in the discipline. While interest in SEA and its various forms of environmental accounting, social accounting and sustainability reporting has become widespread, and corporate sustainability reporting moves towards the mandatory, a feminist dimension is largely lacking. Certainly, ecofeminism has been rarely addressed in relation to accounting.

Ecofeminism and accounting

Given that contemporary ecofeminism tends to focus on relationships between environmental degradation, the position of women, climate change and capitalism, there are clear implications for the role of accounting. Accounting is a mechanism associated with the perpetuation of neoliberalism and marketised capitalist systems (Annisette & Prasad, 2017; Lehman, Annisette, & Agyemang, 2016; Morales, Gendron, & Guénin-Paracini, 2014). Accounting can also shed light on environmental degradation (Bebbington & Larrinaga, 2024; Jones, 2010) or gendered inequalities (Haynes, 2017; Lehman, 2019). Yet, ecofeminist accounting has not developed to its full potential in addressing these interlinkages, although there are some exceptional studies which bring feminism to bear on these relationships between accounting and the environment, or in relation to SEA.

A critical explanation for the lack of the social and gendered perspectives within SEA arises from the nature of accounting itself. Christine Cooper's distinctive and powerful early work draws from the work of Cixous, who had argued that language fixes meanings of the masculine and feminine, which results in entrenched patriarchal systems (Cooper, 1992). Cooper (1992) applied the binary opposites inherent in accounting, such as debit/credit or profit/loss (see also Chapter 2), to a critique of accounting, particularly in relation to the environment. She suggests that the masculine nature of accounting privileges 'the *masculine* over the *feminine*' which means 'forcing nature's multiplicity into accounting's binary oppositions, which is a violence against nature, a denial of her multiplicity' (Cooper, 1992, pp. 25–26) and actually damages the environment further. For Cooper (1992, p. 28), environmental accounting is founded on 'phallogocentric understandings', which derives from Derrida's notion that language privileges the masculine, and 'will be unable to bring about revolutionary change despite the high hopes and desires of some of its proponents', a view which seems prescient given the corporate capture of much of sustainability reporting.

Building on Cooper's early use of Cixous (Cooper, 1992), Cooper and Senkl's (2016) analysis of KPMG's True Value statement suggests that binary dualisms are deeply embedded in accounting and business practice, serving 'to frame problems like climate change as being disconnected from the problems of business' (p. 502) and ignoring any critiques of inequality. They draw attention to the prevalent phallocentric symbolic order which gives an impression of solving environmental problems while actually cementing their threats. Furthermore, they argue that symbolic and ideological signifiers within language reinforce the gendered symbolic order of accounting and its interaction with the dominant capitalist and patriarchal social order, resulting in an absence of recognition of the effects of climate change on humans and a reduction of the climate problem to matters of risk management (Senkl & Cooper, 2023). While Cixous is widely defined as a poststructural feminist (see Chapter 6) with her emphasis on language and deconstruction, rather than an ecofeminist, Cooper and Senkl's work illustrates how critiquing relationships between accounting, the environment and patriarchy can draw from feminist theorising.

Gallhofer (2018) takes an explicitly ecofeminist position to critique the continuing nature of binary oppositions within accounting, based on what she terms Western dualisms, which shape the interrelationship between humans and nature. For Gallhofer (2018), ecofeminism positions humans as part of nature rather than in domination of it, allowing for a holistic and inclusive approach to thinking about the nature-human interaction that transcends social systems of domination and dichotomous thinking. She applies her ecofeminist theorising to the development of new accountings for nature, termed as corporate nature responsibility reporting, that create visibility, awareness and action on the well-being of both humans and nature. Gallhofer suggests that these new forms of accounting will help to overcome binary, Westernised ways of thinking and accounting.

What these articles have in common is a recognition of the interaction between accounting, gender, climate change and capitalism. They also posit that a feminist approach offers a nuanced and theorised critique of current corporate masculinist practices, while also offering a feminine alternative. However, other than Gallhofer (2018) and an early unpublished paper (Buhr & Reiter, 2000), explicit ecofeminist perspectives have rarely translated into accounting.

Yet, ecofeminist perspectives hold potential for accounting because of their explicit concern with the interaction of climate change and environmental degradation, patriarchy and capitalism. Accounting is associated with the perpetuation of all three areas. Its underpinning of all of business interactions and reporting renders it a central tool of capitalism, which itself is implicated in contributing to climate change through emissions. The use of fossil fuels and the extractive industries, such as oil and gas in particular, take primacy in industrialised economies, despite putative moves towards more environmentally sustainable sources of power. Our economies also commodify and exploit non-human species, such as animals and forests, resulting in species degradation, violence and extinction. Moreover, systems of patriarchy underpin capitalism and capitalist means of production though divisions of labour, employment practices, supply chain compositions and representation in leadership and power systems. Accounting as a calculative practice underpins these attributes and constructs of capitalism, and accounting as a profession supports their development and continuation.

Taking an ecofeminist perspective on accounting requires an ontological shift from anthropocentric paradigms of value to holistic and integrated perspectives on humanity and nature. It requires consideration of what we choose to measure and report on using forms of accounting and more importantly what we choose not to measure and value. For example, accounting's instrumental rationality provides economic justification for environmental destruction and war (Chwastiak & Lehman, 2008) but often fails to account for measures of human well-being (Laurent, 2017). SEA emerged from a concern with proposing new forms of accounting and accountability that addressed the externalities which businesses fail to account for, a concern that has not been resolved despite the advent of sustainability reporting, CSR reporting and various other measures, such as natural capital accounting (Sullivan, 2018) and the financialisaton of nature (Arjaliès & Gibassier, 2023). What it did not address was the role of gender, race or other human dimensions in the interaction with nature, which ecofeminism explicitly addresses. The underpinning of capitalism with patriarchy and binary relations is a central focus of ecofeminism that can be applied both to a critique of accounting and to an exploration of new forms of accounting for the future. For this, a form of accounting which blends feminism and care for humanity and nature is necessary; it is to accounting and the ethics of care which I now turn.

Ethics of care

Carol Gilligan is said to be the originator of the concept of the ethics of care when she criticised the work of Lawrence Kohlberg, a psychologist proposing a theory of moral development, which he argued went through six stages (Tronto, 1993). As an associate of Kohlberg, Gilligan critiqued his work for the fact that the subjects of his longitudinal study were all male and his research therefore resulted in incomplete findings and biased results, resulting in a hierarchical ordering of moral principles based on a male elite (Gilligan, 1977). Proposing to view morality 'in a different voice', from a woman's perspective, Gilligan (1977, 1982) argues that conceptions of morality are incomplete if they focus on principles of justice rather than compassion and care, which she argues are more at the centre of women's moral development. Although Gilligan's work was influential in raising awareness of gendered perceptions of psychological development, she was critiqued by feminists as being essentialist and for ignoring other intersectional identities by basing her own research on White, middle-class women, and for ostensibly influencing the privileging of the private over the public context in relation to women's roles, which feminists were trying to break away from (Robinson, 2019). Nonetheless, the ethics of care concept has since proliferated into many disciplines beyond psychology, into philosophy, politics, international relations and, as I will go on to illustrate, potentially into accounting.

Debates centre on 'the difference between an ethic of justice and rights and an ethic of care and relationship' (Tronto, 1993, p. 78). Held distinguishes between the emphasis of each approach as follows:

> In the dominant moral theories of the ethics of justice, the values of equality, impartiality, fair distribution, and noninterference have priority; in practices of justice, individual rights are protected, impartial judgments are arrived at, punishments are deserved, and equal treatment is sought. In contrast, in the ethics of care, the values of trust, solidarity, mutual concern, and empathetic responsiveness have priority; in practices of care, relationships are cultivated, needs are responded to, and sensitivity is demonstrated.
>
> *(Held, 2006, pp. 15–16)*

Held (2006) argues that both perspectives are valuable, but how they relate together may depend on the context or domain in which they have priority; for example, in the realm of law, she argues that justice has priority, although the humanity of care should always be present. I tend to think of the Covid-19 pandemic when there was a clear emergency and urgency to deal with, during which it was important that universal human rights were respected, meaning that governments had to step in to provide social, civil, political and economic support. However, these also had to be combined with the ethics of care in promoting care for the vulnerable, resulting in restriction of some rights such as freedom of movement to protect others, and importantly promoting caring across global and local societies by ensuring access to vaccines in poorer communities or less developed countries. Such a balance of rights and care is difficult to agree for both governments and individuals, potentially resulting in critical consequences, such as excess deaths during the pandemic (Haynes, 2020).

Definition and features of ethics of care

Despite the critique of Gilligan's early work, feminists have since embraced the wider concept of the ethics of care and it has become central to much feminist theorising and practice. A definition of care, which has become widely accepted, arises from the work of feminist political scientist Joan Tronto:

> On the most general level, we suggest that caring be viewed as a *species activity that includes everything that we do to maintain, continue, and repair our 'world' so that we can live in it as well as possible*. That world includes our bodies, our selves, our environment, all of which we seek to interweave in a complex life-sustaining web.
>
> *(Fisher & Tronto, 1991, cited in Tronto, 1993, italics in original)*

What I find appealing about this definition is its active focus on current and future well-being, while acknowledging the degree of interconnectivity between people, environment and the wider world. The definition encompasses the necessity for caring actions of human beings interacting with the social and environmental worlds, and as such resonates with some of the features of both ecofeminist thinking and SEA. What is not explicit in the definition is to place the ethics of care within a political and feminist argument, although Tronto's (1993) *Moral Boundaries* is a vehement argument for the political dimension of the ethics of care, in which she suggests care reveals relations of power relating to gender, privilege, race and class. Tronto's argument can be taken further, as according to Barnes:

> If care is a species activity, it encompasses relationships that are not only intimate, like personal care, or interpersonal relationships, but relationships that are also political and stretching across boundaries of identity, geography, race, religion, relationships that are global.
>
> *(Barnes, 2015, p. 35)*

Hence, the ethics of care concept is powerful in revealing the interconnectedness of people across many modes of apparent difference, while situating them in a global context.

From a feminist perspective, the ethics of care has some distinctive features. Held (2006) argues it encompasses a central focus on meeting the needs of others for whom we have responsibility, the value of emotional rather than rationalistic responses in understanding an ethics of care and a reconceptualisation of how we understand the public and private domains, since caring occurs across both. Yet, it is important to note that these facets do not relegate caring only to women, to the domestic or home environment or to the irrational/emotional conceptualisations of women that feminists have tried to break away from. Held (2006) argues for these features of the ethics of care to pertain to civil society, the rule of law, the political economy and the market economy as a transformative moral approach. Robinson (2011) stresses that the central feature of the ethics of care is relational ontology, since the self is always understood in relation to others as people are interdependent in their social relations and requirements for care, but an effect of this has been to distort the experiences of women since they are more socially associated with care. She rejects the notion of care as a women's issue arguing that 'when care is constructed more broadly to include a structural critique of relations of dependence, perceptions of difference, and patterns of exclusion, these valid concerns about care ethics confining women to subordinate, undervalued positions in society may be overcome' (Robinson, 1997, p. 122). Indeed, a feminist conceptualisation of the ethics of care has been applied to broaden dominant notions of masculinity, such as in fatherhood, albeit noting that destabilising traditional masculinity is complex (Jordan, 2020). The political nature of the ethics of care draws attention to embedded concepts of gender and power relations that, while framing the concept firmly as a feminist ethic, take it beyond a female perspective to a broader definition of affective relations underpinned by care rather than universal individualism. The ethics of care is therefore a concept that can apply to humanity as a whole rather than being embodied in women.

Ethics of care and neoliberalism

However, although the ethics of care representing a philosophy of caring relations can apply widely to numerous private and public scenarios, care as a practice or an act is often embedded in the neoliberal principles of a marketised economy. Healthcare and personal care are increasingly privatised or subjected to elements of a paid service provision in many countries, including the UK. This can have the effect of depersonalising and commodifying care, and, significantly, increasing inequalities in the provision of and access to care. For example, in periods of austerity affecting individual and public spending, only the wealthier have recourse to their preferences in privatised forms of care, as others have to make do what they can afford or what is offered by the state. Ultimately, this market mechanism erodes state provision and creates or exacerbates inequalities, as neoliberalism favours the individualised rather than the collective approach to responsibility.

Under neoliberalism, care as a practice and form of labour has become a globalised commodity. Migrant care workers (predominantly women but also some men), often from poorer nations, who provide child, elder, nursing, personal and cleaning care, enable other more affluent nations to operate more productively under global capitalism and the free market. Robinson (2011) discusses the means by which some entire families are linked in a 'global care chain' consisting of those who migrate or are trafficked to other nations to perform care work, those in the family they support who are left behind and those in other countries for whom they provide care. She argues that 'these relationships must be understood as embedded in both the institutions and structures of the global care economy and in the gender and racial norms and hierarchies that feminize and devalue caring labor' (Robinson, 2011, p. 65). Despite feminist efforts to move away from essentialism, care and caring tends to continue to be associated with social norms related to women, and particularly with those who are 'othered' by race and class. In other words, although caring as a general role (of children, of the sick, of the home) tends to be disproportionately carried out by women, paid care work in the global economy is often the remit of poorer, sometimes migrant, sometimes less educated women with fewer opportunities due to their race and class positioning. Hence, when evaluating the role of neoliberalism and care in our economies, it is necessary not only to consider gender but to take an intersectional lens to evaluate structural forces and power inequities beyond patriarchy (Hankivsky, 2014). Indeed, the global market for care workers is rooted in postcoloniality as a constitutive element of global capitalism which supports the wheels of global commerce by ensuring basic care needs are met, but which also sustains inequalities.

During the period of the Covid-19 pandemic,[5] I highlighted that structural inequalities relating to age, health, poverty, disability, race and gender in the UK were a significant factor in pandemic outcomes, exposing a need for the ethics of care to be embedded in accounting mechanisms to combat such societal challenges (Haynes, 2020). The government's underpinning belief in the private sector model of new public management had the effect of fragmenting services between public and private providers before and during the pandemic, resulting in a lack of political accountability across a complex system of care delivery and an erosion of trust from the public (Broadbent, 2020). Moreover, the role of government in making unethical decisions within their own model of neoliberalism resulted in the offering of questionable contracts for personal protective equipment, causing huge losses of public money.[6] Through the experience of the Covid-19 pandemic, at a time when caring relations between individuals, states and nations were essential, and despite the many caring actions of those on the frontline of healthcare, neoliberal ideologies and practices undermined the effectiveness of the response.

During the pandemic, it was also pertinent to note how the interaction of patriarchy, care and neoliberalism was evident. During this period, persistent gendered norms rose to the surface of locked-down family life, as women took on more of the burden of additional childcare and homeschooling; in the UK, this was for an average of more than three additional hours per day, compared to two hours for men, with 34% of women reporting that the challenge of balancing work and childcare affected their mental health, compared to 20% of men (Office for National Statistics, 2020a, 2020b). The pandemic regressed some of the positioning gained for women in the workforce as, whether parent or not, the burden of unpaid care, disproportionate loss of employment or re-evaluation of possibilities caused women's unequal position in the workplace to be exacerbated (McKinsey & Co., 2020; PWC, 2021). Numerous articles evidence the unrealistic expectations of productivity and invisible service work being served on women academics (Górska et al., 2021; Parlak, Cakiroglu, & Gul, 2021; Utoft, 2020). Moreover, gender-based violence around the world increased during the pandemic as people were limited in their movements and confined to their homes, giving abusers more opportunity for violence and those who are abused no opportunity to avoid it (Piquero et al., 2021). According to Yardley (2021), domestic abuse is a neoliberal manifestation of patriarchy, where perpetrators assert a right to possess and control that is driven by market-based individualism validated by their own sense of entitlement and freedom. Given that neoliberalism is an individualistic notion rather than a collective notion, it interacts with patriarchal attitudes and structures to promote a demand for care while offering no reciprocal caring. The ethics of care is therefore potentially eroded by our economic systems.

Ethics of care within accounting

The theoretical approach of the ethics of care has not been extensively addressed within the accounting discipline. This is perhaps because of the inherently commercial underpinning of accounting as a technology and the dominant ideology of the maximisation of shareholder value economic model. As I discuss further below, accounting is dominated by rights and responsibilities rather than approaches underpinned by care. Although there is a multiplicity of research on the ethics of professional accountants and the merits of teaching ethics within accounting education (for examples, see, Cameron & O'Leary, 2015; Seifert, LaMothe, & Schmitt, 2023), which are beyond the scope of a feminist approach, ethics of care are largely absent.

Research by Reiter some decades ago is an exception, where she argues that accounting ethics education could be enriched by applying an ethics of care perspective, enabling students to acquire conflict resolution skills by understanding others, developing 'caretaking abilities' (Reiter, 1996, p. 62). Furthermore, she argues for a feminist ethics of care in reconceptualising the audit process, where auditor independence is a key ethical issue within accounting practice but is 'organized around a central ethical conflict' where the auditor is hired and paid by the client while supposedly being independent from the client in a separatist model (Reiter, 1997, p. 306). Reiter argues that an ethics of care perspective would allow auditors to focus on relational and contextual issues suggesting that:

> The implication for accounting of the care view of moral maturity is that the ideal state for professional judgement is a set of appropriately embedded relationships, rather than a mythic independence of mind.
>
> *(Reiter, 1997, p. 303)*

However, such concepts as the ethics of care have not mainstreamed in accounting research or practice, although others have argued for a different perspective on ethics in accounting. For example, Dillard has promulgated the 'ethic of accountability' concept, which is the reciprocal relationship between society and the management of organisations, where management is 'accountable for the use of society's economic assets' and 'society accepts its responsibility for holding organizational management to account for its actions' (Dillard, 2008, p. 4). Shearer (2002) argues for a radical accountability that seriously considers 'obligation to the Other' (p. 565) rather than the 'ethical deficiencies [of] the interpersonal relationship of economic accountability' (p. 544). While neither of these conceptualisations of moral accountability are explicitly underpinned by feminist concepts of ethics of care, they both critique the underpinning economic logic of rendering an account within accounting practice, in favour of one which acknowledges power relations, contextualisation and the importance of relationality within the rendering of an account. These concepts are also important within ethics of care.

In one of the few recent accounting studies that considers an ethics of care, although he does not consider it as a feminist perspective, Dellaportas (2019) argues that the calculative practices of accounting lead to the separation of moral consequences from behaviour, resulting in the objectification and dehumanisation of people and the inability of managers to feel empathy for others. Drawing from early work on care ethics (Gilligan, 1977, 1982; Noddings, 1984), he argues for accounting to be underpinned by concern for others in which the role of emotion is key in making moral judgements, arguing that 'notions of care, empathy and emotion are de-emphasised in the traditions of accounting that stress objectivity and arm's length relationships' (Dellaportas, 2019, p. 1622). To counter this approach, he coins the term 'connected accounting' underpinned by an ethics of care perspective, which he argues increases accounting's connection and proximity to stakeholders, resulting in a transition from a limited 'caring-about' to a helping 'caring-for' based on compassion, concern and care for others (Dellaportas, 2019, p. 1629). Dellaportas' work is an important contribution to the mediating effect of care within accounting.

However, my interpretation of the ethics of care is as a broader, more politicised, feminist concept that counters some of the ideological power of accounting. As I argued previously in this book (see Chapter 1), accounting is a socio-political construct implicated in inequality through its association with neoliberal market capitalism, its underpinning calculative practices that serve the modern organisation and the global positioning of its professional bodies and firms. The feminist theorisation and application of the ethics of care within accounting holds the possibilities for a relational, rather than individualised, form of ethics underpinning accounting. In the next sections I will address the potential for integrating an ecofeminist care ethic in accounting, and finally present my argument for moving from accounting for care to accounting as care.

Integrating ecofeminism and ethics of care in accounting

Going back to Fisher and Tronto's definition of care, a key point is that caring centres on repairing 'our world', which includes 'our environment' and 'a life-sustaining web' (Fisher & Tronto, 1991, cited in Tronto, 1993). The theory of the ethics of care can be applied whether that world is a small, contained social context or the planetary boundaries. Since climate change is a matter of record and environmental degradation is problematic around the globe, approaching the problem through an ethics of care lens is one way of shifting a mindset that is largely failing to address the unsustainability of human activities. In this sense it is fruitful to consider the interaction of ecofeminism and ethics of care in addressing these problems.

Both ecofeminism and ethics of care have been accused of an underpinning essentialism since both are associated with ostensibly 'feminine' binaries and values of being close to nature and of caring. Some ecofeminists have been associated with the somewhat derogatory concept of 'motherhood environmentalism' that situates their concern for the environment in their literal care of babies and children, and reduces women's views to their reproductive status, as if only mothers can understand and worry about their children's future. However, recognising the interaction between caring for nature and caring for people as a holistic moral position allows for a relational, affective feminist positioning that goes beyond literal embodiment or identification as mother or as carer.

When concepts of care ethics are placed in a wider critique of globalisation, which recognises the marketisation of care under neoliberal ideologies and the widespread impact of market mechanisms and human activity on the unsustainability of the planet, the interaction of ecofeminism and ethics of care becomes clearer. Ecofeminism is concerned with the material and political effects of oppressive power relations, particularly patriarchy, and their relations with the environment. Ethics of care in its broadest sense is concerned with relations of care within private, public, institutional and global settings that are influenced by and have the potential to influence globalisation, economic models, neoliberalism and international relations. Both have a political dimension that critiques neoliberal capitalism and the impact of gendered power relations on social and environmental well-being, although increasingly both ecofeminism and care ethics look beyond gender to other forms of intersectional oppressions.

The recognition within ecofeminism and ethics of care of other values and characteristics beyond gender enables them to offer a yet more powerful critique of, and potential alternative to, current societal systems. The legacy of colonialism, for example, lingers in the raced and classed dimensions of migration, where workers from poorer countries provide caring services for those of more affluent countries, as discussed earlier. Understanding this phenomenon through an ecofeminist ethics of care lens illuminates the commodification of care under globalised capitalism (Robinson, 2011), while also highlighting the challenges facing people in developing countries whose livelihoods and economic stability is threatened by climate change, which contributes to that migratory impulse (Kaczan & Orgill-Meyer, 2020). Similarly, Indigenous values with powerful connections to land, the environment and the earth are disrupted and overridden by marketised worldviews, which can be challenged through incorporating ecological care ethics (Boulton & Brannelly, 2015).

In other words, contemporary theorisations of both ecofeminism and ethics of care share some components of feminist critique that place neoliberal globalised capitalism at their centre, under power relations of patriarchy as well as other systems of domination. They then consider their effects on relations with the social and the environmental, with humanity and the planet, offering alternative perspectives on society. In terms of their relevance to accounting, I next go on to develop a conceptualisation of accounting that incorporates relations of social and planetary care.

From accounting for care to accounting as care

Our current accounting model is one that accounts *for* things, assigning values to items that are accounted for in a transactional process. In accounting technology, double-entry bookkeeping uses debits and credits as measures to underpin the overarching financial account that is given, resulting in a balance sheet or statement of financial affairs, and an income statement, also known as a profit and loss account. Debits and credits are equal yet opposite entries that come into balance in the statement of financial affairs, signifying assets (debits) as stores of value and liabilities (credits) as obligations or things owing. These double entries interrelate with the income (credits) and expenditure (debits) of the income statement. It is worth noting that debits and credits are not always literal, tangible items, such as buildings or cash, or even descriptive items such as a mortgage or a debt. Since accounting is a social construction, debits and credits may also be socially constructed and monetised items that are symbolic of a benefit or a responsibility; for example, a right to have, hold or own something (debits) and a responsibility to make good, make right or hold a contingency against future problems (credits). They may represent an acknowledgement of use or degradation, such as amortisation or depreciation (debits) or a longer-term investment or commitment, for example, reserves (credits). Such items are not a tangible asset or item that we can literally see or count but are a constructed representation of value or diminution of value.

Accounting, therefore, tends towards these artificial binaries of debit and credit, broadly representing rights and responsibilities. For example, an asset is defined by the International Accounting Standard Board's newly revised conceptual framework as:

> A present economic resource controlled by the entity as a result of past events. An economic resource is a *right* that has the potential to produce economic benefits.[7]
>
> *(emphasis in italics is mine)*

In other words, accounting, as it currently stands, emphasises the right to value in the future through control of an asset in the present that became ours through some kind of action or transaction in the past. Accounting emphasises the rights that accrue to an entity giving an account and the responsibilities it owes in return. The resulting account that is rendered accounts *for* these rights and responsibilities. Hence, when accounting *for* care, it emphasises the costs and monies owed rather than any underlying philosophy of care.

Ethics of care theory transcends a transactional approach to care and caring. It is a feminist philosophy that pertains to wider aspects of human and non-human activity. Care and caring relates to our interconnected relationality with others, with humanity, animals, and the environment. It invokes the need to consider and underpin accounting with empathy, compassion and concern for others, embedded in stakeholder relationships (Dellaportas, 2019). However, taking a feminist perspective on the ethics of care, as I have discussed above, involves considering not only emotional rather than rationalistic connections within the care relationship, but also the political dimensions of power relations. It goes beyond the practice of care in interpersonal relationships and centres care within the global economy. Although I have argued that ethics of care apply to humanity as whole rather than being a feminine concept embodied solely in women, I continue to mobilise it as a feminist concept since feminism fights against gendered power relations, structures and institutions. Care and caring within a globalised neoliberal capitalist economy is imbued with gendered power relations, as well as power relations relating to other intersectional characteristics such as race, class or age, and the wider political dimensions of postcoloniality and geopolitical tensions. Moreover, if ecofeminism is integrated with feminist ethics of care, the underpinning relationality also includes caring for the environment, for non-human life and for the earth. This broader concept of the ethics of care involves taking positions on feminism, racism, class, violence and war, and the planet.

Taking an ecofeminist ethics of care perspective does not suggest or necessitate the abandonment of rights and responsibilities. Emphasising care and caring is a political question that raises the importance of rights to education, healthcare, employment and equality (Tronto, 1993). It also raises issues of the rights and responsibilities of humanity to sustain the planetary environment, where the impacts of climate change are unequally felt across the globe. Moreover, human rights are not incompatible with ethics of care and thinking differently about care ethics underpinned by intersectionality can bring:

> ...unique opportunities for building stronger alliances among diverse social justice organizations, women's organizations, disability and civil rights activists, labour unions, indigenous organizations, human rights organizations, faith-based organizations, and immigrant advocacy groups.
> *(Hankivsky, 2014, p. 261)*

Held (2006) also argues for the interaction of rights and care, suggesting that 'care involves moral considerations at least as important as those of justice', although 'justice should be incorporated into morally acceptable practices of care' (Held, 2006, p. 158). She argues for a cultural shift whereby the values of care are embedded more closely within the actions and practices of civil society, economic systems, democratic governments and political institutions (Held, 2006).

In relation to accounting, the question is then how existing accounting systems, based on rights and responsibilities, can reflect these dimensions of ethics of care. In a commentary on the Covid-19 pandemic and the systemic social inequalities based on race, gender, class and age that it highlighted, I argued that 'We need an accounting that enables us to care and *care better*' (Haynes, 2020, p. 640, my emphasis). I stated:

> The pandemic has shown how connected we are with each other. We are not separate or independent, everyone is vulnerable, but the impact

> has shown us that some lives appear to be held in less value than others. Requirement for care is more evident than ever, whether caring for ourselves, for others, mutually for each other and for non-human life that sustains us. Care is not just for people defined as carers or as needing care. Care is caring for humanity. Care is what makes possible to survive as humans on this planet. Neglect of caring shows that we cannot survive, if we were ever in doubt.
>
> *(Haynes, 2020, p. 640)*

Accounting expresses a right to receive, balanced with associated responsibilities, and it highlights the costs involved. Accounting for care may reflect a right to receive care balanced with responsibility to offer care. This need not be dyadic or simply two-way where the carer and cared for both offer and receive care. Instead, it can reflect the multidimensionality and multifaceted nature of care, as both individuals and organisations or institutions are multiple receivers and givers of care in some form. When we think of accounting *for* care, this assumes an underpinning by the extant binaries inherent in accounting technologies, of ownership and control, representing power relations and domination. However, if we think of accounting *as* care, those binaries may continue to represent rights and responsibilities, but they are countered by an understanding of relational ethical connection. Moreover, integrating an ecofeminist ethic within ethics of care supports an ontological movement from anthropocentric paradigms of value to more holistic and integrated perspectives on relationships between humanity and nature.

I therefore end this chapter with a call for a conceptual and practical re-evaluation of accounting *for* care to accounting *as* care.

Practising accounting as care

Conceptualising accounting *as* care acknowledges the role of accounting technologies in underpinning the unequal power relations within our global societies, facilitated by state, commercial, public, private and even civil society organisations. However, importantly, conceptualising accounting *as* care promotes the possibility and opportunity for accounting to take a more caring and relational approach to defining value, reporting on that value and holding the practice of caring to account. Underpinning accounting with feminist ethics of care emphasises the need for accounting and reporting entities to reflect on the relationships inherent in their activities as well as the impact of their actions on wider relations with the environment, political systems, democracy and geopolitics. Embedding ethics of care in accounting to promote accounting *as* care is not the same as following a CSR agenda, which focuses on the perceived responsibilities of a firm to wider stakeholders, but which is often critiqued for its partiality or greenwashing (Sundarasen, Zyznarska-Dworczak, & Goel, 2024), and use of legitimation strategies to justify firm behaviour (Bebbington, Larrinaga, & Moneva, 2008; Dhandhania & O'Higgins, 2022). Rather, accounting as care reflects the need for a new morality of care and responsive relations between individuals, communities, companies, government and states. Given the environmental crises facing the planet, accounting as care also incorporates relations between humanity and non-human species, and with wider ecological relations.

Of course, this conceptualisation of accounting as care is an ambitious, some might think naïve, way of rethinking the role and practice of accounting. Cultural and ethical change is profoundly difficult to attain, especially when dominant power relations persist in societies, violence and war is endemic and climate change is creeping towards critical levels. Yet all of these factors make different ways of thinking all the more morally imperative. As feminists of many theoretical perspectives have long known, political change requires new arguments and critical perspectives to challenge the status quo. Hence, I argue for accounting as care in ways that enable us to challenge neoliberal globalised capitalist practices that specifically undermine relations of care.

Despite these grand challenges, there are specific ways of beginning to move towards an accounting that embeds relations of caring and care in its value systems. Some suggestions for practices that can be implemented by companies and state systems, which incorporate ecofeminist ethics of care, are as follows:

- Robust data in public accounting is essential, as I previously argued: 'Supporting decision makers and activists with appropriate data to counter poverty, age, racial, gendered and dis/ableist discrimination, inequality and lack of care is therefore an important driver for accounting metrics and research' (Haynes, 2020, p. 640);
- Investment in infrastructure for health, education and housing can be balanced with investment in renewable energy and sustainable building, potentially with taxation incentives to encourage sustainable practices;
- Organisations can move away from unwarranted short-term, zero-hours contracts which fuel poverty and precarity towards offering more caring flexible working hours and costs;
- A living wage, which offers sufficient care to enable people to be fairly compensated and afford to live in a humane way, can be seen as an investment by organisations in people rather than a cost;
- Much care work and caring are performed by unpaid carers or family members; therefore, more flexible social security or welfare models that enable unpaid carers to take up employment, if they wish and are able to do so, without being financially penalised, can support carers and those cared for;

- Reform and regulation of markets is essential if the ethics of care is to influence globalised financial systems.
- There is a role for accountability when conceptualising accounting as care. Within organisations, accounting metrics, and the profession more broadly, can aid holding businesses and organisations to account for the care they offer to their employees, stakeholders and communities, and for their impact on the wider environment and planetary ecology.

Conclusion

This chapter has explored the relevance of ecofeminism and the ethics of care concept to accounting. It has addressed the early origins of both concepts together with their more contemporary political feminist orientations which sees ecofeminism critiquing capitalism and climate change and the ethics of care exposing a lack of caring under neoliberalism. Despite the prevalence of SEA and forms of sustainability reporting in the accounting discipline, ecofeminism has been little utilised in any contemporary critique of accounting. Yet, the chapter argued that integrating ecofeminism and ethics of care in accounting holds promise for a feminist approach to accounting. It argued for going beyond accounting *for* care to an approach that reconceptualises accounting *as* care in an attempt to reframe accounting technologies with an underpinning ecofeminist care ethic. The chapter culminates with some pragmatic suggestions for practising accounting as care.

Notes

1 https://climate.copernicus.eu/global-climate-highlights-2023
2 https://csear.co.uk/
3 https://finance.ec.europa.eu/capital-markets-union-and-financial-markets/company-reporting-and-auditing/company-reporting/corporate-sustainability-reporting_en
4 The epoch of human-induced effects on the planet and climate.
5 The WHO declared a public health emergency of international concern on 30th January 2020 which was rescinded on 5th May 2023, although the Covid-19 virus remained a global health threat. Wise, J. (2023). Covid-19: WHO declares end of global health emergency. *British Medical Journal*, *381*, 1041. https://doi.org/10.1136/bmj.p1041
6 For details of the PPE scandal in the UK, see the Public Accounts Committee report of June 2022 https://committees.parliament.uk/committee/127/public-accounts-committee/news/171306/4-billion-of-unusable-ppe-bought-in-first-year-of-pandemic-will-be-burnt-to-generate-power/ and https://www.theguardian.com/uk-news/2022/dec/09/revealed-the-full-inside-story-of-the-michelle-mone-ppe-scandal
7 International Financial Reporting Framework (IFRS) conceptual framework project summary, revised March 2018, available at https://www.ifrs.org/content/dam/ifrs/project/conceptual-framework/fact-sheet-project-summary-and-feedback-statement/conceptual-framework-project-summary.pdf

References

Adams, C. A. (2004). The ethical, social and environmental reporting-performance portrayal gap. *Accounting, Auditing & Accountability Journal*, *17*(5), 731–757. https://doi.org/10.1108/09513570410567791

Angotti, M., Ferreira, A. C. d. S., Eugénio, T., & Branco, M. C. (2024). A narrative approach for reporting social and environmental accounting impacts in the mining sector – Giving marginalized communities a voice. *Meditari Accountancy Research*, *32*(1), 42–63. https://doi.org/10.1108/MEDAR-11-2021-1513

Annisette, M., & Prasad, A. (2017). Critical accounting research in hyper-racial times. *Critical Perspectives on Accounting*, *43*, 5–19. https://doi.org/10.1016/j.cpa.2016.06.002

Arjaliès, D.-L., & Gibassier, D. (2023). Can financialization save nature? The case of endangered species. *Contemporary Accounting Research*, *40*(1), 488–525. https://doi.org/10.1111/1911-3846.12810

Barnes, M. (2015). Beyond the Dyad: Exploring the Multidimensionality of Care. In M. Barnes, T. Brannelly, L. Ward, & N. Ward (Eds.), *Ethics of Care. Critical Advances in International Perspective* (pp. 31–43). Bristol: Policy Press.

Bebbington, J., & Larrinaga, C. (2014). Accounting and sustainable development: An exploration. *Accounting, Organizations and Society*, *39*(6), 395–413. https://doi.org/10.1016/j.aos.2014.01.003

Bebbington, J., & Larrinaga, C. (2024). The influence of Power's audit society in environmental and sustainability accounting. *Qualitative Research in Accounting & Management*, *21*(1), 21–28. https://doi.org/10.1108/QRAM-01-2022-0007

Bebbington, J., Larrinaga, C., & Moneva, J. M. (2008). Corporate social reporting and reputation risk management. *Accounting, Auditing & Accountability Journal*, *21*(3), 337–361. https://doi.org/10.1108/09513570810863932

Bebbington, J., Österblom, H., Crona, B., Jouffray, J.-B., Larrinaga, C., Russell, S., & Scholtens, B. (2020). Accounting and accountability in the Anthropocene. *Accounting, Auditing & Accountability Journal*, *33*(1), 152–177. https://doi.org/10.1108/AAAJ-11-2018-3745

Bebbington, J., & Unerman, J. (2020). Advancing research into accounting and the UN Sustainable Development Goals. *Accounting, Auditing & Accountability Journal*, *33*(7), 1657–1670. https://doi.org/10.1108/AAAJ-05-2020-4556

Blowfield, M., & Murray, A. (2019). *Corporate Social Responsibility* (4th ed.). Abingdon: Oxford University Press.

Boulton, A., & Brannelly, T. (2015). Care Ethics and Indigenous Values: Political, Tribal and Personal. In M. Barnes, T. Brannelly, L. Ward, & N. Ward (Eds.), *Ethics of Care. Critical Advances in International Perspective* (pp. 69–82). Bristol: Policy Press.

Braidotti, R. (2016). Posthuman Feminist Theory. In L. Disch & M. Hawkesworth (Eds.), *The Oxford Handbook of Feminist Theory* (pp. 673–698). Oxford University Press. https://doi.org/10.1093/oxfordhb/9780199328581.013.35

Braidotti, R., Charkiewicz, E., Hausler, S., & Wieringa, S. (1994). *Women, the Environment and Sustainable Development: Towards a Theoretical Synthesis*. London: Zed Books.

Broadbent, J. (2020). The response to Covid-19 in England: Political accountability and loss of trust. *Journal of Accounting & Organizational Change*, *16*(4), 527–532. https://doi.org/10.1108/JAOC-07-2020-0093

Brown, J., & Dillard, J. (2013). Agonizing over engagement: SEA and the "death of environmentalism" debates. *Critical Perspectives on Accounting*, *24*(1), 1–18. https://doi.org/10.1016/j.cpa.2012.09.001

Brown, J., Dillard, J., & Hopper, T. (2015). Accounting, accountants and accountability regimes in pluralistic societies: Taking multiple perspectives seriously. *Accounting, Auditing & Accountability Journal*, *28*(5), 626–650. https://doi.org/10.1108/AAAJ-03-2015-1996

Buhr, N., & Reiter, S. (2000). Environmental disclosure and accountability: An ecofeminist perspective. Proceedings of the Sixth Interdisciplinary Perspectives on Accounting Conference. Manchester: University of Manchester,

Cameron, R. A., & O'Leary, C. (2015). Improving ethical attitudes or simply teaching ethical codes? The reality of accounting ethics education. *Accounting Education*, *24*(4), 275–290. https://doi.org/10.1080/09639284.2015.1036893

Carson, R. (2022). *The Silent Spring*. London: Penguin.

Chwastiak, M., & Lehman, G. (2008). Accounting for war. *Accounting Forum*, *32*(4), 313–326. https://doi.org/10.1016/j.accfor.2008.09.001

Cooper, C. (1992). The non and nom of accounting for (M)other nature. *Accounting, Auditing & Accountability Journal*, *5*(3), 16–39. https://doi.org/10.1108/09513579210017361

Cooper, C., & Senkl, D. (2016). An (other) truth: A feminist perspective on KPMG's true value. *Sustainability Accounting, Management and Policy Journal*, *7*(4), 494–516. https://doi.org/10.1108/SAMPJ-08-2016-0049

Coulson, A. B., Adams, C. A., Nugent, M. N., & Haynes, K. (2015). Exploring metaphors of capitals and the framing of multiple capitals: Challenges and opportunities for < IR >. *Sustainability Accounting, Management and Policy Journal*, *6*(3), 290–314. https://doi.org/10.1108/SAMPJ-05-2015-0032

Cuckston, T. (2018a). Making accounting for biodiversity research a force for conservation. *Social and Environmental Accountability Journal*, *38*(3), 218–226. https://doi.org/10.1080/0969160X.2018.1516559

Cuckston, T. (2018b). Making extinction calculable. *Accounting, Auditing & Accountability Journal*, *31*(3), 849–874. https://doi.org/10.1108/AAAJ-10-2015-2264

Cuckston, T. (2019). Seeking an ecologically defensible calculation of net loss/gain of biodiversity. *Accounting, Auditing & Accountability Journal*, *32*(5), 1358–1383. https://doi.org/10.1108/AAAJ-01-2018-3339

Deegan, C. (2017). Twenty five years of social and environmental accounting research within Critical Perspectives of Accounting: Hits, misses and ways forward. *Critical Perspectives on Accounting*, *43*, 65–87. https://doi.org/10.1016/j.cpa.2016.06.005

Dellaportas, S. (2019). The role of accounting in mediating empathic care for the "other". *Accounting, Auditing & Accountability Journal*, *32*(6), 1617–1635. https://doi.org/10.1108/AAAJ-02-2017-2860

Dhandhania, A., & O'Higgins, E. (2022). Can "sin industries" prove their legitimacy through CSR reporting? A study of UK tobacco and gambling companies. *Accounting, Auditing & Accountability Journal*, *35*(4), 1009–1034. https://doi.org/10.1108/AAAJ-11-2019-4239

Dillard, J. (2008). An Ethic of Accountability. In C. Jeffrey (Ed.), *Research on Professional Responsibility and Ethics in Accounting* (Vol. 13, pp. 1–18). Leeds: Emerald.

Donovan, J. (2001). *Feminist Theory: The Intellectual Traditions* (3rd ed.). New York: Continuum.

Federici, S. (2009). The Devaluation of Women's Labour. In A. Salleh (Ed.), *Eco-Sufficiency and Global Justice* (pp. 43–65). London: Pluto Press.

Ferreira, C. (2017). The contested instruments of a new governance regime: Accounting for nature and building markets for biodiversity offsets. *Accounting, Auditing & Accountability Journal*, *30*(7), 1568–1590. https://doi.org/10.1108/AAAJ-12-2015-2336

Fisher, B., & Tronto, J. C. (1991). Towards a Feminist Theory of Care. In E. Abel & M. Nelson (Eds.), *Circles of Care: Work and Identity in Women's Lives* (p. 40). Albany: State University of New York Press.

Fotaki, M., & Pullen, A. (2024). Feminist theories and activist practices in organization studies. *Organization Studies*, *45*(4), 593–616. https://doi.org/10.1177/01708406231209861

Gaard, G. (2011). Ecofeminism revisited: Rejecting essentialism and re-placing species in a material feminist environmentalism. *Feminist Formations*, *23*(2), 26–53. https://doi.org/10.1353/ff.2011.0017

Gaard, G. (2015). Ecofeminism and climate change. *Women's Studies International Forum*, *49*, 20–33. https://doi.org/10.1016/j.wsif.2015.02.004

Gallhofer, S. (2018). Going beyond Western dualism: Towards corporate nature responsibility reporting. *Accounting, Auditing & Accountability Journal*, *31*(8), 2110–2134. https://doi.org/10.1108/AAAJ-12-2015-2358

Gallhofer, S., Haslam, J., & van der Walt, S. (2011). Accountability and transparency in relation to human rights: A critical perspective reflecting upon accounting, corporate responsibility and ways forward in the context of globalisation. *Critical Perspectives on Accounting*, *22*(8), 765–780. https://doi.org/10.1016/j.cpa.2011.07.002

Gilligan, C. (1977). In a different voice: Women's conceptions of self and of morality. *Harvard Educational Review*, *47*(4), 481–517.

Gilligan, C. (1982). *In a Different Voice: Psychological Theory and Women's Development*. Harvard: Harvard University Press.

Górska, A. M., Kulicka, K., Staniszewska, Z., & Dobija, D. (2021). Deepening inequalities: What did COVID-19 reveal about the gendered nature of academic work? *Gender, Work & Organization*, *28*(4), 1546–1561. https://doi.org/10.1111/gwao.12696

Gray, R., Brennan, A., & Malpas, J. (2014). New accounts: Towards a reframing of social accounting. *Accounting Forum*, *38*(4), 258–273. https://doi.org/10.1016/j.accfor.2013.10.005

Gray, R., Owen, D., & Adams, C. A. (1996). *Accounting & Accountability. Changes and Challenges in Corporate Social and Environmental Reporting*. Hemel Hempstead: Prentice Hall.

Grosser, K., & Moon, J. (2019). CSR and feminist organization studies: Towards an integrated theorization for the analysis of gender issues. *Journal of Business Ethics*, *155*(2), 321–342. https://doi.org/10.1007/s10551-017-3510-x

Hankivsky, O. (2014). Rethinking care ethics: On the promise and potential of an intersectional analysis. *American Political Science Review*, *108*(2), 252–264. https://doi.org/10.1017/S0003055414000094

Haynes, K. (2017). Accounting as gendering and gendered: A review of 25 years of critical accounting research on gender. *Critical Perspectives on Accounting*, *43*, 110–124. https://doi.org/10.1016/j.cpa.2016.06.004

Haynes, K. (2020). Structural inequalities exposed by COVID-19 in the UK: The need for an accounting for care. *Journal of Accounting & Organizational Change*, *16*(4), 637–642. https://doi.org/10.1108/JAOC-08-2020-0099

Haynes, K., & Murray, A. (2015). Sustainability as a Lens to Explore Gender Equality: A Missed Opportunity for Responsible Management. In P. M. Flynn, K. Haynes, & M. A. Kilgour (Eds.), *Integrating Gender Equality into Management Education* (pp. 55–80). Sheffield: Greenleaf.

Held, V. (2006). *The Ethics of Care: Personal, Political, Global*. New York: Oxford University Press. https://doi.org/https://doi.org/10.1093/0195180992.001.0001

IPCC. (2007). *Fourth Assessment Report*. Geneva: WMO/Intergovernmental Panel on Climate Change.

IPCC. (2013). *Fifth Assessment Report*. Geneva: WMO/Intergovernmental Panel on Climate Change.

IPCC. (2023). *Climate Change 2023 – Synthesis Report*. Geneva: Intergovernmental Panel on Climate Change.

Irving, S., & Helin, J. (2018). A world for sale? An ecofeminist reading of sustainable development discourse. *Gender, Work & Organization*, *25*(3), 264–278. https://doi.org/10.1111/gwao.12196

Jayasinghe, K., & Thomas, D. (2009). The preservation of Indigenous accounting systems in a subaltern community. *Accounting, Auditing & Accountability Journal*, *22*(3), 351–378. https://doi.org/10.1108/09513570910945651

Jones, M. (2014). *Accounting for Biodiversity*. Abingdon: Taylor & Francis.

Jones, M. J. (2010). Accounting for the environment: Towards a theoretical perspective for environmental accounting and reporting. *Accounting Forum*, *34*(2), 123–138. https://doi.org/10.1016/j.accfor.2010.03.001

Jordan, A. (2020). Masculinizing care? Gender, ethics of care, and fathers' rights groups. *Men and Masculinities*, *23*(1), 20–41. https://doi.org/10.1177/1097184X18776364

Kaczan, D. J., & Orgill-Meyer, J. (2020). The impact of climate change on migration: A synthesis of recent empirical insights. *Climatic Change*, *158*(3), 281–300. https://doi.org/10.1007/s10584-019-02560-0

Kaur, A., & Lodhia, S. K. (2017). The Extent of Stakeholder Engagement in Sustainability Accounting and Reporting: Does Empowerment of Stakeholders Really Exist? In *Modern Organisational Governance* (Vol. 12, pp. 129–145). Leeds: Emerald Publishing Limited. https://doi.org/10.1108/S2043-052320170000012007

King, Y. (2018). Healing the Wounds: Feminism, Ecology, and Nature/Culture Dualism. In N. Tuana & R. Putnam Tong (Eds.), *Feminism and Philosophy* (pp. 353–373). Abingdon: Routledge.

Laurent, É. (2017). *Measuring Tomorrow: Accounting for Well-Being, Resilience, and Sustainability in the Twenty-First Century*. Princeton: Princeton University Press.

Lehman, C., Annisette, M., & Agyemang, G. (2016). Immigration and neoliberalism: Three cases and counter accounts. *Accounting, Auditing & Accountability Journal*, *29*(1), 43–79. https://doi.org/10.1108/AAAJ-09-2013-1470

Lehman, C. R. (2019). Reflecting on now more than ever: Feminism in accounting. *Critical Perspectives on Accounting*, *65*, 102080. https://doi.org/10.1016/j.cpa.2019.04.001

Lennard, J. B., & Roberts, R. W. (2023). Chapter 3: The Accounting Profession, Corporate Social Responsibility, and Ethics. In M. Brivot & C. Cho (Eds.), *Research*

Handbook on Accounting and Ethics (pp. 35–49). Cheltenham: Edward Elgar Publishing. https://doi.org/10.4337/9781800881020.00011

Mallory, C. (2018). What's in a name? In defense of *Ecofeminism* (not ecological feminisms, feminist ecology, or gender and the environment): Or "why ecofeminism need not be ecofeminine – But so what if it is?". *Ethics and the Environment*, *23*(2), 11–35. https://doi.org/10.2979/ethicsenviro.23.2.03

McKinsey & Co. (2020). *COVID-19 and Gender Equality: Countering the Regressive Effects*. https://www.mckinsey.com/featured-insights/future-of-work/covid-19-and-gender-equality-countering-the-regressive-effects/

McPhail, K., & Ferguson, J. (2016). The past, the present and the future of accounting for human rights. *Accounting, Auditing & Accountability Journal*, *29*(4), 526–541. https://doi.org/10.1108/AAAJ-03-2016-2441

Mellor, M. (1997). *Feminism and Ecology*. Cambridge: Polity Press.

Mies, M., & Shiva, V. (2014 [1993]). *Ecofeminism*. London and New York: Zed Books.

Morales, J., Gendron, Y., & Guénin-Paracini, H. (2014). State privatization and the unrelenting expansion of neoliberalism: The case of the Greek financial crisis. *Critical Perspectives on Accounting*, *25*(6), 423–445. https://doi.org/10.1016/j.cpa.2013.08.007

Murray, A., Sinclair, D., Power, D., & Gray, R. H. (2006). Do financial markets care about social and environmental disclosure? Further evidence and exploration from the UK. *Accounting, Auditing & Accountability Journal*, *19*(2), 228–255. https://doi.org/10.1108/09513570610656105

Murray, A., Skene, K., & Haynes, K. (2017). The circular economy: An interdisciplinary exploration of the concept and application in a global context. *Journal of Business Ethics*, *140*(3), 369–380. https://doi.org/10.1007/s10551-015-2693-2

Noddings, N. (1984). *Caring: A Feminine Approach to Ethics and Moral Education*. Oakland, CA: University of California Press.

Office for National Statistics. (2020a). *Coronavirus and Homeschooling in Great Britain: April to* ***June 2020***. London. https://www.ons.gov.uk/peoplepopulationandcommunity/educationandchildcare/articles/coronavirusandhomeschoolingingreatbritain/apriltojune2020#parents-who-were-homeschooling-in-april

Office for National Statistics. (2020b). *Parenting in Lockdown: Coronavirus and the Effects on Work-Life Balance*. London. https://www.ons.gov.uk/peoplepopulationandcommunity/healthandsocialcare/conditionsanddiseases/articles/parentinginlockdowncoronavirusandtheeffectsonworklifebalance/2020-07-22

Oksala, J. (2018). Feminism, capitalism, and ecology. *Hypatia*, *33*(2), 216–234. https://doi.org/10.1111/hypa.12395

Parlak, S., Cakiroglu, O. C., & Gul, F. O. (2021). Gender roles during COVID-19 pandemic: The experiences of Turkish female academics. *Gender, Work & Organization*, *28*(S2), 461–483. https://doi.org/10.1111/gwao.12655

Pearse, R. (2017). Gender and climate change. *Wiley Interdisciplinary Reviews: Climate Change*, *8*(2), e451.

Piquero, A. R., Jennings, W. G., Jemison, E., Kaukinen, C., & Knaul, F. M. (2021). Domestic violence during the COVID-19 pandemic – Evidence from a systematic review and meta-analysis. *Journal of Criminal Justice*, *74*, 101806. https://doi.org/10.1016/j.jcrimjus.2021.101806

PWC. (2021). *COVID-19 Is Reversing the Important Gains Made over the Last Decade for Women in the Workforce – PwC Women in Work Index*. https://www.pwc.com/gx/en/news-room/press-releases/2021/women-in-work-index-2021.html

Reiter, S. (1997). The ethics of care and new paradigms for accounting practice. *Accounting, Auditing & Accountability Journal*, *10*(3), 299–324. https://doi.org/10.1108/09513579710178098

Reiter, S. A. (1996). The Kohlberg–Gilligan controversy: Lessons for accounting ethics education. *Critical Perspectives on Accounting*, *7*(1), 33–51.

Robinson, F. (1997). Globalizing care: Ethics, feminist theory, and international relations. *Alternatives*, *22*(1), 113–133.

Robinson, F. (2011). *The Ethics of Care: A Feminist Approach to Human Security*. Philadelphia: Temple University Press.

Robinson, F. (2019). Resisting hierarchies through relationality in the ethics of care. *International Journal of Care and Caring*, *4*(1), 11–23. https://doi.org/10.1332/239788219X15659215344772

Russell, S., Milne, M. J., & Dey, C. (2017). Accounts of nature and the nature of accounts. *Accounting, Auditing & Accountability Journal*, *30*(7), 1426–1458. https://doi.org/10.1108/AAAJ-07-2017-3010

Salleh, A. (2009). Ecological Debt: Embodied Debt. In A. Salleh (Ed.), *Eco-Sufficiency and Global Justice* (pp. 1–40). London: Pluto Press.

Salleh, A. (2017). *Ecofeminism as Politics: Nature, Marx and the Postmodern*. London: Zed Books Ltd.

Seifert, S. G., LaMothe, E. G., & Schmitt, D. B. (2023). Perceptions of the ethical infrastructure, professional autonomy, and ethical judgments in accounting work environments. *Journal of Business Ethics*, *182*(3), 821–850. https://doi.org/10.1007/s10551-021-05001-0

Senkl, D., & Cooper, C. (2023). On valuing (m)other nature in times of climate crises – A reflection on the non and nom of accounting for (m)other nature. *Critical Perspectives on Accounting*, *91*, 102430. https://doi.org/10.1016/j.cpa.2022.102430

Shearer, T. (2002). Ethics and accountability: From the for-itself to the for-the-other. *Accounting, Organizations and Society*, *27*(6), 541–573. https://doi.org/10.1016/S0361-3682(01)00036-8

Shiva, V. (1988). *Staying Alive: Women, Ecology and Development*. London: Zed Books.

Spence, C. (2009). Social and environmental reporting and the corporate ego. *Business Strategy and the Environment*, *18*(4), 254–265. https://doi.org/10.1002/bse.600

Spence, L. J., & Taylor, S. (2024). Feminist corporate social responsibility: Reframing CSR as a critical force for good. *British Journal of Management*, *35*(3), 1198–1208. https://doi.org/10.1111/1467-8551.12798

Sullivan, S. (2018). Making nature investable: From legibility to leverageability in fabricating 'Nature' as 'Natural-Capital'. *Science & Technology Studies*, *31*(3), 47–76. https://doi.org/10.23987/sts.58040

Sundarasen, S., Zyznarska-Dworczak, B., & Goel, S. (2024). Sustainability reporting and greenwashing: A bibliometrics assessment in G7 and non-G7 nations. *Cogent Business & Management*, *11*(1), 2320812. https://doi.org/10.1080/23311975.2024.2320812

Thompson, C. (2006). Back to nature? Resurrecting ecofeminism after poststructuralist and third-wave Feminisms. *Isis*, *97*(3), 505–512. https://doi.org/10.1086/508080
Thomson, I. (2014). Responsible social accounting communities, symbolic activism and the reframing of social accounting. A commentary on new accounts: Towards a reframing of social accounting. *Accounting Forum*, *38*(4), 274–277. https://doi.org/10.1016/j.accfor.2014.05.002
Tinker, T., Neimark, M., & Lehman, C. (1991). Falling down the hole in the middle of the road: Political quietism in corporate social reporting. *Accounting, Auditing & Accountability Journal*, *4*(2), 28–54. https://doi.org/10.1108/09513579110000504
Tronto, J. C. (1993). *Moral Boundaries A Political Argument for an Ethic of Care*. London: Routledge.
United Nations Economic Commission for Africa. (2009). *Gender and Climate Change – Women Matter*. https://repository.uneca.org/handle/10855/15345
Utoft, E. H. (2020). 'All the single ladies' as the ideal academic during times of COVID-19? *Gender, Work & Organization*, *27*(5), 778–787. https://doi.org/10.1111/gwao.12478
Vollmer, H. (2021). Public value and the planet: Accounting in ecological reconstitution. *Accounting, Auditing & Accountability Journal*, *34*(7), 1527–1554. https://doi.org/10.1108/AAAJ-11-2019-4283
WCED. (1987). *Our Common Future*. Oxford: Oxford University Press.
Wise, J. (2023). Covid-19: WHO declares end of global health emergency. *British Medical Journal*, *381*, p1041. https://doi.org/10.1136/bmj.p1041
Yardley, E. (2021). Technology-facilitated domestic abuse in political economy: A new theoretical framework. *Violence against Women*, *27*(10), 1479–1498. https://doi.org/10.1177/1077801220947172
Zoloth, L. (2017). At the last well on Earth: Climate change is a feminist issue. *Journal of Feminist Studies in Religion*, *33*(2), 139–151. https://doi.org/10.2979/jfemistudreli.33.2.14

8

INTEGRATING FEMINIST THEORIES, METHODOLOGIES AND ACTIVISM

The emancipatory potential of feminist accounting

Introduction

This final chapter synthesises the potential of the multiple feminisms considered in this book into a multifaceted emancipatory project interconnected with the power and role of accounting in society, as a profession and as a technology. The overarching aim of the book was to examine the relationship between contemporary feminisms and accounting and thereby consider the emancipatory potential of feminist accounting. This chapter brings these arguments together.

I first discuss the continuing real and present need for, and relevance of, feminism in contemporary societies and academia, together with some further reflections on my positioning as a feminist accounting academic (Haynes, 2023), which may resonate with others. I summarise the comprehensive overview of contemporary feminist theories applied to accounting which this text has addressed, including the issues addressed by multiple feminisms, their theoretical position, application to accounting and their emancipatory potential. The intention is to advance feminist theorisations of accounting and give new insights into their relevance.

However, I then address two further interrelated areas of feminist theory and practice: feminist methodology and feminist activism. Feminist methodologies work in conjunction with feminist theories to produce knowledge in, and of, the numerous challenges and oppressions that feminism seeks to address. Producing feminist knowledge requires strong links between epistemology, methodology and ontological positioning to produce knowledge that counters the 'malestream'. Hence, I discuss how feminist methodologies represent different ways of knowing and writing that include reflexivity and

DOI: 10.4324/9781032636603-8

ethics of care. Activism in its various forms is a central tenet of feminism. The chapter addresses the power of activism and resistance within accounting, including utilising accounting technologies, within social movements and accounting academia.

Finally, I argue that feminist accounting, through blending theory, key concepts of feminist methodology and activist practice in an integrative approach synthesises the emancipatory potential of feminism within the accounting context. It produces rich, critical understandings of the operationalisation of accounting technologies and the accounting profession in gendered power relations and domination. It enables us to understand how inequalities are created, perpetuated and potentially overcome in and through accounting (Haynes, 2025). However, as I illustrated in the earlier chapters of this text, applying feminism to accounting can generate new principles and conceptualisations that address some of the grand challenges and injustices of our time, thus offering hope for a better future and a more just world.

The continuing relevance of feminism

Feminism is concerned with addressing inequities, structural inequalities, oppressions, sexism and violence against women. The emphasis placed on these issues by feminists and others will depend on numerous issues: their geopolitical contextualisation; social, political and economic orientation and status; individual and collective characteristics and experiences of gender, race, class or sexuality; or understandings and experience of sexism, violence and discrimination. This helps to explain why there are so many theoretical approaches to feminist issues, which take different perspectives on these challenges.

However, I want to explain three points in clarifying my approach to feminism. The first is that I take an inclusive approach to feminism, but I do not assume that women are all the same, as their experiences and the challenges they face may be radically different. Where I have stated feminism is concerned with women, I include trans women in that statement, who are also women. Indeed, feminists have many solidarities with other people who are gender-fluid or non-binary genders, in terms of their experience of marginalisation, violence or oppression. I will address men and feminism in more detail later in this chapter. Second, in highlighting some of the issues that feminism challenges, I do not suggest that one has to experience issues such as violence and discrimination, gendered forms of poverty or domination in order to fight against it. In addition, feminists may not all share the same characteristics of race, class, sexuality or religion as other women, but can potentially offer support. Feminism can be born of personal experience, but it can also involve taking a stand in solidarity and allyship for others. This may involve some uncomfortable personal reflections on our own privilege, for instance, in my case as a White, middle-class Westerner, in relation to others who are raced and classed differently or live in different geopolitical locations. However, part of the process of allyship can include decolonising the self and involve enhanced reflexivity that brings new insights and actions (see Haynes, 2023, 2025). Third, I do not presume that there is one 'best' theoretical approach to feminism. Choice of feminist theory to elucidate feminist issues will depend on the contextual issues noted above, as well as the positioning of the researcher.

I discussed the numerous issues that feminism seeks to challenge and overcome in depth in Chapter 1 and throughout each chapter of this text. By way of recap, these might include basic human rights and the aims reflected in the sustainable development goals (SDGs), such as education, health and reproductive care, political representation and decision-making, safe and meaningful work, and access to clean environments and action on climate change. These are issues affecting men and women globally but have particular resonance to women's lives, where women's rights and needs may be overlooked (UN Women, 2015). Systemic challenges also include sexism, discrimination, stereotyping, endemic gender-based violence, sexual violence and misogyny, which is sometimes so extreme it becomes a terrorist act. Further challenges pertain to inequalities inherent in women's roles, parenting and employment. The feminist mantra that the 'personal is political' was coined by the radical feminist movement of the 1960–1970s in the USA to draw attention to women's lives in the private, home environment, arguing that the home and the family is a political space as much as is the public space (Nicholson, 1981). Although, as seen in Chapter 4, this movement was rightly critiqued as being too White and middle-class-focused, the sentiment that women's personal experiences of ordinary life, such as at home, in relationships, when caring or parenting, occur in a social, cultural and political space continues to be highly pertinent to feminist agendas. However, 'personal' issues interact with 'public' in legislative, civic, institutional, organisational and professional spaces, which are equally politicised. Hence, I suggest it is a false dichotomy to try to separate private and public challenges for women, as they interact across different contexts. The identity of a woman is subjected to gendered social, cultural and economic norms and perceptions in whatever context she is situated. These are the issues that feminism, of whatever orientation, seeks to fight against and overturn. This is the role of feminism as an emancipatory practice, which seeks to challenge these norms, overturn oppressions and challenge systemic inequalities.

There is a discourse, particularly in Western countries, that feminism has lost its relevance, as women increasingly enter higher education and the workplace, play a role in leadership positions and in public life. In the so-called postfeminist era of contemporary modernity, women are perceived as successful, exercising choice and deploying their sexualities to suit themselves (Butler, 2013). The concept of postfeminism reflects a number of discursive tropes: that gender inequality is a thing of the past; that it relates to other countries or contexts; that women now have numerous advantages and that organisational cultures as accepted as how things are (Gill, Kelan, & Scharff, 2017). As McRobbie (2009, p. 1) argues:

> The 'post' of postfeminism does not signify feminism's death. Rather, postfeminism becomes a kind of substitute for, or displacement of, feminism as a radical political movement in which earlier feminist demands for equal rights, collective activism, and the eradication of gender inequality are taken into account and then displaced by the postfeminist ideals of individualism, choice, and empowerment.

Postfeminism emerges from neoliberalism as an individualist agenda, putting the onus on individual women to shape their own destiny with resilience and confidence (Gill, 2017), while conforming to norms of femininity, including stable, heterosexual relationships and career progression (Adamson, 2017). In this way neoliberal capitalism has co-opted feminism, as a means of commodifying elements of women's lives through a focus on products and services related to individual well-being, and as a means of avoiding wider structural, cultural and organisational change. Accounting's role as a technology underpins these effects and the role of the accounting profession perpetuates this postfeminist rhetoric, which is why the reform of organisational norms, cultures and structures supported by liberal feminist agendas has been largely ineffective in making more widespread change, as was discussed in Chapter 3.

Feminism and accounting

Given the issues above, I argue for the continuing relevance of feminism on a global scale which interacts with the challenges posed by accounting, both as a technology and as a profession. I have offered a comprehensive overview of contemporary feminist theories applied to accounting, together with a discussion of how they have been applied in feminist research in accounting, and, importantly, where there is potential to apply feminist theorisation further. Feminist theories, I argue, have emancipatory potential in and *for* accounting by enabling a richer understanding of accounting's role in gendered and other inequalities. Feminist theories challenge the perceptions, domination and oppression inherent in those inequalities and invoke a means of addressing them, thus having emancipatory potential.

A summary of these feminist theories, their applications to accounting and their emancipatory potential is shown in Table 8.1.

In summary, I began with a historical overview of the development of the accounting profession and its interaction with early feminism in Chapter 2 because it helps to explain the underlying masculine norms embedded in the profession from its very inception, as well as how they continue to influence contemporary practice. Indeed, as was argued, accounting technologies and calculative practices themselves are based on socially constructed dualisms. Liberal feminism (see Chapter 3), with its neoliberal reformist agenda, has been the dominant mode of reform within the accounting profession, as reflected in research on segregation and stratification, socialisation and work-life balance issues. Yet, despite the failure of liberal feminism to generate more radical reform, there is still emancipatory potential in understanding and addressing further the lack of gender neutrality in the profession, embedded privileges and outmoded archetypes and ways of working. Chapter 4 addressed many of the omissions of liberal feminism in addressing difference, in class, race and intersectionality, discussed through the lens of more radical, Marxist and Black feminisms. The distinct emancipatory potential for these feminisms is to challenge accounting's calculative role in perpetuating power relations and difference, challenging the accounting profession on its record on race and class, and more broadly addressing the role of accounting in racial justice.

Postcolonial, decolonial, transnational, Islamic and Muslim feminisms (Chapter 5) allow us to embrace wider global feminist insights in the interest of social justice, particularly the role of accounting technologies in colonising practices. These feminisms offer great emancipatory potential for understanding and addressing the decolonisation of accounting research, rationality and systems and the accounting profession globally. In their critique of neoliberalist capitalism, these feminisms offer multiple opportunities to address commodification and exploitation, while accounting as a research field can also benefit from the feminist principles outlined in the chapter that support its scholarly decolonisation. Applying concepts from poststructuralist feminism (see Chapter 6) in relation to accounting highlights the significance of dominant discourses on gender, performativity, identity and cis-heteronormativity. Further research offers the potential for dual analysis of discursive, cultural representation *and* lived experience that has particular resonance for understanding gendered performativity, embodiment and affect. An agenda for queering accounting, whether considering identity, gender and sexuality in the profession, or as a means of disrupting and subverting, is emerging as an area of focus that has resonance with this area of feminist theory. Finally, ecofeminist theory addresses exploitation and violence against nature and women. By linking concepts of ecofeminism with concepts from the ethics of care theory, highlighting the political and relational dimension of ethics

TABLE 8.1 Summary of feminist theories, their applications to accounting and emancipatory potential

Chapter	*Theoretical positions*	*Key focus/key attributes*	*Applications to accounting*	*Emancipatory potential by understanding, challenging and addressing:*
2	Early feminisms	• Women's suffrage/entry to professions • Masculine norms and practice • Patriarchy	• Professionalisation • Social/professional closure • Gendered accounting logics	• Differences between Western and non-Western contexts • How history influences present norms or giving a *Herstory* • How accounting technologies and calculative practices are socially constructed and politically influential
3	Liberal feminism	• Equality legislation/equal opportunities • Moderate • Reformative • Neoliberal • Tendency to individualised responsibility for action • Limited influence on cultural norms	• Overcoming barriers to entry • Normative socialisation • Segregation of types of work • Stratification in career hierarchies • Parenting and work-life balance issues	• The lack of gender neutrality in institutions and professions • The embedded privilege within the masculine binary and the White middle class • Highlighting the outmoded ideal, archetypal accountant career model • Enabling fair/transparent choices in parenting and WLB issues
4	Radical, Marxist, Black feminisms. Feminist approaches using Bourdieu	• Class/race/intersectionality • Structures of privilege • Interaction with capitalism • Political struggle • Difference • Resistance	• Structural inequalities • Calculative practices/accounting technologies as gendered, raced and classed • Experiences of accountants	• Accounting's calculative role in power relations/ violence/ inequalities • Influence of class in professions and support for more social mobility • More focus on racial justice

5	Postcolonial, decolonial, transnational, Islamic and Muslim feminisms	• Colonisation/oppression of Indigenous Peoples • Domination of Indigenous knowledge/power • The 'gendered subaltern' • Inequities of modern globalised capitalism • Going beyond borders of nation states • Contextualised meanings of feminism under Islam and in non-Western contexts	• Role of calculative practices/ accounting technologies in colonialism/slavery • Postcolonial influences on profession • Decolonising accounting research, language and profession • Accounting and racialisation/ marginalisation	• Persistence of postcolonial European dominance of accounting rationality and systems • More postcolonial research on gender • Further decolonisation of accounting research, language and profession • Focus on global commodified misogyny; exploitative supply chains; neoliberalism; marginalisation
6	Poststructuralist feminism	• Gender as product of language systems and discourses • Subverting the 'binary logic of gender' • Gender is fluid, multiple, discursive and subjective • Performativity v. 'doing gender' • Queer theory	• Language of accounting represents dominant discourses • 'Doing gender' and gendering in profession • Influence of identity as multiple and fluid • Queering identity, gender and sexuality in profession Role of calculative practices and profession in constituting and experiencing the body	• Possibilities for analysis of discursive, cultural representation *and* lived experience • More focus on gendered performativity in profession • Queering (disrupting, subverting) accounting • Considering cis-heteronormativity of accounting • More focus on embodiment and affect
7	Ecofeminism Ethics of care (EoC)	• Links between exploitation of nature and oppression of women • Violence against nature and women • Gendered effects of climate change • EoC = relational ontology • Both theories subject to critique of essentialism	• The role of calculative practices/ accounting technologies in valuing nature • SEA tends to omit gender issues except in neoliberal reporting • EoC rarely addressed in accounting • Potential for more political dimension to EoC	• Potential of a feminist approach to SEA • More focus on environmental justice • Focus on critiquing role of accounting in driving neoliberal capitalism • Embedding relational ethics (regarding nature and people) into accounting • Move from accounting *for* care to accounting *as* care

of care, Chapter 7 argues for their emancipatory potential. I focus on the need and opportunity to focus on environmental justice, to critique the role of accounting in driving inequalities within neoliberal capitalism and to embed more relational ethics regarding nature and people into accounting. This chapter conceptualises accounting from an ecofeminist/ethics of care perspective that mobilises accounting *as* care.

Each of the chapters shows how feminist theories can invigorate a renewed, interrogative, critical approach to understanding the role of accounting technologies and the accounting profession in gendered power relations, domination and oppression. Yet they also address how these feminisms have the further potential to resist these challenges.

Further scope for feminist theories and accounting

My aim in this text was to provide an insight into numerous feminist theories and their application to accounting technologies and the accounting profession in the hope that both new and established scholars of accounting would find your own inspiration to apply feminist theories and feminist intent to your own work. For feminist scholars, expert in specific theories, I hope that you will find their application to the gendered nature and culture of accounting of interest, while I acknowledge that in many cases I have had to brief in addressing various feminisms. In a text such as this which ranges widely across different feminisms, it is also inevitable that there are some feminist positions that I have been unable to cover. I chose those where there is a strong resonance and potential for application to accounting, but other scholars may expand this range.

For instance, there are feminist theories and positions that may relate to specific racial or Indigenous groups that I have not been able to include. Chicana feminism emerged from within the Chicano movement in the 1960s by women of Mexican heritage fighting for rights and against machismo (Garcia, 1989), and there may still be a relevance to contemporary gender relations within accounting in Mexico. Within contemporary Big Four firms in Mexico, paternalistic masculinity characterises approaches to management, which prevents women accountants from complying with time demands and inhibits their career progression (Ruiz Castro, 2012). Insights into other Indigenous feminisms and Indigenous accounting would be a welcome addition to the field of feminist accounting.

Similarly, I have not been able to address psychoanalytical feminisms in any detail, although they are not widely applied in accounting. As exceptions, Shearer and Arrington (1993) apply Luce Irigaray's feminist deconstruction of Freudian and Lacanian notions of sexual difference, and her own notion of the feminine imaginary, to deconstruct some dominant notions of accounting's relationship with value, but few others have done the same. More recently, Baker and Brewis (2020) produced a potential psychoanalytical explanation for why women accountants struggle to attain and embody the identity of the 'perfect worker' in the profession, which is an idealised, masculine subject. Drawing on Freud's theory of melancholia, they argue that neoliberalism works in consort with the psyche to reinforce gender oppression at the level of the unconscious through self-blame and shame (Baker & Brewis, 2020). These examples illustrate the further potential for applying psychoanalytical feminist approaches to understanding accounting.

Finally, although I discuss various forms of activism, including mention of digital activism, later in this chapter, I have not gone into detail on the nature of digital feminism. This type of feminism makes use of digital platforms, social media and internet forums to connect, debate and protest using technology (Lange & Pérez-Moreno, 2020). Digital feminism, or what has been termed hashtag activism, reflecting its preponderance on X (formerly Twitter) is concerned with commentary and connection. It is often initiated by outrage and anger at specific events and a desire for experiences to be acknowledged (Mendes & Ringrose, 2019). For example, digital movements like #MeToo, protesting against sexual assault, represent online activism that becomes highly visible, though this is not without risks to those involved, who may find the very act of posting online raises vulnerabilities as well as offers solidarities, and puts them at risk of being trolled and abused (Clark-Parsons, 2021). The multiple hashtag movements which represent specific causes – #MeToo, #BlackLivesMatter, #SayHerName amongst others – represent important means of speaking out and solidarity, where 'global reach, speed, immediacy, dialogue, visibility, engagement, contact, connection, collectivity and shared understanding' are paramount for participants (Mendes, Ringrose, & Keller, 2018, p. 240).

However, digital feminism represents a form of activism rather than a feminist theory, although it can be theorised in numerous ways as a communicative practice, a response to power, forms of storytelling or processes of de/politicisation under neoliberalism amongst others (see, for example, Baer, 2016; Clark, 2016; Scharff, Smith-Prei, & Stehle, 2016). As an activism, although accountants may have engaged with digital feminism, it is not clear how it relates to accounting technologies and the accounting profession. If there were examples of digital feminisms or specific movements within accounting, they might represent forms of counter or shadow account; however, currently there is no research or evidence of this. Nonetheless, although I have omitted any detailed discussion of digital feminism in this text as it does not represent a feminist theory, there are potential opportunities for the future if it were possible to apply techniques of netnography (Jeacle, 2021) to feminist discussion on digital platforms. Research might address the interconnection of individualisation under neoliberalism with social connections and solidarities.

Feminist methodologies: ways of knowing and writing in accounting

Hand in hand with feminist theories are feminist methodologies or feminist approaches to methodology and method. Feminist theories are a means of understanding, interpreting and addressing various forms of inequality and oppression against women. Achieving feminist epistemology – feminist knowledge – requires a methodological approach to underpin the means of producing such contributions to knowledge. Feminist methodology goes beyond addressing gender as a binary variable, as in so many approaches to gender research, especially in the more positivist dimensions of accounting or business research, as discussed in Chapter 1. Such research is not feminist in its ontological orientation. As Hardies and Khalifa (2018) point out, addressing gender as a 'dummy variable' often obscures the nuances of gender and its social construction, positions women as 'other' to men and fails to address additional characteristics. In contrast, a feminist approach uses a feminist theoretical framework or methodological orientation, going beyond an interest in gender as an object of study, to contest gender divisions, challenge inequalities and overcome oppressions and sexisms (Haynes, 2008a). In other words, feminist methodology and theory have a political and emancipatory intent. Feminist methodology provides a means of challenging and rethinking the means of knowledge production (Bell et al., 2020).

While feminists may make use of various methods of research, in terms of how the research is designed and data collected, the underpinning philosophy of feminist methodology tends to contain various tenets which go beyond a specific method, which I now discuss in this section. In doing so, I build on an earlier article on the relevance of feminist research methodologies to accounting research (Haynes, 2008a), while integrating more recent discussion on feminist ways of knowing and writing. Drawing together perspectives on feminist methodology from earlier feminist researchers (Harding, 1987; Letherby, 2003; Ramazanoglu & Holland, 2002; Reinharz, 1992), I argued:

> The central facets of feminist research methodology would include challenging objectivity and valuing subjectivity; recognising the links between ontology and epistemology, and between research process and product; developing non exploitative relationships within the research; aiming to bring about change for women; valuing the personal and private as worthy of study; and using reflexivity as a source of insight.
>
> *(Haynes, 2008a, p. 545)*

These facets remain relevant in feminist approaches to research. For example, the value of enhancing knowledge on the subjectivity of women's experiences and their everyday lives, within and in relation to accounting, remains as necessary as ever in the face of the various challenges that this book has addressed. These include sexism, stereotyping or challenges in career progression, intersections of gender and race, geopolitical and social positioning, relations with the environment and roles in society, amongst others. Accounting, as I have argued in this book thus far, is implicated in all of these areas, as a profession or as a technology. Hence, treating people as the 'object' of research, without questioning the mode of production of knowledge about them, can obfuscate the politicised nature of knowledge with its problematic assumptions of objectivity. An objectivist approach to research, which is common in accounting, considers only the method rather than its underlying ontological and epistemological assumptions (Haynes, 2012, 2023), whereas as Letiche et al. (2023, p. 4) point out:

> There is no such thing as the 'real object of research'; the 'object' is always entwined in a machinery of representation, production and experimentation.

Moreover, in feminist research, the researcher themselves may be both object and subject of the research, part of the phenomenon under study and both insider and outsider in the process. For example, some of my early research on the interaction of accounting and motherhood drew from my personal experiences of being both an accountant and a mother and trying to understand the various difficulties and juxtapositions that this entailed both for myself and for others (Haynes, 2008b, 2008c). Despite the purpose of the research being to extend knowledge and understanding of women's lived experiences, including my own, in the interpretive process I noted the contradiction occurring in deepening private knowledge of the women accountants in the study while generating more instrumental public outcomes that serve career outcomes and publications as well as serve social justice for women (Haynes, 2010). Yet, with critical reflexivity and mitigation of power relations in research through an ethic of care, the two positions are not mutually exclusive. As Bell et al. (2020, p. 184) attest:

> Within the politics of knowledge production, feminist scholars often position themselves as reflexive actors within structures and practices of inequality and oppression, rather than as neutral observers.

Such a positioning allows for feminist researchers' political intent – addressing the oppression of women (albeit from numerous theoretical positions as illustrated in this book). It therefore links our ontological and epistemological positioning, as feminist values underpin the knowledge produced.

Reflexivity in feminist research

Reflexivity in research goes beyond simple reflection to question critically the effects of the researcher's prior knowledge, assumptions, positioning and own role in the design, conduct, interpretation and writing of the research (Cunliffe, 2016; Haynes, 2017c, 2023; Hibbert, Coupland, & MacIntosh, 2010). Feminist researchers tend towards more explicit openness on our positioning within the processes of knowledge production, such as feminist-motivated research questions (Vachhani & Pullen, 2019), as well as the phenomenon under study. For example, reflecting on the methodological process within a study of women on boards in Egypt, Amal Abdellatif and I wrote reflexive positioning statements about how our personal, yet quite different, background experiences of marginalisation informed the interpretive phenomenological analysis within the study, showing how reflexivity, reciprocity, mutual learning and political intent informed our 'multidimensional feminist hermeneutic process' (Abdellatif & Haynes, 2025).

Furthermore, within accounting research, other scholars have reflexively addressed their positioning as members of the accounting academy, and their situatedness in knowledge production. Dambrin and Lambert (2012), for example, reflexively analyse the illusory neutrality of accounting research on gender, while illustrating how they felt compelled to moderate pragmatically their own academic identities and scholarship away from overtly being seen as feminists, to avoid alienating other peers and to ensure their research outcomes were heard. Similarly, Tanima and George (2024, p. 109) reflexively offer a personal account of their lived experience in accounting academia and invoking the feminist mantra of the 'personal is political' to show that their 'personal experiences as educators are shaped by societal norms, gender and racial hierarchies'. Drawing from Cunliffe's (2003, 2004) notion of 'radical reflexivity', which suggests that reflexivity encompasses a lived moral and ethical project, I further conceptualised feminist academic identity as intersubjective identity work (Haynes, 2023). I suggest that identity work as a feminist academic is an ongoing practice of questioning our social, cultural, political and ethical positioning in relation to others, requiring awareness of global oppressions of women or marginalised others; addressing power, privilege and decolonisation in knowledge production; and negotiating feminist positions and emancipatory possibilities as both insider and outsider in academic contexts (Haynes, 2023).

Ethics of care in research practice

Yet, if the researcher is reflexively located in feminist research methodology and applies a feminist approach to method, this often reveals positionalities, emotions and vulnerabilities. Moreover, engagement with research participants often means that their vulnerabilities are also exposed, especially when addressing sensitive subjects around oppression and domination. To counter these issues, feminist researchers often consciously apply ethics of care to their research process. Ethics of care as a feminist methodological approach originate from the theoretical construct of ethics of care discussed in Chapter 7. With its origins in feminist ethics of care theory, it draws upon relationality and relational ontology, concern with the needs of others and the value of emotionality in epistemology (Held, 2006; Robinson, 2011; Tronto, 1993). As Brannelly and Barnes (2022, p. 6) suggest:

> The feminist ethics of care is a critical approach that seeks to understand the necessity of care to wellbeing, to understanding marginalisation and identifying responsibility to remedy social injustices.

When applied to feminist methodology, ethics of care require making informed and political choices about the questions we ask in research, thinking about who those questions are for and whose interests are being served by the research (Brannelly & Barnes, 2022), since, as feminists, those questions often address issues of inequality, domination and discrimination in the interests of social justice. To this end, feminist research:

> ...has a political purpose to challenge mainstream or 'malestream' knowledge (Letherby, 2003), to enable rather than disable understanding, counteract rather than ignore injustice, open rather than close areas investigation in all aspects of women's lives.
>
> *(Haynes, 2008a, p. 546)*

An ethics of care approach to research practice commits to respect relationality between researchers and participants and between researchers themselves. In relation to participants, this requires acknowledging the positioning and contextualisation of the participants, addressing their marginalisation, treating them as co-constructors within the research process, considering their emotional needs and minimising hierarchical power relations between researcher and participant, resulting in a non-exploitative approach to research (Abdellatif & Haynes, 2025; Sai et al., 2024). As an example of how this approach might be carried out, in her study of women on boards in Egypt, Amal Abdellatif, as lead researcher and conductor of the interviews, sought to build trust with participants through reciprocal sharing of mutual vulnerabilities and identities as Egyptian women, although not all their positionalities were identical (Abdellatif & Haynes, 2025). To embed feminist ethics of care and reciprocity in the research process, she also arranged for a local entity that promotes women on boards in the MENA region to share information with the participants on their available support, and for the sharing of experiences of those participants who consented, so that through 'sharing, reciprocity and relationality' participants found the experience 'to be empowering, emancipating and comforting' (Abdellatif & Haynes, 2025, p. 75).

However, feminist ethics of care embedded in research practice prioritise notions of care between the self and the other, whether the 'other' are participants or other researchers (Preissle, 2007). Hence there is a movement in feminist research to consider relationality between researchers themselves, in the interests of moving away from hierarchical, functionalist relationships towards collective, ethical approaches that enable multiple voices and positionalities, allow for vulnerabilities and challenge academic hegemonies in knowledge production (Abdellatif et al., 2024; Clavijo & Mandalaki, 2024; Johansson et al., 2024; Sai et al., 2024). By way of example, Sai et al. (2024) explore the potential for transforming the pervasive neoliberal culture underpinning research production through a relational approach rooted in ethics of care, addressing self-care and care for others, which they argue can change the prevailing managerial discourse towards more caring values and practices. Moreover, trauma-informed research methods, which focus on safeguarding the dignity, security and well-being of participants to ensure that they are not retraumatised by research encounters, blend well with feminist methodologies and principles of ethics of care (Taylor-Dunn, 2023).

In considering feminist ethics of care in research, there is also a need to reflect on collaborative research between researchers of the Global North and the Global South, or between Indigenous and non-Indigenous researchers, to understand how principles of decoloniality might influence the ethical caring process (Brannelly & Barnes, 2022). The decolonisation of accounting research and academia was addressed in more detail in Chapter 5. It is an area where feminist methodologies combined with feminist epistemologies have a role to play in the decolonisation process. In this sense, principles of the ethics of care require combining with feminist critical self-reflexivity to acknowledge and address power and privilege with academic communities, by incorporating alternative ways of knowing, embracing intersubjective collaborative learning from others and avoiding power relations in research processes (Haynes, 2023). It also requires broader ethics of care in our academic reviewing practices, anticipating vulnerabilities, avoiding gate-keeping of knowledge in international journals and extending political decolonisation in academic research (Haynes, 2025).

Writing feminist research differently

Feminist methodologies address the critical questions and challenges posed by feminism, in relation to the oppression and domination of women and others marginalised by non-binary genders, to produce feminist emancipatory knowledge. When producing and writing that research, many feminists aim to write it 'differently' in ways that encompass the relationality, reflexivity and ethics of care underpinning feminist methodologies. Traditional academic writing in the disciplines of accounting, business and management, much of the social sciences, as well as the sciences, is ostensibly based on a masculinist paradigm of rationality, objectivity and rationality which can obscure the messiness, emotionality and subjectivity embedded in academic writing. While rejecting any essentialist assumptions behind ways of writing, since such writing norms are socially constructed, many feminists are resisting the normative constraints of research presentation to write themselves into their research and to write differently. The scientific norms of much academic writing 'are restrictive [and] inhibit the development of knowledge and excise much of what it is to be human from our learning, teaching and research' (Gilmore et al., 2019, p. 3).

Writing differently enables feminist scholars 'to respect difference, to embrace own and others' vulnerabilities, to resist the "linear", masculine, patriarchal knowledge, and to reflect on the ethical and political dimensions of knowledge production' (Abdellatif & Haynes, 2025, p. 71). For example, Boncori (2022) situates the need for feminist research and writing in resistance to neoliberal and masculine approaches to academic work, arguing it represents a political and feminist project, a critical perspective and a means for change. Writing differently requires rejecting academic reductionism to embrace the personal, experiential in a form of conversation with a chosen audience (Kostera, 2023). It conveys feeling as well as meaning and is aligned with feminist sensibilities, while challenging academic orthodoxy and conformity (Kociatkiewicz & Kostera, 2023).

In a visceral yet vulnerable example of such writing, Pullen (2018, p. 123) likens conventional academic writing to labiaplasty, in the way it silences and constrains women's writing – 'embodied writing, leaky writing, dirty writing, feminine writing' – by the need to conform to patriarchal cultural norms in neoliberal academia. Her writing is both a protest and a call to resist being silenced and erased:

> I write to speak. Writing extends me, it reaches well beyond the confines of myself. At a very basic level, I would like my writing to speak from me, of me, when I am able to.
>
> *(Pullen, 2018, p. 123)*

Embodied writing reflects an embodied researcher with emotions, corporeality and physical responses. In feminist writing it reflects a feminine or non-binary, non-masculine body that is constrained into disembodied, masculine, competitive ways of writing. Paying attention to the body in research yields embodied knowledge that pays attention to the body and the self (Ellingson, 2006).

In the accounting discipline, accounting research tends to be dominated by functionalist paradigms. While, as I have shown in this text, researchers are addressing feminist challenges and using feminist theories to some extent, explicit feminist methodologies are mentioned more rarely. Moreover, 'writing differently' is only beginning to emerge. Some feminist accounting researchers write with passion and feeling that engages with reader with their commitment (see, for example, Lehman, 2012, 2019). Emotion and embodied difference are present in accounts of research practices and processes related to accounting (see, for example, Annisette & Prasad, 2017; Círico, 2024; Clavijo, Perray-Redslob, & Mandalaki, 2024; da Silva, 2016; Tanima & George, 2024). Where embodied writing is seen more prevalently is in autoethnographical accounting research where emotion and embodiment can be embedded into accounts and vignettes, although not all such research in accounting takes an explicitly emotive approach (Haynes, 2017b). Zou (2021, p. 695), for example, gives an emotive, embodied account of her fieldwork experiences, giving voice to their 'flesh and blood', which generate additional insights and enable the reader to feel her shock and struggles in the field, thus challenging 'a disembodied and disengaged way of practicing fieldwork'.

Similarly, in two further examples, I invoke the emotion and effect on the body of various practices and experiences related to accounting academia. In the first (Haynes, 2011), I illustrate the situated tensions arising when presenting feminist, emotive work on experiences in the accounting profession in different academic contexts, which has potential professional consequences These tensions and challenges include the difficulties in dealing with sensitive and personal subjects, the balance between theory and emotive writing, how to find the right 'voice' to speak of experience and dealing with emotion. Since feminist writing, and presentation of that writing, often addresses personal, profound and oppressive issues, whether experienced by the researcher or not, it does not necessarily fit the mould of traditional rationalistic scientific presentation of research. The embodied effects on me were multiple, given the vulnerability exposed by such writing: 'I am reticent'...'I feel myself tensing up'... 'my body takes over'... 'I feel pummelled'... 'My body, eyes, head, and heart, all ache' (Haynes, 2011, pp. 138 & 143). Yet, such an 'embodied encounter... stimulates the imagination towards new ways of thinking far more effective than repeated rationalistic displays' (Inckle, 2010, p. 28). In the second example, addressing three incidents in academic leadership, I explore the effects on my identity and my body of sexism, aggression and burnout (Haynes, 2024). The effects are visceral – 'My heart sinks'... 'He shouts louder over my voice. He will not stop asserting, yelling, waving his arms'....'Emotions whirling. Shock, fear, guilt'. However, the point is to discuss how to resist and change prevailing cultures of neoliberal managerialism in academia that perpetuate gendered assumptions and negate embodied affect and needs for care (Haynes, 2024).

In summary, feminist research methodologies allow for ways of knowing that address the challenges and questions that feminism raises, and to which the theories addressed in this text are applied. There is no one fixed feminist method since this will depend on the approach and focus of the research (Haynes, 2008a, 2010). However, feminist research is politicised, reflexive, embodied and sometimes vulnerable, although all of these can be supported and mitigated as necessary through an ethic of care for the self and others in the process. Feminist embodied writing need not directly focus on the body, but it is written from the body. In other words, it represents a 'feminine' alternative to the instrumental rationality of much academic writing, recognising the interaction of bodies and identities with research, and placing affect and care at its centre. Such forms of feminist methodology and 'writing differently' can potentially involve vulnerability and risk for those carrying it out. Yet it can also be emancipatory, joyful, meaningful and invoke transformation at micro, meso and macro levels, where change is needed (Haynes, 2017a).

Activism, resistance and accounting

Activism is a central part of feminism, given the focus on transforming and overturning structures and cultures of domination. This section addresses the potential and incidence of feminist activism in the discipline of accounting or practised by accountants. Critical accounting has long been a form of counterpoint to the traditional mainstream research of functionalist and positivist accounting, with an intent to challenge the role of accounting in society's structures, norms and cultures. In this sense, it illustrates a desire for social and political change. However, the line between critique and activism is fairly hard, with most research tending towards critique rather than active engagement with change. Dey (2024), however, argues that what can be considered as accounting activism is broadening in scope, with recognition that activism encompasses many forms and scales of actions, and can be associated with different forms of engagement rather than outright political praxis. Nonetheless, Thomson (2014), argues that social accounting research, for example, has not produced the transformation of social accounting required to produce more sustainable societies and corporate practices. He argues for it to go further to facilitate the development of transformative social accounting praxis requiring targeted interventions in the form of social accounting communities and transformative educative practice.

There are examples of specific activist practice that mobilises accounting technologies in the interests of social justice or political change. For instance, Martinez and Himick's (2023) study of the Occupy Edmonton movement, a grass-roots protest against financial capitalist exploitation and greed, showed that activists utilised simple yet functional accounting calculations to monitor cash inflows and outflows in ways that were useful for non-experts and compatible with non-hierarchical self-organising. Cooper and Coulson (2014) illustrate how a group of academics and activists collaborated to produce evidence of health and safety breaches in a large-scale industry disaster where employees were killed, by scrutinising accounting disclosures to identify lack of transparency and entrenched power relations. These examples illustrate that accounting technologies can be utilised for activist praxis.

None of these examples, however, are feminist in orientation. Feminist activism, making use of accounting technologies, is apparently elusive. Corporate social responsibility (CSR) practice, which is arguably related to accountability practices, CSR disclosures and governance, all of which tangentially relate to accounting theories and systems, addresses gender issues, albeit rarely feminist. However, CSR theorisation and research on gender could be enhanced by more explicit reference to feminist theories (Grosser & Moon, 2019). Spence and Taylor (2024, p. 1201) call for a feminist CSR research agenda, drawing from Judith Butler's concept of critique as practice of values in order for CSR to be an 'effective force for good for all'. This, they argue, would support an ethical justification and the reflexive questioning of what is important, why and how norms have been developed, encouraging researchers to question forms of CSR and dismantle power relations by adopting a feminist lens to 'emancipate the disadvantaged by diffusing inequalities, including those along gender lines' (Spence & Taylor, 2024, p. 1204)

Further potential for feminist activism relates to feminist social movements (Grosser & McCarthy, 2019), where their role in challenging norms, structures and inequalities could potentially be related to the broader role of accounting in perpetuating neoliberalist constructs. Counter accounting, or shadow accounts, offer the potential to open spaces for democratic contestation and to advance progressive change against neoliberalism (George, Brown, & Dillard, 2021). Producing feminist shadow accounts is a form of feminist activism, exposing injustice and inequality. I discussed shadow accounts in much more detail in Chapter 4 when I discussed more radical approaches to feminism. For example, I argued in Chapter 4 that the #MeToo movement as discussed in relation to accounting in Goncharenko's (2023a, 2023b) research can reflect a form of shadow account to counter unspoken stories of hidden violence. Similarly, Lehman (2016, p. 89) argues that accounting makes 'things governable, thinkable and knowable' including the experiences of incarcerated women, suggesting that counter accounts will make visible race, gender and class in mythologising, institutionalising and normalising the criminal. As was discussed in Chapters 4 and 5, Black feminist writers such as Collins (2022 [1990]) and Lorde (2018, 2019) frame activism very much as part of their feminist rationale, and similarly transnational feminism focuses heavily on intersectionality, social justice and activism. There is a great deal of potential, therefore, for feminist in accounting to address activism in more detail or for shadow accounts to focus on feminist issues.

Feminist activism in accounting academia

Where we do see more discussion of feminist activism is in relation to accounting academia. Debates about the need for higher education to change towards more responsible and holistic approaches to education have come to the fore particularly since the financial crisis of 2008 and as the challenges of climate change became more entrenched (Cho & Costa, 2024; Connell, 2019; Dyllick, 2015). It is beyond the scope of this book to address accounting curricula and pedagogy. As I have discussed throughout this text, accounting research offers great potential for feminism, and conducting research that challenges norms, ideas and mindsets is a form of feminist transformative practice. However, in this section relating to accounting academia I am addressing the scope to apply feminist activism in addressing academe's own oppressions.

Like many institutions, as seen in the critique of the accounting profession in this text, universities are widely considered as gendered organisations (Benschop & Brouns, 2003; Fagan & Teasdale, 2021). The organisation of academic work is around an 'ideal academic', based on a masculinised norm of being constantly available for work, with no caring responsibilities, engaging in competitive performance (Ivancheva, Lynch, & Keating, 2019; Martinovic & Verkuyten, 2013). Academics are faced with a publish or perish culture that drives competition and performance management (Gebreiter, 2022; Malsch & Tessier, 2015). Career progression in academia is problematic for those who do not meet this idealisation (Bleijenbergh, Van, & Vinkenburg, 2012), which may include anyone gendered, raced or classed as 'other' to the norm. Hence, it is not surprising that women academics struggle when returning to work after maternity leave (Davies et al., 2022), suffer disproportionately with precarity in contractual status (Ivancheva et al., 2019) and experience dissonance between academic and family life (Toffoletti & Starr, 2016). The commerciality of modern higher education institutions drives out egalitarian and caring approaches to work (Lynch, 2006). Moreover, sexism appears to be rife in business schools in which many accounting departments are situated (Lima, Casa Nova, & Vendramin, 2024; Shymko et al., 2024; Yarrow & Davies, 2024).

The gendered challenges within accounting academia often present similar challenges globally in terms of balancing work and family responsibilities or facing gendered models of success (Haynes, 2025). However, they are not entirely homogeneous, and contextualisation offers understanding of localised norms and cultures. For example, Italian female accounting academics face persistent patriarchal structures and cultures that heavily influence their roles and opportunities in academia (Galizzi, McBride, & Siboni, 2023). As noted in Chapter 5, Colombian women accounting academics are a significant minority with continuing barriers to progression (Chamorro González, Jacinto, & Peñaloza, 2020), and are also subjected to significant pay gaps (Restrepo Quintero & Isaza Castro, 2019). In Brazil, while women accounting academics face gendered challenges (Casa Nova, 2022), they are also heavily racialised and sexualised, which brings additional inequalities (da Silva, 2016). Moreover, given that Brazil is one of the most transphobic countries in the world with high rates of gender violence (Círico, 2024; Círico, Galvão, & Casa Nova, 2024), wider inclusion of trans, queer or non-binary identities in accounting academia (not limited to Brazil) raises a further need for interventions towards gender justice.

The question is then how can feminist academics resist these inequities through feminist activism? Through addressing my own identity as a feminist academic, I have reflected on how active engagement in intersubjective identity work can bring about a reflexive understanding of academic praxis in such a turbulent academic context (Haynes, 2023). This enables my feminist identity to be underpinned by a reflexive awareness of the need to learn from and work with others, to be aware of power and privilege (including my own) and to address further the need for decolonisation in knowledge production (Haynes, 2023). Reflecting on these issues then enables a broader understanding of what we might stand for as feminists and how we might effect change. My daughter, Florence Reedy, and I engaged in a discussion on this very issue in a public dialogue representing private discussions, where we sought to understand how we could enact feminist praxis while trying to maintain a career in gendered university institutions at different positions on the career spectrum (Reedy & Haynes, 2023). Drawing from Sara Ahmed's (2017) powerful work on *Living a Feminist Life*, we discussed how Florence is vocally and digitally engaged in addressing sexism and committed to feminist research in which she enacts her feminist principles, highlighting feminist voices, giving feminist narratives, following a feminist methodology, whereas I, from a position of senior management, try to influence and lead institutional agendas which I believe could improve academic life for women and marginalised others and counter more neoliberal university objectives. As Florence noted:

> Yeah, you are more likely to try quietly to persuade and influence, whereas I'm more outspoken and direct. We are different, but we both stand up to sexism, discrimination, racism and misogyny when we see it.
>
> *(Reedy & Haynes, 2023, p. 186)*

When faced with sexism, my personal strategy was to maintain embodied affective authenticity, using my body as a place of comfort and resistance, rejecting masculine symbolism and refusing to project a rational, authoritarian, managerial form of academic leadership which seemed to be required by the institution; this, however, was only made possible by forming solidarities and support networks with colleagues (Haynes, 2024). I offer these personal reflections not as ideal instances of feminist activism but as examples of the kind of praxis that can be made by feminist academics amongst the many that others are undertaking. Feminist resistance can be both individualised and collective; it can be subversive, using legitimisation conferred by leadership roles, as well as overt (Haynes, 2024).

Other strategies for feminist solidarity and activism draw on feminist consciousness raising which, McCarthy and Grosser (2023) argue, can co-opt neoliberal individualism by reconceptualising what role people can play in social change. Feminist activism in an academic organisation can take the form of shifting policies, strategies and goals over time, achieved through networks, micro-politics and everyday practices rather than collective large-scale movements (Bendl, Danowitz, & Schmidt, 2014). However, collectivism and feminist solidarity is a central part of feminist activism, whether through providing a supportive space for women's writing (Sharp & Messuri, 2023), through building feminist networks that encompass feminist values (Lima et al., 2024) or through mobilising more formally established feminist organisations within academia to build collective action to challenge sexism through the nexus of research, support and advocacy (Gurrieri et al., 2024).

The role of men in feminism

In such processes of change it is worth considering the role of men in feminist action. Tienari and Taylor (2019) argue that it is essential for men as well as women to engage with feminist theory and activism, as pro-feminists, although they suggest this may also entail risks for men as it also does for women, in the interests of reducing the effects of misogyny, patriarchy and sexism for all (Bell et al., 2020). As I noted in considering accounting research on gender:

> Just as women are not a unitary category, neither are men. Men also experience social and economic deprivation, poverty, violence, and exploitation under global capitalism... To position men as a binary opposed to women in gender research ignores the complex nature of issues which relate to men and women alike: the reorganisation and precariousness of family and working life; the economic and cultural resources needed for the making of identity; and the commodification of emotional and intimate life under capitalism. Accounting's relationship with all of these areas is worthy of further study. This is not to argue for the reassertion of male dominance but the acknowledgement of male gendering in order to subvert and overturn gendered constructs.
>
> *(Haynes, 2017a, pp. 120–121)*

Men, Kelan (2023) argues, can be centrally involved in creating gender-inclusive cultures in organisations. Given the discussions in this text, especially in Chapter 6 on cis-heteronormativity, masculinity, queering and identities, drawing men into pro-feminist activism may support a more diverse culture. However, if men are to be allies or directly involved in activism to promote inclusive academic cultures, it is essential that heteropatriarchal norms are not inadvertently or consciously reproduced.

The emancipatory potential of feminist accounting

My aim in this book was to provide a comprehensive overview of contemporary feminist theories applied to accounting, in terms of both accounting technologies and the accounting profession. Feminist theorisations of accounting offer rich insights into how accounting technologies are embedded in gendered power relations and processes of domination underpinned by neoliberal capitalism. These theories also illustrate and interpret how various aspects of gender relations, as well as race and class, are experienced, performed and embedded in cultures and structures of the accounting profession. Applying feminist theories to understanding the challenges and issues raised by feminists expands our interpretation of, and action against, inequalities, silences, violence and oppression of women. The multiple feminist theorisations and their applications to accounting were summarised in Table 8.1 and discussed earlier in this chapter.

However, I go further to argue that feminist theories blend with feminist methodologies and feminist activism to form an integrative approach to feminist accounting which has emancipatory potential. Blending theory, key concepts of feminist methodology and activist practice allows for the interaction of epistemology, methodology and ontology with feminist political intent and emancipatory outcomes.

The interaction of feminist theories, methodologies and activism as an integrative model for feminist accounting is shown in Figure 8.1.

Figure 8.1 illustrates the many *Feminist Issues in Accounting* that concern feminists in the way that they interact with accounting technologies and the accounting profession. The feminist theories addressed in this text, also summarised as *Feminist Theories for Accounting*, offer critical lenses that take account of varying social, political and global contextualisations, which can be applied to any of the issues concerning feminists. *Feminist Methodologies for Accounting* recognise that contributions to knowledge – epistemology – are closely associated with the means of that knowledge production – methodology. Hence, if we are to produce knowledge with, of, and for women, to addresses the challenges faced, applying key principles of feminist methodology will ensure that ways of thinking, participating, doing and writing research represent and reflect feminist values.

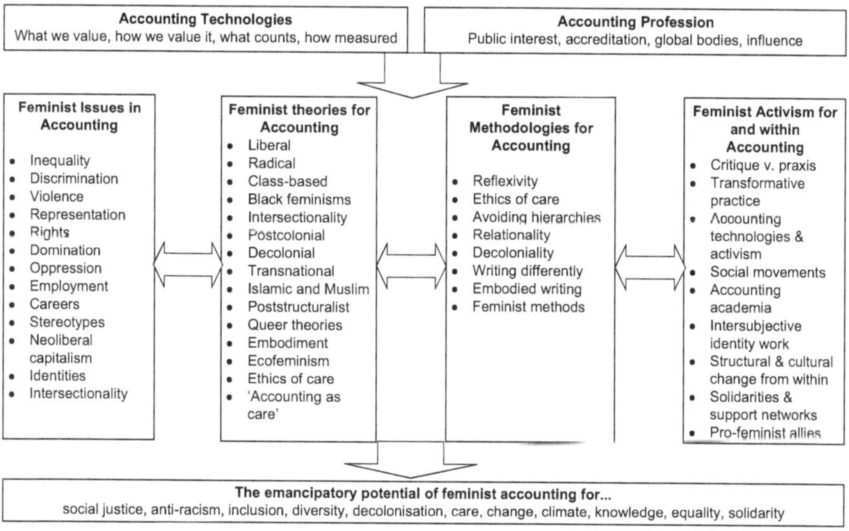

FIGURE 8.1 The emancipatory potential of feminist accounting.

Feminism is an ontological position as well as a theoretical perspective – a way of being or living in the world (Ahmed, 2017; Haynes, 2023; Stanley, 1990).

Moreover, feminism engenders various forms of activism. Research into issues concerning feminists is itself a form of activism, especially as overt positioning as a feminist can invoke a degree of risk. The challenges faced by feminists are locally and globally unequal, as in some areas feminist ideologies are accepted and in others feminist challenges to misogyny and patriarchy are met with backlash and violence (Fotaki & Pullen, 2024). As summarised in Figure 8.1, in *Feminist Activism for and within Accounting*, activist practice can involve both critique and praxis. It addresses transformative action supported by collectivities, networks and solidarities, or social movements. In relation to the accounting discipline, it can involve change from within which attempts to change cultures and structures.

I have illustrated how accounting technologies have been used to justify abhorrent actions in colonialism, in slavery and in the simple maintenance of a neoliberal status quo. Yet they have also been used to support activism and transformation. Even within current accounting systems, accounting technologies can be used to try to bring about positive change, albeit with mixed results. For example, concepts of gender mainstreaming, whereby gender and its effects are considered at every step of decision-making processes by organisations and governments have gained some recent traction in relation to management accounting and control systems (Wittbom, 2015; Wittbom & Häyrén, 2021). Similarly, gender-responsive budgeting, primarily implemented in public sector organisations or government departments, aims to have a gender-equitable distribution of resources, thus promoting equality (Jorge & Pimentel, 2021; Khalifa & Scarparo, 2021; Steccolini, 2019). These mechanisms work within existing accounting paradigms and practices rather than developing new conceptualisations of accounting.

I propose that feminist accounting has emancipatory potential because it transcends existing ways of thinking about accounting, as a technology and as a profession. Putting together feminist issues, theories, methodologies and activism into an integrative approach to feminist accounting highlights these possibilities. As I discussed in Chapter 1 when introducing feminist accounting as an emancipatory project, I use the term emancipation to refer to freedom from oppression, exploitation, violence, disadvantage, power relations, sexism and inequalities. It does not suggest that people, particularly women, do not have agency, although the degree of personal freedom that women have varies round the world. What it recognises is that gender oppressions are rooted in social, political and economic structures, with varying effects at micro, meso and macro levels. Neoliberal capitalism influences these areas of feminist struggle because many are associated with commodification, labour and employment, economic inequalities and exploitation. Accounting technologies used by organisations, multinational companies and governments, whether historically or contemporaneously, underpin not only what we measure and how we measure it, but the actual value systems inherent in those measures. As I have discussed in this text, accounting is not a neutral phenomenon, nor is it gender-neutral in conceptualisation and potentially in how it is applied. The accounting profession represents a powerful body of influence with its extensive accreditation of and direct employment of accountants globally. The profession's own record on gender and inclusivity is therefore subject to scrutiny.

Feminist critique of accounting's role in gendered power relations, social structures and neoliberal economies is essential to challenge current norms and social relations. The breadth of feminist theorisation from numerous different perspectives, contextualisations and positions illustrated in this text provides a means of understanding, interpreting and challenging how those structures and norms came about, and, importantly, how they uncover new ways of thinking and knowing that move accounting away from its traditional functionalist paradigm towards a feminist agenda for social justice. The integrative blend of feminist theory, methodology and activism becomes an emancipatory project that opens up the potential to conceptualise, embrace and organise new accounting technologies and apply them differently using feminist ethics of care and principles of decolonisation with the profession and within accounting academia. Multiple reconceptualisations of accounting, through the lens of a feminist approach and the multiple feminist theories, have been proposed in the earlier chapters.

Hence, as summarised in Figure 8.1, feminist accounting as an emancipatory project offers hope by challenging inequalities of gender, race and class amongst others; embracing inclusion, diversity and equality; challenging racism, exclusion and violence; supporting decolonisation of academia and ourselves; protecting the climate, planet and animal and human life; and forming new collectivities and solidarities to overturn oppression and domination.

Conclusion

By way of concluding remarks, I hope this text provides a rich theoretical and practical resource to advance knowledge and application of feminist theories within accounting, encourages feminist methodologies and activism and stimulates further feminist research in the interests of social justice.

References

Abdellatif, A., Gatto, M., O'Shea, S., & Yarrow, E. (2024). Ties that bind: An inclusive feminist approach to subvert gendered "othering" in times of crisis. *Gender, Work & Organization*, *31*(4), 1463–1478. https://doi.org/10.1111/gwao.12752

Abdellatif, A., & Haynes, K. (2025). Be-ing seen: Towards a feminist interpretative phenomenological analysis to researching the marginalised. *Culture and Organization*, *31*(1), 64–85. https://doi.org/10.1080/14759551.2024.2378789

Adamson, M. (2017). Postfeminism, neoliberalism and a 'successfully' balanced femininity in celebrity CEO autobiographies. *Gender, Work & Organization*, *24*(3), 314–327. https://doi.org/10.1111/gwao.12167

Ahmed, S. (2017). *Living a Feminist Life*. Durham: Duke University Press.

Annisette, M., & Prasad, A. (2017). Critical accounting research in hyper-racial times. *Critical Perspectives on Accounting*, *43*, 5–19. https://doi.org/10.1016/j.cpa.2016.06.002

Baer, H. (2016). Redoing feminism: Digital activism, body politics, and neoliberalism. *Feminist Media Studies*, *16*(1), 17–34. https://doi.org/10.1080/14680777.2015.1093070

Baker, D. T., & Brewis, D. N. (2020). The melancholic subject: A study of self-blame as a gendered and neoliberal psychic response to loss of the 'perfect worker'. *Accounting, Organizations and Society*, *82*, 101093. https://doi.org/10.1016/j.aos.2019.101093

Bell, E., Meriläinen, S., Taylor, S., & Tienari, J. (2020). Dangerous knowledge: The political, personal, and epistemological promise of feminist research in Management and Organization Studies. *International Journal of Management Reviews*, *22*(2), 177–192. https://doi.org/10.1111/ijmr.12221

Bendl, R., Danowitz, M. A., & Schmidt, A. (2014). Recalibrating management: Feminist activism to achieve equality in an evolving university. *British Journal of Management*, *25*(2), 320–334. https://doi.org/10.1111/1467-8551.12008

Benschop, Y., & Brouns, M. (2003). Crumbling ivory towers: Academic organizing and its gender effects. *Gender, Work & Organization*, *10*(2), 194–212. https://doi.org/10.1111/1468-0432.t01-1-00011

Bleijenbergh, I. L., Van, M. L., & Vinkenburg, C. J. (2012). Othering women: Fluid images of the ideal academic. *Equality, Diversity and Inclusion: An International Journal*, *32*(1), 22–35. https://doi.org/10.1108/02610151311305597

Boncori, I. (2022). *Researching and Writing Differently*. Bristol: Policy Press.

Brannelly, T., & Barnes, M. (2022). *Researching with Care. Applying Feminist Care Ethics to Research Practice*. Bristol: Policy Press.

Butler, J. (2013). For White girls only? Postfeminism and the politics of inclusion. *Feminist Formations*, 35–58. https://doi.org/10.1353/ff.2013.0009

Casa Nova, S. P. d. C. (2022). "Ridin' down the highway" – Reflections on the trajectories of women professors in academia. *Advances in Scientific and Applied Accounting*, *15*(2), 030–046/047–062. https://doi.org/10.14392/asaa.2022150202

Chamorro González, C., Jacinto, R. A. P., & Peñaloza, L. V. (2020). Women Accountants in Academic and Research Spaces in Colombia. In C. R. Lehman (Ed.), *Resistance and Accountability* (Vol. 22, pp. 23–34). Emerald Publishing Limited. https://doi.org/10.1108/S1041-706020200000022002

Cho, C. H., & Costa, E. (2024). Sustainability accounting education: Challenges and outlook. *International Journal of Sustainability in Higher Education*, *25*(7), 1412–1425. https://doi.org/10.1108/IJSHE-02-2024-0152

Círico, J. (2024). *Vozes da resistência: vivências de pessoas transgêneras e travestis na contabilidade brasileira [Voices of resistance: experiences of transgender and transvestite people in Brazilian accounting]* [PhD, Universidade Federal de Uberlândia]. Uberlândia, Brazil.

Círico, J., Galvão, A. A., & Casa Nova, S. P. d. C. (2024). Carta Aberta: (In)visibilizing transgender bodies in organizations. *Organization*, in press, 13505084241275780. https://doi.org/10.1177/13505084241275780

Clark, R. (2016). "Hope in a hashtag": The discursive activism of# WhyIStayed. *Feminist Media Studies*, *16*(5), 788–804. https://doi.org/10.1080/14680777.2016.1138235

Clark-Parsons, R. (2021). "I see you, I believe you, I stand with you":# MeToo and the performance of networked feminist visibility. *Feminist Media Studies*, *21*(3), 362–380. https://doi.org/10.1080/14680777.2019.1628797

Clavijo, N., & Mandalaki, E. (2024). The wor(l)d is out – You are not alone: Toward a healing organizational autoethnography in/through feminist reading and writing. *Organization*, in press, 13505084241238285. https://doi.org/10.1177/13505084241238285

Clavijo, N., Perray-Redslob, L., & Mandalaki, E. (2024). Cracking a brick in the master's house: Counter practices as counter-accounts of difference and survival. *Accounting, Auditing & Accountability Journal*, *37*(4), 1153–1177. https://doi.org/10.1108/AAAJ-07-2022-5936

Collins, P. H. (2022 [1990]). *Black Feminist Thought. Knowledge, Consciousness, and the Politics of Empowerment* (30th Anniversary Edition ed.). Abingdon: Routledge.

Connell, R. (2019). *The Good University. What Universities Actually Do and Why Its Time for Radical Change*. London: Zed Books.

Cooper, C., & Coulson, A. B. (2014). Accounting activism and Bourdieu's 'collective intellectual' – Reflections on the ICL case. *Critical Perspectives on Accounting*, *25*(3), 237–254. https://doi.org/10.1016/j.cpa.2013.01.002

Cunliffe, A. L. (2003). Reflexive inquiry in organizational research: Questions and possibilities. *Human Relations*, *56*(8), 983–1003. https://doi.org/10.1177/00187267030568004

Cunliffe, A. L. (2004). On becoming a critically reflexive practitioner. *Journal of Management Education*, *28*(4), 407–426. https://doi.org/10.1177/1052562904264440
Cunliffe, A. L. (2016). "On Becoming a Critically Reflexive Practitioner" redux: What does it mean to be reflexive? *Journal of Management Education*, *40*(6), 740–746. https://doi.org/10.1177/1052562916668919
da Silva, S. M. C. (2016). *Tetos de vitrais: Gênero e raça na contabilidade no Brasil* [Tese de Doutorado em Controladoria e Contabilidade: Contabilidade, Universidade de São Paulo]. Faculdade de Economia, Administração e Contabilidade.
Dambrin, C., & Lambert, C. (2012). Who is she and who are we? A reflexive journey in research into the rarity of women in the highest ranks of accounting. *Critical Perspectives on Accounting*, *23*(1), 1–16. https://doi.org/10.1016/j.cpa.2011.06.006
Davies, J. M., Brighton, L. J., Reedy, F., & Bajwah, S. (2022). Maternity provision, contract status, and likelihood of returning to work: Evidence from research intensive universities in the UK. *Gender, Work & Organization*, *29*(5), 1495–1510. https://doi.org/10.1111/gwao.12843
Dey, C. (2024). Activism and Accounting. In H. Vollmer (Ed.), *Handbook of Accounting in Society* (pp. 280–293). Cheltenham: Edward Elgar Publishing.
Dyllick, T. (2015). Responsible management education for a sustainable world. *Journal of Management Development*, *34*(1), 16–33. https://doi.org/10.1108/JMD-02-2013-0022
Ellingson, L. L. (2006). Embodied knowledge: Writing researchers' bodies into qualitative health research. *Qualitative Health Research*, *16*(2), 298–310. https://doi.org/10.1177/1049732305281944
Fagan, C., & Teasdale, N. (2021). Women professors across STEMM and non-STEMM Disciplines: Navigating gendered spaces and playing the academic game. *Work, Employment and Society*, *35*(4), 774–792. https://doi.org/10.1177/0950017020916182
Fotaki, M., & Pullen, A. (2024). Feminist theories and activist practices in Organization Studies. *Organization Studies*, *45*(4), 593–616. https://doi.org/10.1177/01708406231209861
Galizzi, G., McBride, K., & Siboni, B. (2023). Patriarchy persists: Experiences of barriers to women's career progression in Italian accounting academia. *Critical Perspectives on Accounting*, 102625. https://doi.org/10.1016/j.cpa.2023.102625
Garcia, A. M. (1989). The development of Chicana feminist discourse, 1970–1980. *Gender and Society*, *3*(2), 217–238. https://doi.org/10.1177/089124389003002004
Gebreiter, F. (2022). A profession in peril? University corporatization, performance measurement and the sustainability of accounting academia. *Critical Perspectives on Accounting*, *87*,(102292). https://doi.org/10.1016/j.cpa.2021.102292
George, S., Brown, J., & Dillard, J. (2021). Social movement activists' conceptions of political action and counter-accounting through a critical dialogic accounting and accountability lens. *Critical Perspectives on Accounting*, *91*, 102408. https://doi.org/10.1016/j.cpa.2021.102408
Gill, R. (2017). The affective, cultural and psychic life of postfeminism: A postfeminist sensibility 10 years on. *European Journal of Cultural Studies*, *20*(6), 606–626. https://doi.org/10.1177/1367549417733003
Gill, R., Kelan, E., & Scharff, C. (2017). A postfeminist sensibility at work. *Gender, Work & Organization*, *24*(3), 226–244. https://doi.org/10.1111/gwao.12132
Gilmore, S., Harding, N., Helin, J., & Pullen, A. (2019). Writing differently. *Management Learning*, *50*(1), 3–10. https://doi.org/10.1177/1350507618811027

Goncharenko, G. (2023a). In the spotlight: Rethinking NGO accountability in the #MeToo era. *Critical Perspectives on Accounting*, *92*, 102308. https://doi.org/10.1016/j.cpa.2021.102308
Goncharenko, G. (2023b). The #MeToo legacy and "the Collective Us": Conceptualising accountability for sexual misconduct at work. *Accounting, Auditing & Accountability Journal*, *36*(7/8), 1814–1838. https://doi.org/10.1108/AAAJ-01-2022-5642
Grosser, K., & McCarthy, L. (2019). Imagining new feminist futures: How feminist social movements contest the neoliberalization of feminism in an increasingly corporate-dominated world. *Gender, Work & Organization*, *26*(8), 1100–1116. https://doi.org/10.1111/gwao.12267
Grosser, K., & Moon, J. (2019). CSR and feminist organization studies: Towards an integrated theorization for the analysis of gender issues. *Journal of Business Ethics*, *155*(2), 321–342. https://doi.org/10.1007/s10551-017-3510-x
Gurrieri, L., Prothero, A., Bettany, S., Dobscha, S., Drenten, J., Ferguson, S., Finkelstein, S., McVey, L., Ourahmoune, N., Steinfield, L., & Tuncay Zayer, L. (2024). Feminist academic organizations: Challenging sexism through collective mobilizing across research, support, and advocacy. *Gender, Work & Organization*, *31*(5), 2158–2179. https://doi.org/10.1111/gwao.12912
Hardies, K., & Khalifa, R. (2018). Gender is not "a dummy variable": A discussion of current gender research in accounting. *Qualitative Research in Accounting & Management*, *15*(3), 385–407. https://doi.org/10.1108/QRAM-08-2017-0083
Harding, S. (1987). Is There A Feminist Method? In S. Harding (Ed.), *Feminism and Methodology* (pp. 1–13). Milton Keynes: Open University Press.
Haynes, K. (2008a). Moving the gender agenda or stirring chicken's entrails?: Where next for feminist methodologies in accounting? *Accounting, Auditing & Accountability Journal*, *21*(4), 539–555. https://doi.org/10.1108/09513570810872914
Haynes, K. (2008b). (Re)figuring accounting and maternal bodies: The gendered embodiment of accounting professionals. *Accounting, Organizations and Society*, *33*(4–5), 328–348. https://doi.org/10.1016/j.aos.2007.04.003
Haynes, K. (2008c). Transforming identities: Accounting professionals and the transition to motherhood. *Critical Perspectives on Accounting*, *19*(5), 620–642. https://doi.org/10.1016/j.cpa.2006.10.003
Haynes, K. (2010). Other lives in accounting: Critical reflections on oral history methodology in action. *Critical Perspectives on Accounting*, *21*(3), 221–231. https://doi.org/10.1016/j.cpa.2009.11.002
Haynes, K. (2011). Tensions in (re)presenting the self in reflexive autoethnographical research. *Qualitative Research in Organizations and Management*, *6*(2), 134–149. https://doi.org/10.1108/17465641111159125
Haynes, K. (2012). Reflexivity. In C. Cassell & G. Symon (Eds.), *The Practice of Qualitative Organizational Research: Core Methods and Current Challenges* (pp. 77–95). London: Sage.
Haynes, K. (2017a). Accounting as gendering and gendered: A review of 25 years of critical accounting research on gender. *Critical Perspectives on Accounting*, *43*, 110–124. https://doi.org/10.1016/j.cpa.2016.06.004
Haynes, K. (2017b). Autoethnography in Accounting Research. In Z. Hoque, L. D. Parker, M. A. Covaleski, & K. Haynes (Eds.), *The Routledge Companion to Qualitative Accounting Research Methods* (pp. 215–230). Abingdon: Routledge.
Haynes, K. (2017c). Reflexivity in Accounting Research. In Z. Hoque, L. D. Parker, M. A. Covaleski, & K. Haynes (Eds.), *The Routledge Companion to Qualitative Accounting Research methods* (pp. 284–298). London: Routledge.

Haynes, K. (2023). Reflexivity and academic identity in accounting: Intersubjective reflexive identity work as a feminist academic. *Accounting, Auditing & Accountability Journal*, *36*(5), 1379–1395. https://doi.org/10.1108/AAAJ-10-2022-6099

Haynes, K. (2024). Resisting sexisms, aggression, and burnout in academic leadership: Surviving in the gendered managerial academy. *Gender, Work & Organization*, *31*(5), 2286–2302. https://doi.org/10.1111/gwao.13137

Haynes, K. (2025). The role of accounting in creating, perpetuating and overcoming inequalities: Going beyond discipline, borders and stasis towards accounting as activism. *Gender, Work & Organization*, *32*(2), 912–928. https://doi.org/10.1111/gwao.13191

Held, V. (2006). *The Ethics of Care: Personal, Political, Global.* New York: Oxford University Press.

Hibbert, P., Coupland, C., & MacIntosh, R. (2010). Reflexivity: Recursion and relationality in organizational research processes. *Qualitative Research in Organizations and Management: An International Journal*, *5*(1), 47–62. https://doi.org/10.1108/17465641011042026

Inckle, K. (2010). Telling Tales? Using ethnographic fictions to speak embodied 'truth'. *Qualitative Research*, *10*(1), 27–47. https://doi.org/10.1177/1468794109348681

Ivancheva, M., Lynch, K., & Keating, K. (2019). Precarity, gender and care in the neoliberal academy. *Gender, Work & Organization*, *26*(4), 448–462. https://doi.org/10.1111/gwao.12350

Jeacle, I. (2021). Navigating netnography: A guide for the accounting researcher. *Financial Accountability & Management*, *37*(1), 88–101. https://doi.org/10.1111/faam.12237

Johansson, J., Gao, G., Sölvell, I., & Wigren-Kristoferson, C. (2024). Exploring caring collaborations in academia through feminist reflexive dialogs. *Gender, Work & Organization*, *31*(5), 2241–2263. https://doi.org/10.1111/gwao.13115

Jorge, S., & Pimentel, L. (2021). Debate: On the 'why' of gender budgeting. *Public Money & Management*, *41*(7), 504–505. https://doi.org/10.1080/09540962.2021.1936935

Kelan, E. (2023). *Men Stepping Forward. Leading Your Organization on the Path to Inclusion.* Bristol: Bristol University Press.

Khalifa, R., & Scarparo, S. (2021). Gender Responsive Budgeting: A tool for gender equality. *Critical Perspectives on Accounting*, *79*, 102183. https://doi.org/10.1016/j.cpa.2020.102183

Kociatkiewicz, J., & Kostera, M. (2023). Writing differently: On the constraints and possibilities of presenting research rooted in feminist epistemologies. *Gender,* **Work & Organization,** *31*(1), 284–304. https://doi.org/10.1111/gwao.13072

Kostera, M. (2023). Introduction. In M. Kostera (Ed.), *How to Write Differently. A Quest for Meaningful Academic Writing* (pp. 1–7). Cheltenham: Edward Elgar Publishing.

Lange, T., & Pérez-Moreno, L. C. (2020). Architectural historiography and Fourth Wave feminism. *Architectural Histories*, *8*(1), 26. https://doi.org/10.5334/ah.563

Lehman, C. R. (2012). We've come a long way! Maybe! Re-imagining gender and accounting. *Accounting, Auditing & Accountability Journal*, *25*(2), 256–294. https://doi.org/10.1108/09513571211198764

Lehman, C. R. (2016). Unshackling Accounting in Prisons: Race, Gender, and Class. In C. R. Lehman (Ed.), *Accounting in Conflict: Globalization, Gender, Race and Class* (Vol. 19, pp. 89–112). Leeds: Emerald Group Publishing Limited. https://doi.org/10.1108/S1041-706020160000019006

Lehman, C. R. (2019). Reflecting on now more than ever: Feminism in accounting. *Critical Perspectives on Accounting*, *65*, 102080. https://doi.org/10.1016/j.cpa.2019.04.001

Letherby, G. (2003). *Feminist Research in Theory and Practice*. Buckingham: Open University Press.

Letiche, H., De Loo, I., Lowe, A., & Yates, D. (2023). Meeting the research(er) and the researched halfway. *Critical Perspectives on Accounting*, *94*, 102452. https://doi.org/10.1016/j.cpa.2022.102452

Lima, J. P. R. d., Casa Nova, S. P. d. C., & Vendramin, E. d. O. (2024). Sexist academic socialization and feminist resistance: (De)constructing women's (dis)placement in Brazilian accounting academia. *Critical Perspectives on Accounting*, *99*, 102600. https://doi.org/10.1016/j.cpa.2023.102600

Lorde, A. (2018). *The Master's Tools Will Never Dismantle the Master's House*. London, UK: Penguin.

Lorde, A. (2019). *Sister Outsider*. London, UK: Penguin.

Lynch, K. (2006). Neo-liberalism and marketisation: The implications for higher education. *European Educational Research Journal*, *5*(1), 1–17. https://doi.org/10.2304/eerj.2006.5.1.1

Malsch, B., & Tessier, S. (2015). Journal ranking effects on junior academics: Identity fragmentation and politicization. *Critical Perspectives on Accounting*, *26*, 84–98. https://doi.org/10.1016/j.cpa.2014.02.006

Martinez, D., & Himick, D. (2023). Accounting in (direct) action: Prefiguring emancipation in accounting research. *Critical Perspectives on Accounting*, *93*, 102476. https://doi.org/10.1016/j.cpa.2022.102476

Martinovic, B., & Verkuyten, M. (2013). 'We were here first, so we determine the rules of the game': Autochthony and prejudice towards out-groups. *European Journal of Social Psychology*, *43*(7), 637–647. https://doi.org/10.1002/ejsp.1980

McCarthy, L., & Grosser, K. (2023). Breaking isolation: Consciousness-raising as a methodology for academic activism. *Organization*, *30*(5), 1152–1167. https://doi.org/10.1177/13505084231166172

McRobbie, A. (2009). *The Aftermath of Feminism: Gender, Culture and Social Change*. Los Angeles and London: Sage.

Mendes, K., & Ringrose, J. (2019). Digital Feminist Activism: #MeToo and the Everyday Experiences of Challenging Rape Culture. In B. Fileborn & R. Loney-Howes (Eds.), *#MeToo and the Politics of Social Change* (pp. 37–51). Cham: Springer International Publishing.

Mendes, K., Ringrose, J., & Keller, J. (2018). #MeToo and the promise and pitfalls of challenging rape culture through digital feminist activism. *European Journal of Women's Studies*, *25*(2), 236–246. https://doi.org/10.1177/1350506818765318

Nicholson, L. J. (1981). "The Personal is Political": An analysis in retrospect. *Social Theory and Practice*, *7*(1), 85–98. https://doi.org/10.5840/soctheorpract1981714

Preissle, J. (2007). Feminist Research Ethics. In S. Hesse-Biber (Ed.), *Handbook of Feminist Research: Theory and Praxis* (pp. 515–534). Thousand Oaks: Sage.

Pullen, A. (2018). Writing as labiaplasty. *Organization*, *25*(1), 123–130. https://doi.org/10.1177/1350508417735537

Ramazanoglu, C., & Holland, J. (2002). *Feminist Methodology: Challenges and Choices*. London: Sage.

Reedy, F., & Haynes, K. (2023). Daughter-mother perspectives on feminist activism in the academy. *Organization*, *30*(1), 181–192. https://doi.org/10.1177/13505084211061237

Reinharz, S. (1992). *Feminist Methods in Social Research*. Oxford: Oxford University Press.

Restrepo Quintero, K., & Isaza Castro, J. G. (2019). ¿De lo masculino a lo femenino? Reflexiones sobre el mercado laboral de la contaduría pública. *Revista Científica General José María Córdova*, *17*(27), 527–553. https://doi.org/10.21830/19006586.385

Robinson, F. (2011). *The Ethics of Care: A Feminist Approach to Human Security*. Philadelphia: Temple University Press.

Ruiz Castro, M. (2012). Time Demands and Gender Roles: The Case of a Big Four Firm in Mexico. *Gender, Work & Organization*, *19*(5), 532–554. https://doi.org/10.1111/j.1468-0432.2012.00606.x

Sai, L., Gao, G., Mandalaki, E., Zhang, L. E., & Williams, J. (2024). Co-constructing new ways of working: Relationality and care in post-pandemic academia. *Culture and Organization*, in press, 1–16. https://doi.org/10.1080/14759551.2024.2323726

Scharff, C., Smith-Prei, C., & Stehle, M. (2016). Digital feminisms: Transnational activism in German protest cultures. *Feminist Media Studies*, *16*(1), 1–16. https://doi.org/10.1080/14680777.2015.1093069

Sharp, E. A., & Messuri, K. (2023). A reprieve from academia's chilly climate and misogyny: The power of feminist, women-centered faculty writing program. *Gender, Work & Organization*, *30*(4), 1236–1253. https://doi.org/10.1111/gwao.12967

Shearer, T. L., & Arrington, E. C. (1993). Accounting in other wor(l)ds: A feminism without reserve. *Accounting, Organizations and Society*, *18*(2), 253–272. https://doi.org/10.1016/0361-3682(93)90036-6

Shymko, Y., Vershinina, N., Daskalaki, M., Azevedo, G., & Quental, C. (2024). From the cocoon to la chape de plomb: The birth and persistence of silence around sexism in academia. *Gender, Work & Organization*, *31*(5), 2113–2137. https://doi.org/10.1111/gwao.13025

Spence, L. J., & Taylor, S. (2024). Feminist corporate social responsibility: Reframing CSR as a critical force for good. *British Journal of Management*, *35*(3), 1198–1208. https://doi.org/10.1111/1467-8551.12798

Stanley, L. (Ed.) (1990). *Feminist Praxis: Research, Theory and Epistemology*. London: Routledge.

Steccolini, I. (2019). New development: Gender (responsive) budgeting—A reflection on critical issues and future challenges. *Public Money & Management*, *39*(5), 379–383. https://doi.org/10.1080/09540962.2019.1578538

Tanima, F. A., & George, S. (2024). When the personal is political: Sharing – As insight – Our lived experiences as women of colour in accounting academia. *Social and Environmental Accountability Journal*, *44*(2), 93–111. https://doi.org/10.1080/0969160X.2024.2320304

Taylor-Dunn, H. (2023). Researching Domestic Abuse and Sexual Violence – Ethical and Methodological Considerations. In C. McLoone-Richards (Ed.), *Researching Domestic Abuse and Sexual Violence. Critical Perspectives for Student-Practitioner Researchers*. (pp. 2018–2023). Abingdon: Routledge.

Thomson, I. (2014). Responsible social accounting communities, symbolic activism and the reframing of social accounting. A commentary on new accounts: Towards a reframing of social accounting. *Accounting Forum*, *38*(4), 274–277. https://doi.org/10.1016/j.accfor.2014.05.002

Tienari, J., & Taylor, S. (2019). Feminism and men: Ambivalent space for acting up. *Organization*, *26*(6), 948–960. https://doi.org/10.1177/1350508418805287

Toffoletti, K., & Starr, K. (2016). Women academics and work–life balance: Gendered discourses of work and care. *Gender, Work & Organization*, *23*(5), 489–504. https://doi.org/10.1111/gwao.12133

Tronto, J. C. (1993). *Moral Boundaries A Political Argument for an Ethic of Care*. London: Routledge.

UN Women. (2015). *Progress of the World's Women 2015–2016. Transforming Economies, Realizing Rights*. New York. https://www.unwomen.org/en/digital-library/publications/2015/4/progress-of-the-worlds-women-2015

Vachhani, S. J., & Pullen, A. (2019). Ethics, politics and feminist organizing: Writing feminist infrapolitics and affective solidarity into everyday sexism. *Human Relations*, 72(1), 23–47. https://doi.org/10.1177/0018726718780988

Wittbom, E. E. (2015). Management control for gender mainstreaming—A quest of transformative norm breaking. *Journal of Accounting & Organizational Change*, *11*(4), 527–545. https://doi.org/10.1108/JAOC-08-2012-0069

Wittbom, E. E., & Häyrén, A. I. (2021). Post-NPM gender accounting—Can public value management enhance gender mainstreaming? *Public Money & Management*, *41*(7), 507–515. https://doi.org/10.1080/09540962.2021.1929432

Yarrow, E., & Davies, J. (2024). A typology of sexism in contemporary business schools: Belligerent, benevolent, ambivalent, and oblivious sexism. *Gender, Work & Organization*, *31*(5), 2019–2039. https://onlinelibrary.wiley.com/doi/abs/10.1111/gwao.12914

Zou, Y. (2021). Methodological Insights – Experiencing and knowing in the field: An autoethnographic account of conducting audit fieldwork in China. *Accounting, Auditing & Accountability Journal*, *34*(3), 680–698. https://doi.org/10.1108/AAAJ-07-2020-4706

APPENDIX 1

The 30 Audit Firms with PIE clients responding to the FRC survey 2023

(Listed in order of fee income from audit)

PwC
KPMG
Deloitte
EY UK
BDO
Grant Thornton UK
KPMG (Ireland)
EY (Ireland)
RSM
Mazars
Crowe UK
MHA Macintyre Hudson
PKF Littlejohn
Haysmacintyre
Moore Kingston Smith
Johnston Carmichael
Kreston Reeves
Price Bailey
Beever and Struthers
Hazlewoods
Shipleys
Gerald Edelman
Grant Thornton (NI)
Carter Backer Winter
LB Group
Bennett Brooks & Co

Johnsons Financial Management
BSG Valentine
Royce Peeling Green
Begbies

Source: Key Facts and Trends in the Accountancy Profession, Professional Oversight Board for Accountancy, Financial Reporting Council annual report 2023

INDEX

Note: **Bold** page numbers refer to tables; *italic* page numbers refer to figures and page numbers followed by "n" denote endnotes.

Kolibri 360 GmbH
Ferdinand-Jühlke-Straße 7
99095 Erfurt, Deutschland
produktsicherheit@kolibri360.de